Understanding
Computer-Based
Education

Understanding Computer-Based Education

MARTIN A. SIEGEL
DENNIS M. DAVIS

*University of Illinois
at Urbana-Champaign*

Random House  New York

First Edition

987654321

Library of Congress Cataloging in Publication Data
Siegel, Martin A.
    Understanding computer-based education.
    Includes bibliographies and index.
    1. Computer-assisted instruction.   I. Davis,
Dennis M.   II. Title.
LB1028.5.S493   1986   371.3'9445   85-2030
ISBN: 0-394-33474-4

IBM is a registered trademark of International
Business Machines Corporation.

Apple is a registered trademark of Apple
Computer, Inc.

The Plato® system is a development of the
University of Illinois. Plato® is a service mark of
Control Data Corporation.

Text Design: Jo Stein

Cover Design: Nadja Furlan–Lorbek

Manufactured in the United States of America

For
Linda, Adam, and Mara

Preface

This book has a simple purpose. We think of our audience as educators—teachers, prospective teachers, and teacher trainers—who know little or nothing about computers and computer-based education (CBE), are uncomfortable with the technical aspects of educational computing, but feel that the field is rapidly becoming so important that they need to find out something about it. This book supplies the information you need. When you find out what that is, you may be surprised—pleasantly, we hope.

You will not find any discussion of bits and bytes, of RAM and ROM, or CP/M, I/O ports, or S-100 buses here. This book is not "everything you always wanted to know about computers." In fact, it is not about *computers* at all. It is about the *use* of computers in education by nonspecialists.

It does not take the lid off your Apple and provide a guided tour of its electronic components. Instead, it talks about how patterns of computer use in our culture are changing and orients the educational user within the new culture.

It does not talk about binary arithmetic, Boolean logic, or the ASCII character codes. Instead, it talks about the ways computers are used in education and compares the various uses from the teacher's point of view.

In short, this book concentrates on *people*—not on machines.

It represents the distillation of twelve years' experience working with computer nonspecialists in CBE in a wide variety of capacities. With our colleagues at the Computer-based Education Research Laboratory at the University of Illinois, we have developed over 500 hours of computer-based instructional lessons. That experience has given us a good feel for educational users. A large part of the instruction we have developed includes basic skills lessons for learning-disadvantaged adults in the Illinois prison system. Teachers who have no previous computer training deliver daily instruction easily and reliably to hundreds of students all over Illinois at locations far from our laboratory. The relative inaccessibility of our sites demands instruction that fully accommodates the user. It would not work if we expected users to conform to the computer when we are hundreds of miles away and cannot guide them, help them, or do it for them. Necessity has made us "nonspecialist specialists"—we know how teachers and students unfamiliar with computers think, what they want, and what they need.

While our university work has centered on instructional development and research on the PLATO system, we have also developed several instructional packages for microcomputers, which is the hardware configuration most schools can expect to have—at least for the next few years. In this book, we compare the particular strengths of different sized educational computer systems, so you will benefit from the diversity of our development experience. Of equal importance, because we have worked in several different computer environments—including elementary and secondary public schools—we have been able to crystallize insights about computer-based instruction that transcend the restricted viewpoints of those who work with any single hardware configuration. We share those insights with you in this book.

Finally, we have consulted and lectured extensively on the educational uses for computers. Our audiences have included teachers and other nonspecialist computer users. We know the questions educational users frequently ask. We also understand what bothers, confuses, and frustrates them. We address those concerns in this book.

Taken together, these experiences have taught us that the main problem new educational computer users face is not so much one of *finding out* information as one of *making sense* of the profusion of complex, confusing, often contradictory facts, opinions, and advice that abounds on the subjects of computers and computer-based education. For that reason we strive here to create in our readers not computer literacy but a condition we might call "conceptual literacy." Our goal is to adopt an outlook that is somewhat different from many introductory texts, which often take a "smorgasbord" approach and present the full range of options, opinions, and directions in a field without attempting to evaluate, compare, or coordinate them. Given the state of confusion most beginning educational computer users experience, we determined it would be more helpful to present a single, clear perspective of the field of CBE. We do not just *describe* the central issues but evaluate them and explore their interrelationships from one carefully articulated point of view.

Beginning in the early chapters with broader issues, which concern the changing nature of computer users in our culture, we move to increasingly specific discussions of CBE instructional approaches in Chapters 5 through 8. Then we widen the scope again in the later chapters, applying key insights from the microscopic treatment of the central section in broader contexts— first to the classroom and then to education generally. We hope that this treatment will increase your knowledge of the field of CBE, but we hope even more that it will increase your understanding.

Without wishing to hold them in any way responsible for any blunders we might make, we must extend our thanks to several people for their invaluable insights and efforts. Their support aided us both in writing this book and in the formation of our thinking on the subject of computer-based education. Literally, we could not have done it without them.

We thank our colleagues, past and present, in the PLATO Education Group, University of Illinois: J. Michael Felty, Robert Dixon, Elizabeth Clapp, Lindsay Reichmann, John Bryan, Albert Liu, Dorothy Silver, John Gilpin, Elaine Bruner, Ethan Edwards, Catherine Daubard, Dorothy O'Connell, Sharon Dugdale, David Kibbey, Stephen Alessi, David Fuller, Mariellen Gilpin, Joan Phebus, Connie Kyse, Walter Brooks, Louis DiBello, James Bowery, and Tim Halvorsen.

We received strong support from Daniel Alpert, Director, Center for Advanced Study, University of Illinois; from Franklin Propst, Associate Director, Computer-based Education Research Laboratory, University of Illinois; and from our good friends and colleagues, A. Lynn Misselt, Steven Clapp, and Edward Bruner. Nor can we mention the topic of support without expressing our gratitude to our parents and families, whose care and concern have always sustained us.

We owe a special debt of gratitude to the State of Illinois Department of Corrections for sponsoring much of the curriculum development that has enabled us to formulate and implement our thinking on computers in education—particularly to Richard Hinckley and J. Clark Esarey, past superintendents, with whom we worked closely for many years.

Dorothy O'Connell, the administrative assistant of our project, deserves special recognition for the countless hours she devoted to the task of beating our turgid prose into whatever degree of readability it now possesses, as do Judy Rothman and Lucy Rosendahl, our Random House editors, and our friend, Ethan Edwards, who read the manuscript carefully and provided many helpful comments and criticisms. An unsung heroine, our project secretary, Joan Phebus, did the typing and displayed great patience with the sometimes recalcitrant text editor on which this manuscript was produced.

Finally, we gratefully acknowledge our mentors and teachers, Siegfried Engelmann, now at the University of Oregon, and Donald L. Bitzer, Director, Computer-based Education Research Laboratory, University of Illinois and PLATO's founder, who, more than any others, have shaped our thinking and to whom we owe an eternal debt of gratitude.

Martin A. Siegel
Dennis M. Davis

Urbana, Illinois

Contents

1 The Educational Computing Context — 1

The Changing Role of the Computer in Our
Society — 1

A Social History of Computers — 2

Third Wave Computing — 6

Hardware and Software — 7

Cautions for Educational Computer Users — 10

Unfriendly Software — 10

Hobbyism — 13

Computer Literacy — 16

2 How Computers Teach — 19

Can Computers Really Teach? — 19

How Computers Work — 20

People Thinking versus Computer "Thinking" — 21

Computer "Thinking"/Computer Teaching — 22

Instructional Strengths of the Computer — 24

Range of Adaptivity — 25

Adaptive Instruction and the Student — 26

Adaptive Instruction and the Teacher — 27

Why Use Computers to Deliver Instruction? — 27

Individualized Instruction — 28

Getting the Computer's "Best Effort" — 32

Shaping Long-Term Retention — 32

The Computer as an Instructional Medium — 34

Computers versus Human Teachers — 34

Computers versus Books   35
Computers versus Film   36
The Danger of Imitation   37

3   Approaches to Computer-Based Education I   41
Many Points of View   42
Defining the Range of Approaches   43
  The Logo Program   43
  The PLATO Curriculum Project   44
The Global System of Classification   47
  Computer-Based Testing (CBT)   49
  Computer-Managed Instruction (CMI)   50
  Features of a Fully Automated CMI System   52
  Complete Teaching   56

4   Approaches to Computer-Based Education II   59
The Instruction-Oriented System of Classification   59
  Implications of the Instruction-Oriented System   65
The Goal-Oriented System of Classification   68
  Significance of Taylor's System   69
  Features of CBE Hardware Systems   70
  A Working Perspective   73

5   Logo: A Tutee Approach   77
Introduction to Logo   78
Theory of Logo   78
  Curing Mathophobia   79
  Logo's Roots   80
  The Logo Method   80
Learning with Logo   81
  Drawing   81
  Procedural Approach   83
  Procedures with Inputs   84
  Simple Recursive Procedures   86
  Programs with Text   88

Analysis and Evaluation of Logo 90
Turtle Graphics 91
Inductive Learning Techniques 92
Powerful Ideas 96
Teaching "Applications" 100
The Dictum 102
Logo and Complete Teaching 104

6 Tutee to Tutor: Bridging the Gap   **107**
The Third Wave and Child-Centered Education 108
Keeping the Balance: Education as Communication 110
Resolving the Dilemma: Content-Centered Education 114
Individualizing Instruction 117
Role of the Computer 118

7 The Tutor Approach: Computer Delivery of Instruction   **123**
A Basic Technique for Individualizing Instruction 124
Components of Individualized CBE 128
Accurate Placement 129
Variable Instruction Content 131
Distributed Practice 135
Sequencing of Instruction 137
Critical Remarks and Evaluation 140
Courseware Problems 141
Computer Imagination 141
Limitations of the Lesson Format and Instructional Techniques Discussed in This Chapter 142

8 Educational Software Tools   **147**
A Context for Tools 147
What Is a Software Tool? 148
Second and Third Wave Tools 148

Relationship of Tools to Instruction   149
Product versus Process   151
Machine Tasks versus People Tasks   154
Tools and Computer Imagination   157
Integrating Software Tools   159
The Tip of the Iceberg   165
Computer Management for Integration   166
Power versus Ease of Use   168
Turning Keypress Conventions into
    Generalizations   170
Levels of Access   172

9 The Computer in the Classroom   **177**
First Things First   177
Taking Stock   179
Taking Stock of Your Hardware Situation   180
Taking Stock of Your Instructional
    Requirements   184
Criteria for Evaluating Educational Software   186
Content   186
Programming   187
Computer Imagination   191
Procedure for Evaluating Educational Software   197

10 Attacking the "Courseware Problem"   **203**
The Courseware Problem   203
Understanding the Courseware Problem   206
Schools' Contributions   207
Manufacturers' Contributions   208
Educational Publishers' Contributions   209
University Courseware Developers'
    Contributions   210
Resolving the Courseware Problem   212
CBE Development Centers   215
Goals and Emphases   216
Laboratory School   218

11   Possibilities   **221**
   A Question of Impact   221
   Impact on Curricula   222
   Impact on Schools and Society   228
   Computer Imagination versus Computer Literacy   230

   Index   **233**

Understanding Computer-Based Education

1

The Educational Computing Context

In this chapter we will discuss the "computer revolution" as it affects education. We will examine the history of computer use from a perspective that distinguishes educational computer users and uses from the traditional users, uses, and modes of interaction with computers. And we will examine some implications of this change in computing perspective.

THE CHANGING ROLE OF THE COMPUTER IN OUR SOCIETY

In the preface, we stated that the biggest problem confronting prospective users of educational computers is not finding out what they need to know but making sense of a huge glut of confusing, often conflicting, information about computers and their role in the educational process. Of the many reasons for this confusion, the most fundamental one is probably a failure on the part of the computer industry and those who write about it to recognize that today there are two distinct computer "movements." To borrow the distinction made by Alvin Toffler in his important study *The Third Wave*, we might call them "Second Wave and Third Wave computing."[1]

Second Wave computing is centered mainly in big business, big government, and big science. It is devoted to processing huge amounts of information and making thousands of repetitive calculations—tasks necessary to send bills to millions of phone and power customers, to launch satellites and spacecraft, to run giant nuclear plants, or to compute the nation's income tax. In other words, the value of Second Wave computers is that they do tasks that are simply too big for even roomfuls of actuaries to accomplish working twenty-four hours a day.

Third Wave computing differs both in the kinds and in the size of tasks to which computers are applied. From Pac Man to home finance to educational computing to management information packages for use by office workers, the Third Wave uses of computers are more varied and smaller in scope. Unlike Second Wave computing tasks, most Third Wave tasks *could* be done without computers. Word processing, for example, took place quite adequately with paper, pencil, and typewriter before the advent of the microcomputer, while Second Wave tasks, such as computing the U.S. Census, depend absolutely on the power of giant computers.

Although the nature of Third Wave computer tasks and users may have changed, the basic nature of computers has not. Certainly, we now have small, inexpensive computers where once we had only the hermetically sealed and delicate giants used by big business, government, and science. But the design of small computers commonly dedicated to such Third Wave tasks as computer-based education (CBE)—that is, the ways the computers accept, process, store, and retrieve information—differs only slightly from that of the big Second Wave machines.

It is not surprising, therefore, that the special needs and demands of Third Wave users and uses should oftentimes escape the attention of computer manufacturers (who build the big machines as well as the small ones), computer specialists (who write about both kinds of machines and users), and the popular press (which takes its point of view on computing as well as its information in large part from computer manufacturers and specialists). It is not surprising that these Second Wavers often fail to realize that, while the nature of computers is in large part unchanged, the nature of Third Wave users of and uses for computers differs strongly from their own. The result is the confusion and conflicting information of which we have spoken.

Our first task as Third Wave users is to gain a firm understanding of the computer's changing role in our culture—particularly as it affects education. Let us begin to do that through a brief examination of the history of computing. To arrive at the insight we want, we should focus our attention not on the history of the computer as a machine but on the *social* history of computers. This will enable us to see how computer uses and users have changed.

A SOCIAL HISTORY OF COMPUTERS

You could say that the social history of the computer began with Isaac Newton and with the English philosophers of the seventeenth and eighteenth centuries. None of them, so far as we know, ever had the idea of a computer, but they created the intellectual climate within which the idea of a computer became possible: They ushered in the machine age. Newton's physics, for example, is predicated on a view of the universe as a *mechanical* system. Following his lead, philosophers began to postulate a mechanical model of society to supplant the medieval view of society as a reflection of the divinely created Great Chain of Being. According to the medieval view, as God rules over angels, then humans, animals, plants, and minerals, the king rules over aristocrats, then tradesmen, townsfolk, and peasants who work the land.

By contrast, in a political climate in which the rights of all individuals were coming to be viewed as equal, the notion of a society that worked like a machine—in which people were differentiated by their function rather than their status in the social hierarchy—was quite attractive. Social order came to be seen as a function of the smooth working of the elements of the social machine, and not as a result of the divine investment of authority in a king and class of nobles. The Constitution of the United States represents a pinnacle of such thinking. It is based on the philosophical position that order resides in law, in a mechanical system of built-in checks and balances that function apart from the personalities of those who rule.

In fact, the machine model fit Western man's self-concept so well that it came to predominate much of our thinking, even outside the domains of physics and government. For example, modern medicine is founded on the view of the body as a machine and of the physician as a mechanic. Even in music, the great symphonic composer Ludwig van Beethoven was fascinated throughout his life with such mechanical musical devices as music boxes, mechanical carillons, and Maelzel's invention, the metronome, which has been the scourge of beginning music students ever since. In other words, the idea of patterning human life after the function of machines gradually came to be exalted in Western culture.

Ideas, however, are like people: Their best and worst features seem to come from the same wellspring. So, while the exaltation of the machine ushered in democratic government, modern medicine, and the scientific method, it also caused the mechanization of human life. The machinelike principle of division of labor, formulated by Adam Smith, for example, improved the lifestyle of Europeans, but it also soon led to sweatshops and assembly lines that sharply diminished the satisfaction and sense of accomplishment of preindustrialized labor. In fact, by the nineteenth century, the exaltation of the machine in Western culture created a situation in which the application of the mechanical model, not just to work but to all human activities, became acceptable, even desirable—as unacceptable as that idea seems to us today.

It is within this context of cultural mechanization that the idea for computers first arose among mathematicians of the eighteenth century. They wanted a machine that could perform the thousands of mundane, repetitive calculations necessary to their profession. They reasoned that such a machine would not only be faster and save labor but would eliminate what has come to be known as "human error." And they were right. When it comes to "number crunching" (the modern computer term for running a long series of routine calculations) or for data processing (sorting and tabulating of thousands of bits of information), the computer is unexcelled.

Brainchild of the machine age, then, the idea for computers first emerged as an *assembly line* for information. The goal of the mathematicians who conceived them was not to build an *intelligent* machine but a *beautiful* machine, according to their idea of beauty. The computer was to impose *order* on unruly data, processing it in a regular fashion according to a series of specified operations. (The idea of making computers programmable—that is, of making it possible to change the kind and order of operations they were to perform— was an afterthought, an invention of this century, an adjunct to the basic nature of the machine.)

But an idea is not a working machine. The scientist-engineers who produced the first working computers had to discover how to translate the idea into a functioning reality, and that meant solving some practical, mechanical problems. For one, they had to invent some method by which the computer could remember the correct order of steps to be followed in doing calculations. At that time, the Jaquard loom was receiving a great deal of favorable attention for the way it had revolutionized the weaving of cloth. The Jaquard loom used a stiff punched card to guide the mechanical parts of the loom to each complicated step in the weaving process. It was natural that Jaquard's practical solution was borrowed by the equally practical-minded computer builders, and the grandfather of the IBM card was born.

The engineers who built the first computers also had practical ideas about how to use them. In fact, the first computer to be applied to a practical, real-world problem was Herman Hollerith's amazing tabulating machine. Using the technology of punched cards, Hollerith devised a way to tabulate the 1890 U.S. Census in record time. This accomplishment caused computers to be taken seriously for the first time.

Hollerith's dedication of his computer to data processing prefigured both Second Wave uses and users of computers. In terms of use Second Wave computers depend on large size to gain their usefulness—the larger the better. In this sense size does not refer to how much space the computer takes up. Remember, we are not talking about machines; this is a *social* history. In our terms large size refers to extensive memory and lots of processing power (the ability to store and operate on millions of pieces of information).

It took computer designers many years after Hollerith's idea caught their imaginations to achieve the size and power they wanted. Early computers that occupied whole floors of buildings were often less powerful than many of today's desktop machines. But the commitment to strive for giant-sized memories and powerful processing was present in Second Wave computing from the outset, and the goal was eventually achieved. The computers that calculate, print, and send out millions of phone and credit card bills every month, then process payments and credit your account are the result. So are the mammoth NASA computers that enabled our astronauts to reach the moon. Incidentally, it was the need to pack computer components into a tiny space capsule that provided a major impetus to reducing their *physical* size.

It is easy to see why Second Wave computers had to strive for big memory and big computing power. After all, in the early days of Second Wave computing, clerks could do the same kinds of data processing tasks that computers could do, and for less money since computers were extraordinarily expensive to build, operate, and maintain. The computer's only advantage was that it could do more of them (big memory) faster than clerks (big processing power) and with fewer errors. Thus, Hollerith's idea was taken seriously only when immigration had swelled the country's population by so much in the decade between 1880 and 1890 that it would have taken an army of clerks more than the ten years they had before the next Census to complete the one for 1890. Under these conditions the computer, for all its huge expense, became practical, solely because of the size of tasks it could take on.

Large size, in turn, also had profound effects, not just on the *way* computers were used, but on who used them. Because the big machines were so expensive, their use was restricted to those who needed big jobs done and could afford to pay the cost. As a result big government, big business, and big science (centered in universities) were the sole users of computers.

Because computers were big, costly, delicate, and devoted to such highly specialized tasks, they were used exclusively by carefully trained specialists, not by mere operators or users in the sense that someone uses a typewriter or adding machine. The machines required expertise—and the machine culture in which the computer arose accepted the notion that people should be the servants of such a machine, not the other way around.

The same holds true with the big computers of today. The frequently heard complaint, "I'm just a number in a computer!" is often justified. Few have escaped the frustrations of "computer errors" in billing and the aggravating and demeaning harrassment from a machine that results. When it comes to big computers, the prevailing notion is that people must adjust to the machine. The assembly-line attitude built into the inner workings of the computer reaches out to touch those upon whose lives the computer has an effect. There is little impetus in Second Wave computing to make computers easier to use. Instead, the machine age emphasis is on molding people, standardizing them to the computer's mode of operation.

Then along came the microprocessor. Descendants of the transistor, microprocessors are tiny chips of silicon imprinted with circuitry that makes the chip itself a computer. Though at least as powerful as the components of older computers, microchips are small and inexpensive to produce. At first the new technology was used to reduce the size and cost of Second Wave computers, but before long computer manufacturers began to realize that tiny *microcomputers*, with microprocessors at their hearts, could be produced cheaply enough to attract a mass market.

Sounds wonderful. Since computers no longer had to be big, anyone could interact with them directly to perform any task they wanted. Since they were no longer expensive, anyone could own one. The scions of the computer industry and the journalists and cultural commentators soon began painting pictures of a computer in every home . . . several in every *school!* And their predictions are coming true.

THIRD WAVE COMPUTING

Perhaps you have already detected the flaw in the two preceding paragraphs. We agreed, as we began our history of computers, to make it a social history— to talk about uses and users of computers. But the end of our social history concentrates on chips, microcomputers, and mass markets. The computer people, who envisaged a computer "revolution" based on the widespread availability of small, inexpensive *machines*, failed to recognize either the demands posed by new uses or the needs and nature of new users. Involved with the technology of the new machines, they forgot that the real revolution involves people.

That has caused us some problems—not least among which is the confusion that troubles many prospective users of educational computers. Yet it is not surprising that the computer experts failed to view the computer revolution from our perspective. They are machine oriented, and the new little machines work much like the big ones they are used to. They are specialists, so figuring out how to use the little machines is no problem for them. But it is a big one for us nonspecialists! They view computer tasks as traditional and unvarying, but we do not want to process data and crunch numbers. We want to do different, smaller tasks on computers, but we do not know how. New uses, new users, and small machines that work like big, specialized ones— they are the source of the problems that confront Third Wave computer users and cause the confusion that besets us.

It is reassuring to know why getting involved with educational computing can be confusing and difficult. A certain amount of satisfaction can be derived just from knowing that ours is a "historical" problem—one that has deep roots in the way computers have developed in our culture. After all, history is bigger than all of us! You should take comfort in knowing that it is not your ignorance, ineptitude, or lack of mechanical aptitude that make getting computerized difficult. But however comforting, it does not solve the problem.

Basically, there are two ways out for prospective educational computer users: We can accommodate ourselves to computers on their terms, or we can educate ourselves to make computers work for us. Neither path is easy, but in this book we have chosen the second. That choice requires us to develop some understanding of the function of computers—not from the perspective of the specialist, but from that of a Third Wave user. Specifically, if we want to deepen our insight into how computers may be useful to us as educators, we need to understand how they differ from other machines.

Hardware and Software

The critical difference between computers and other machines, of course, is that computers are programmable. Other machines—air conditioners, for example—have only "hardware" (or machine parts); computers also have "software" (or programs). Both air conditioners and computers are pieces of equipment that do things for people. Calling both of these tools "hardware" makes intuitive sense. These machine parts are, after all, similar to things we might actually find in a hardware store. That intuitive understanding, however, is not quite accurate. It works well enough on its own, but when we try to move from it to a comparable intuitive understanding of "software," we run into problems.

Computer "hardware" really is "hard," but what is "soft" about "software"? The definition of software as "computer programs" does not explain it—even if you know what a computer program is. If a program is defined as "the set of instructions that tell computers what to do," it is still difficult to imagine why such a thing would be called "soft."

To find out, let us continue the analogy by asking whether air conditioners have something that might be equivalent to computer software—to programs that tell the machine what to do. The answer is not as easy as it might seem. The dial or buttons that control the temperature settings, for example, do not qualify as a "program." Even though they control what the machine does, they do not *tell* it what to do. They are just switches. They are hardware. The "program" that tells the machine what to do, that pushes the switches to control temperature settings, is in the head of the user. "I've been mowing the lawn and I'm very hot," you say, and *you* tell the air conditioner to run on high by pushing the appropriate button.

If the air conditioner is a fancier model, its automatic thermostat is more like a real "program," because it is connected to circuits that, depending on data they receive from the environment (temperature of the air), "tell" the air conditioner when to turn on and off. Of course, that is a very simple program. In fact, it can hardly be called a program at all because the term "program" is short for "program of instructions," and the air conditioner's "program" consists of only two instructions:

1. If the air temperature gets above X degrees, turn the machine on.
2. If the air temperature falls below X degrees, turn the machine off.

The air conditioner's "program" is also different from computer software in another respect. It is built into the machine and cannot be changed.

Now we come to the central point of our discussion of the computer as a machine. The reason why an air conditioner and a computer differ in the size of their programs has to do with the *functions* of the machines. An air conditioner's function is to cool a room. What is a computer's function? It is not very helpful to say, "to compute"!

In a literal sense, in fact, the computer has no function—at least no set function like an air conditioner. It is not *for* anything. To put it another way, a computer is for everything. A computer as a machine is pure potential. Its function is to do whatever you want it to do—whatever its program tells it to do. Conversely, without a program to run it, a computer can do nothing. It is in this context that the meaning of "software" becomes clear. Because the function of the computer can change depending on the program it is running, programs are called "soft." Software is soft in the sense that it is changeable; hardware is hard because it is fixed, or unchangeable. The computer must have a complex program because few automatic, fixed functions are built into it. The air conditioner has a very small, *fixed program*, because it has a very specific function. The computer has a large, changeable, *soft program*, because it has no set function.

It is the quality of softness, or the lack of specific, defined function, that makes the computer potentially a transparent *medium* through which information (including education) can flow. Thus, if schools concentrate exclusively or mainly on the hardware component of computers—simply purchasing them for the school, letting kids interact with them as machines, teaching kids to program them—they derive some benefit. But computers are infinitely more valuable to students when the software component is emphasized—when the computer is used as a medium to transmit instruction via software. The true potential of computer-based education (CBE), in other words, derives from the computer's "softness" as a medium. It consists in the machine's capacity *to deliver*, to transmit excellent instruction.

An analogy might help make the concept of transparency of medium more clear. Consider the difference between the way your television repairman looks at your TV set and the way you look at it. To the television repairman, your TV is a machine. He concentrates on it as a machine, and his job is to make the machine work well. As a repairman, he has no interest in what programs the set delivers. However, to the television viewer, the *user* of the TV set, television's purpose is to deliver programs. The only concern he has for the set as a machine is that it keep out of the way. He notices the set itself only when it malfunctions. Under ordinary circumstances, the viewer wants to see *through* the set as a machine to the programs it delivers. He expects it to be "transparent." Computers are very much like televisions. They even look like TV sets. And the nonspecialist computer user is very much like a television viewer.

The example of the TV repairman illustrates the notion of transparency, but it also provides insight into the difference between Second and Third Wave users. Comparing Third Wave users to drivers of cars and Second Wave users to auto mechanics can further deepen that insight. Like the computer, the automobile is an immensely powerful technology with tremendous social impact on our culture. Although cars have been around for decades and millions are on the road, the number of Americans who can build or even repair a car is minuscule. Nor were we ever supposed to be able to build or fix them. Of course, some people like to tinker with them. That is fine, and the knowledge they get from tinkering certainly increases their power over the technology. But we interact with cars primarily as users, and it is in that capacity that they have had their impact on our culture. It is our contention that the same will be true for the computer.

Now we are beginning to develop a useful perspective. Our comparison of the computer to other machines, which led us to consider the softness of software and eventually to see the computer not as a machine but as a transparent medium, has already taken us far from the Second Wave view of the computer as a machine. It shows us clearly why, in education, the computer revolution is centered not in the new machines but in new uses. It shows us that our real concern as educators is not with computers (hardware) but with computer-based education (software).

Consider how we have already begun to clarify the confusion that surrounds the process of getting started in educational computing. Is not one of the biggest sources of confusion the task of mastering and weighing all the differing features of computers? Consider some of the questions that often bedevil the new user:

"Do I need a lot of RAM or is 64K sufficient?"

"Is a color monitor necessary?"

"Must my machine have CP/M?"

"Is one brand of computer best for education?"

Such technical questions simply miss the point. The previous discussion shows clearly that for the educational computer user the questions are simple:

"What do I want to teach?"

"What software delivers that instruction?"

"What computer runs that software?"

There is much more we will have to discuss before we can answer the first two of these questions meaningfully. But once we realize that the answer to the last one comes automatically once the others have been answered, a great deal of confusion vanishes. We know that in Third Wave educational computing, machines are not central in importance. The machine we want is the one that runs the software that delivers the instruction we want. Thus, as we discuss CBE in subsequent chapters, we must focus our attention on educational software.

CAUTIONS FOR EDUCATIONAL COMPUTER USERS

There is another reason why software is the most important concern for educators and other Third Wave users, while hardware capabilities are more important for Second Wave users. Because Second Wave users are computer experts, they can program the software they need. Since they expect to develop software packages as they need them, they do not worry about finding preprogrammed software to do the tasks they want. Instead, they concentrate on finding a machine powerful enough to run their programming.

But we are educators, not computer programmers. Even if we could write our own programs, we would not want to spend time doing so. We want to leave that task to experts and devote ourselves to our own area of expertise—instruction.

The problem, however, is that the very computer experts on whom we Third Wave users depend to develop the software we need are themselves Second Wave users. They have a different attitude toward software, and not surprisingly, some of their unhelpful attitudes often linger in the software they develop for us, creating pitfalls for unwary nonspecialist users. Three of these are important enough to educational users that they bear discussion now, before we begin to examine the content of computer-based educational software in more detail in subsequent chapters. They are unfriendly software, hobbyism, and the notion of computer literacy.

Unfriendly Software

The term "user friendly" is becoming familiar. It is used to describe both hardware and software, but it applies more properly to software. In general terms, it means that a program is easy to use. What are user-friendly programs?

- Programs that interact with you in English instead of indecipherable codes

- Programs that are protected, so that even if you do something dumb or unexpected, you will not destroy the program or lose whatever data you have entered
- Programs that keep you from getting stuck—that will automatically send you somewhere for help, if you try unsuccessfully to do something two or three times
- Programs that place clear directions for using them right on the screen (instead of in a manual—often called "documentation"), and that use consistent conventions to assign program control functions to keys throughout the program

When you stop to think about it, however, the term is actually rather strange. Of all the easy-to-use things we purchase, only computers and software seem to be described by this term. Who ever heard, for example, of a "user-friendly bicycle"? We *expect* things produced for consumption by nonspecialists to be easy to consume. The law of supply and demand usually assures us that they will be.

The market dynamic that assures ease of use is so automatic, in fact, that we are seldom even aware of it. We hardly ever see "unfriendly" consumer products, because, through either market research or the tried-and-true competition of the marketplace, a product's ease of use has been assured.

Actually, the concept has some interesting applications to products other than computerware. For example, when McDonald's was first established, it might well have been described as "user friendly." Unlike old-fashioned restaurants of the sit-down-and-eat variety, McDonald's did not insist that you get dressed up—or even fully dressed! You did not have to worry about whether the kids would behave themselves. And you did not have to wait to be waited on or served. If you cared more about "user friendliness" than quality of food, you chose McDonald's. Americans did . . . to the tune of billions of hamburgers sold!

But McDonald's did not use the term "user friendly," even though they might have. Why do software developers for Third Wave markets like educational computing need to use it? The preceding section of this chapter provides the answer. Failing to recognize the difference between the needs of Second and Third Wave users, the specialists who first developed software for nonspecialist users carried over their own machine age attitude toward computing. The result was unfriendly software.

Some of the user-friendly attributes mentioned in the list above have now become more or less standard in educational software, as specialist software developers begin to recognize the legitimacy of nonspecialist users' demands. But there are still problems. For example, suppose you decide you want to use the computer to teach your students capitalization skills. You find a program, but it is filled with exercises like this:

Press the letter of the sentence that is right:

a. Sue went from Fourth Street to main Avenue on Tuesday.
b. Sue went from Fourth Street to Main Avenue on tuesday.
c. Sue went from Fourth Street to Main Avenue on Tuesday.
d. Sue went from Fourth street to Main Avenue on Tuesday.

You would like to say to the one who programmed the lesson, "This lesson teaches the skill I want, and it uses the computer as a transparent medium through which the instruction flows. I like that. But picking from a multiple choice array like this seems somewhat silly. First, the student might get the question wrong, not because he or she does not know the rule, but just because it is so hard to pick out the right answer among so many similar choices. And second, I want the student to *do* the skill, not merely recognize the error. Couldn't you present a single sentence with a capitalization mistake, like those in the workbooks I now use, and somehow have the student *change* the error?"

If you could put that challenge to the programmer in person, you would probably get an answer like this: "Just how is the student going to *mark* on the computer screen? If you knew more about computers, you wouldn't even ask such a question. Computers have their limitations, but I can't expect you to understand that. Just take my word for it—if you want to do this lesson on computer, you have to do it like this."

That is the kind of user unfriendliness that still lingers, and it is just not acceptable. Computer-based lessons must do more than work smoothly, properly, and easily. If they are to be useful, they must also *teach* well. Instruction delivered on computers must not compete with classroom teachers, nor should it slavishly try to imitate them. Instead, it must take fullest advantage of the strengths of the computer as an educational *medium*, while avoiding its weaknesses. Software that fails to do this is "unfriendly" in a different but equally important way, as the little capitalization example clearly shows.

Making educational software "friendly" in this sense is not easy. It requires a blend of content and pedagogical expertise with programming skill and insight. More, it requires blending them with *imagination*. The problem again stems from the clash between Second Wave and Third Wave computing. Educators—prospective Third Wave users of computers—know content and pedagogy but not the particular strengths of the computer medium. Programmers—Second Wave experts—know well the kinds of nifty things computers can be made to do, but they are familiar only with traditional Second Wave uses. They are as unfamiliar with educational content and method as teachers are with computers.

Programming professionals who are educational amateurs produce slick little software packages with little instructional value. Teachers who are programming amateurs produce good instruction that imitates them, textbooks, or workbooks, but does not exploit the computer medium effectively. *Computer imagination* is necessary to bridge the gap.

Hobbyism

Recently, a local bookstore we frequent had to move its collection of books on computers and computing to a new, special section of the store. There were just too many for the little cubbyhole that had housed them since a few years ago, when the microcomputer craze hit and popular books on computing started to sell well. We took a look at the collection as it is now. Books on how to program seemed to be most numerous. There were at least thirty different books on how to program in the BASIC language, and nearly as many for some of the other popular programming languages.

After programming books, the most popular category seemed to be general introductions. These books often included discussions of names and functions of the parts of a computer, of bits and bytes and binary arithmetic, and even elaborate and complicated discussions of octal and hexadecimal numbers, Boolean logic, and the ASCII character codes. Since we know such books sell in great numbers, we found ourselves admiring the diligence of nonspecialist users willing to tackle such formidable topics. But we also wondered whether, having finished them, readers might ask, "Okay, what do I know? Why did they tell me that? What does it mean, and what am I supposed to do with it?"

If you think about it, there is only one answer to those questions. These "introductory" books on microcomputers proceed on the implicit assumption that because you own or use a microcomputer, you either want—or ought to want—to program it. Why else would you want or need such technical information? Of what use is a knowledge of binary arithmetic?

There is nothing whatever wrong with wanting to learn to program computers. But we were surprised that so few popular books contained guides to commercially available software and that none sought to impart the skills a Third Wave user needs. Clearly that collection implied that the only meaningful way to interact with your microcomputer is to program it—to make yourself into an "amateur specialist." We call that attitude "hobbyism," and it is a classic case of confusion of the roles of old and new users. The idea that an appropriate role for most people who interact with computers is to use them like a driver uses an automobile or like a viewer watches TV seemed to be completely absent.

Just for fun we went to a nearby computer store to check whether hobbyism had as firm a hold there as it did in the bookstore. The salesperson was very willing to show us hardware and explain it in great detail. Then we started the "Will this computer do . . . ?" questions. The fellow we were talking with was honest and straightforward. He carefully explained that while the computer *itself* was capable of performing the tasks we asked, it would need a special *program* to do them, and he did not have one to give us.

Underhandedly, we offered him a little more rope to see if he would hang himself. We asked whether we could not learn how the machine worked on a quasi-technical level, pick up some programming from one of the popular books, and then build the software we wanted ourselves. We were offering to let him sell us the idea of hobbyism. To his credit, the guy at the computer store said, "Sure, but you better not need that software for two or three years. That's how long it will take you to learn enough to build it yourself—and that's if you have a *lot* of time to study programming!"

That degree of honesty is pretty rare. The salesperson had a vested interest in selling us the notion of hobbyism, because if we had believed him, we might have bought a computer, and selling computers is his living. Even though he did not fall for our little trap, his story shows where hobbyism comes from and why it is dangerous. Computer manufacturers are building the powerful little machines we went to see, and they are building them very well. But those who design, manufacture, and distribute them are computer experts. For the most part they are Second Wavers—machine oriented, unconcerned about providing commercially available software, since when *they* need a new program, they just build it themselves. From *their* point of view, what is most important is the *machine's potential* (getting the most power and the greatest number of machine features that aid in programming into the lowest-priced package). As a result we Third Wave users end up with a great little machine and nothing—or mostly bad and unfriendly software—to run on it. And that, in turn, is why so many computers in our schools are standing idle.

To be fair, it is not computer manufacturers' fault that schools are buying computers in large numbers, often only to discover that they cannot make as much good use of them as they had hoped. After all, why should the manufacturers have to act as software *publishers* as well? Publishing is as much out of their league as programming is out of ours. True, we need excellent, easy-to-use educational programs badly, and not having them turns the computers we have bought into expensive white elephants. Still, it is not fair to hold responsible those who built and sold us our computers. They are culpable only to the extent that they promote hobbyism. It is only when they say, in effect, "It's not our fault the computer won't do the job you want. It's *capable* of doing the task. If you are dissatisfied with its performance, do what we do. Learn to program it yourself!"

Hobbyism is bad wherever it prevails because it delays the arrival of *good* software for nonspecialist users and proliferates the number of useless machines in the hands of frustrated Third Wave users. But it is especially bad in educational computing. We need excellent programs now and in large numbers. We do not need a lot of empty talk about how rewarding and fulfilling it can be "to do it ourselves." We want to use the computer as a medium through which instruction flows much as TV programming flows through our TV sets. We do not want to have to hack on the machine itself like a TV repairman. We want to use computers as we use cars, to transport our students to new areas of learning, not to teach them or ourselves to build the car before we get a chance to drive it anywhere! Teachers ought not to think they have to be hobbyist programmers to make good use of computers in their classrooms.

It *can* be fun and exciting to learn some programming if you want to, and there is a place for teacher-developed programs in education. Maybe we should think of them as the computer equivalent of that great institution, the "ditto sheet." In a supplemental role teacher-developed materials are great, and they can add a lot to instruction. But when it comes to the serious delivery of instruction, teachers can no more be expected to develop programs themselves than they can be expected to write their own textbook series.

The insufficiency of hobbyism as a means to acquiring the excellent educational software we need brings up an important question. If teachers are to be users and not programmers, who are the specialists who will develop the educational software we need so badly? Unfortunately, there are very few people right now who can fill the bill. In our universities there are some educators trained as Second Wave programmers who recognize the special needs of educational computing and are developing good programs—but not enough of them. Our need for software is immediate and great. From their Second Wave perspective, computer manufacturers and the popular press have sold us on the educational *potential* of computers as machines. We have acquired them in the hundreds of thousands, and now we desperately need software to use them as transparent media to deliver excellent instruction. We need much more of it, and we need it more quickly than the few university specialists can produce it.

Recognizing the need, many commercial concerns—from tiny cottage industries to major print publishers—are rushing to fill the void. Those who are diligent are finding out that the task is an extremely difficult one. Educational software is a whole new game for everyone. It is not too hard to find good programmers, and we have content experts and curriculum developers enough. It is a bit more difficult, however, to train them to talk one another's languages effectively. The hardest part, as we have already seen in a little example, is figuring out how to do educational tasks in a way that makes sense on computers.

As educational software publishers struggle with this difficult problem, educational computer users looking for software must beware of the large number of unsuccessful attempts to adapt teaching to a new medium. Figuring out what we really want and learning techniques to find it once we know are the two big tasks of the remainder of this book. For now, please realize that the hobbyist ploy—the push to "do it yourself"—is definitely *not* the answer, for the reasons we have discussed in this chapter.

Computer Literacy

There is no question about it: Given the widespread popularity of computers in our society, educators, along with virtually everyone else, need to become "computer literate." But we must also ask what kind of literacy we need. We have already seen that the computer industry and the writers of popular books and pieces about computers for nonspecialists often do not distinguish between the needs of Second Wave and Third Wave users. It is not surprising, therefore, to find that some of them advocate a form of computer literacy that seeks to turn nonspecialist users into hobbyists or to absolve the responsibility of those who develop "unfriendly software" by teaching people how to adapt to the machine. Many computer literacy books make this mistake, and so do many computer literacy courses.

One popular computer literacy text, for example, has twenty-four chapters divided into three main units called, "How Computers Work," "Computers in Our Lives," and "BASIC Programming."[2] Much of the first unit is devoted to naming and describing the functions of the parts of the computer and to introducing concepts (such as binary arithmetic) that programmers need to know (since the last unit teaches some rudiments of programming). The middle unit's name sounds promising, but two of its five chapters merely describe the hardware evolution of computers. The last unit introduces the student to programming.

In all, only thirty pages in the book discuss topics outside the realm of hobbyism, and well over half the book is devoted to teaching programming. We have no quarrel with the book's intrinsic quality. It seems entertaining and readable. The content it teaches can be interesting and fun to know. The problem is that, while a computer literacy course is teaching that, it is *not* teaching what Third Wave users need to know.

To see why computer literacy books so often make this unfortunate choice of contents to teach, let us look at the problem from the perspective of those who write them and teach the courses that use them. Suppose you are a data processing teacher at a local community college. Suddenly, you have a lot of students who are interested in beginning computing courses but who do not intend to enter the computer field as professionals. You probably also have a lot of pressure to accommodate their interest. These students come from the widest variety of fields with a bewildering variety of needs and interests.

"What can I say to all these people?" you ask. "How can I deliver instruction meaningful to all of them?" You do what you can. You decide to take your beginning computer programming course, cut it way back, remove most of the technical stuff, put in some fluff about computer applications, and teach the course that way—slowly and patiently. And you are delighted when you find some textbooks in "computer literacy" that approach the course in the same way.

The frustration and confusion these instructors feel is quite justifiable. In the Second Wave data processing or computer science courses they used to teach, everyone wanted the same kinds of information and the discipline's own approach to computers and programming. But these new students are not just technically unprepared; their interests vary considerably. The hallmark of Third Wave computing, as we have said, is diversity. Thus, one thing that is easy for us to realize within our developing perspective on computing, but that the data processing teacher turned computer literacy instructor often fails to see, is that we do not want a single computer literacy course or group of courses taught in the *computer* department. Because the needs of Third Wave users are so diverse, computer literacy courses need to be split up and transferred to the various divisions of the college.

Rather than a single course or group of courses on computer literacy, we need a range of courses with titles like "Using the Computer in Real Estate" and, most important for us, "Using the Computer in Education." Only when we have them will we be able to shift the emphasis from the Second Wave preoccupation with the computer as machine and begin to address the various needs of Third Wave users. Conversely, until we have that, we have no choice in a single course on computer literacy but to ignore the nonspecialist users' needs and teach about the machine, which is the only common denominator for Third Wave users, even though that information is among the least helpful for their needs.

Granted all this, we face the question of what kinds of knowledge and skills educational users need in their own computer user course. We are not begging the question when we say, "Wait and see." This book contains the kinds of knowledge and skills nonprogramming educational users need. It is truly a computer literacy textbook.

WHAT YOU HAVE LEARNED IN THIS CHAPTER

1. The advent of the microcomputer has created two distinct computer movements. Borrowing Toffler's terms we have called traditional computing uses and users Second Wave, and we have seen how Third Wave computing differs significantly in the kinds of tasks to which it puts computers, the kinds of people who use them, and the attitudes, approaches, and needs of these nonspecialist users.

2. We have seen that educational computing belongs to the Third Wave computing movement, that some Second Wave attitudes have been carried over into Third Wave computing, and that these often cause the confusion teachers feel as they seek to computerize their classrooms and schools.

3. An examination of the social history of computing revealed (1) that the computer "revolution" we are experiencing was brought about not by the

new, small computers but by the change in users and uses of computers; and (2) that the educational utility of the computer as a machine is in large part determined by the quality of educational software available to run on it.

4. We compared Second and Third Wave modes of computer use by means of two analogies. Comparing the computer to a television set, we likened the Second Wave user to a repairman and the Third Wave user to a viewer. Comparing the computer to the automobile, we likened the Second Wave user to a mechanic and the Third Wave user to a driver.

5. Exploring the differences between computers and other machines—through a discussion of hardware and software—we learned that Second Wave users concentrate mainly on computers as machines whereas educational users view computers as a transparent medium through which instruction flows.

6. We learned that because the software needed by Third Wave users is developed by Second Wave computer experts, educational users and the nonspecialist users have to be wary of some attitudinal pitfalls, specifically in the areas of user friendliness, hobbyism, and computer literacy.

7. We saw that educational software is getting more ''friendly'' in the sense that it is increasingly reliable and easy to use. But it is not so ''friendly'' in the sense that much of it is still not very computer imaginative—it does not sufficiently exploit the strengths of the computer as an educational medium.

8. We found that there is still a lot of pressure on Third Wave computer users like teachers to become hobbyists, or ''amateur professionals,'' willing to learn to adapt to software unfriendliness or to ''do it themselves'' when they cannot find good software. We decided that there is a place for teacher programming—for those teachers who want to do it—but to make the use of educational computers maximally effective, we need excellent preprogrammed software we can use the computer to deliver.

9. We saw that, while computer literacy is now a must for teachers and for all nonspecialist computer users, we need more emphasis on the teacher as user, less on teaching teachers about computers as machines.

NOTES

1. Alvin Toffler, *The Third Wave* (New York: William Morrow & Company, 1980).

2. Ellen Richman, *The Random House Book of Computer Literacy* (New York: Vintage Books, 1983).

2

How
Computers Teach

Having established that, from the teacher's perspective, the educational computer is best viewed as an instructional medium rather than as a machine, in this chapter we will examine the medium's strengths and weaknesses. Specifically, we will pose and answer three questions:

1. If computers cannot think, how can they possibly teach?
2. Why would a teacher want to use the computer to deliver instruction?
3. How do computers stack up against other instructional media?

CAN COMPUTERS REALLY TEACH?

Computers have many potential uses in education. They can keep records and do administrative tasks, they can be powerful tools to augment or enhance the learning experience, and they can deliver instruction. Each of these uses is important, and each will be explored in the course of this book.

Perhaps the most intriguing, challenging, even threatening of these uses, however, is the computer's function as a medium to deliver instruction. Teaching, after all, is the job of teachers. Developing a useful perspective of computer-based education (CBE) thus depends on coming to terms with how computers function to deliver instruction. No matter how useful and important, other functions of the educational computer are ancillary to the main purpose of education—teaching and learning. Only when teachers see where the computer fits into *teaching* will it be possible to assess the full impact of the educational computer.

Good teaching often is described as an intuitive activity. Good teachers do not simply present some content, provide students with practice, and then test it. They lead students through the material, pay attention to their questions and responses, figure out intuitively what problems students are having in understanding and applying the material, and offer remediation based on that intuitive understanding. The computer may, after all, be different from other machines, but it is still only a machine. Intuition and understanding are definitely outside its reach, yet these are the central requirements of good teaching. How, then, can a computer teach?

The answer is that it cannot. Computers do not teach; people teach. People build instruction into computer programs, the programs are run on the computer, and the student user receives the human's instruction. The computer is not teaching. As we saw in the last chapter, it is acting as a medium to deliver instruction. In that sense, the computer is very much like textbook, chalkboard, or video media. They also deliver instruction designed and developed by people.

Yet the computer is somehow different. Unlike other teaching media (with the single exception of the human teacher, who in performing some teaching activities may also be viewed as an instructional medium—a deliverer of instruction), the computer can *interact* with students. It can hold the instructional information built into its program in reserve, wait for the student's input to determine what information to supply, and then deliver it contingent upon the student's need. This ability to interact is the computer's greatest strength as an instructional medium. It is also this capacity that sometimes makes the computer appear to be thinking.

You may be familiar with Joseph Weizenbaum's famous program ELIZA. This program startled the counseling profession with its seeming ability to understand patients' questions as it interacted with them. Weizenbaum describes the program and discusses its implications in his fascinating book, *Computer Power and Human Reasoning*,[1] which you may want to read. As Weizenbaum forcefully points out, however much the computer's interactive capacity may make it seem to think, it is not thinking. Still, since CBE utilizes the interactive capacity of computers so integrally, it is important to have a conceptual grasp of what it *is* doing as it interacts with students.

How Computers Work

Any programmer will tell you: "Computers are dumb." In fact, they are capable of doing only four simple tasks:

- *They accept the INPUT of information* in the form of letters, numbers, or symbols.
- *They STORE information* in a form they use and interpret.

- *They MANIPULATE information in several ways:*
    Calculation. Computers add, subtract, multiply, and divide numbers.
    Processing. Computers sort, classify, summarize, and otherwise organize information.
    Comparing. Taking two pieces of information, computers check to see whether or not they are equal, and then do something depending on the result.
- *They give back stored information and/or the results of manipulations (OUTPUT) to the user.*

What is more, computers perform only one of these operations at a time in a given sequence. The sequence is predetermined by the program the computer is running. However, they do the operations very quickly and with a high degree of accuracy. These features of accuracy and speed make the computer good at the number crunching and data processing tasks for which they were originally designed. Our question is : How do these features enable the computer to function as a medium for delivering instruction? We hope the following discussion will make the process clear.

People Thinking versus Computer "Thinking"

If you know someone's name and want to find out his or her phone number, you look it up in the telephone directory. You open the book near where you think the person's name may be found, skip backward or forward to zero in on the right page, and then move down the appropriate column to find the name you want. In looking up the number, you proceed intuitively. You know, for example, that if the person's name begins with P that it is past the middle of the book but probably not by too much. When you get near the right spot, you might use the index entries at the top of the page or you might choose to quickly skim the columns, moving from one to the other rapidly and easily. That is the way people think.

Now, suppose you wanted to program a computer to do the looking for you. The strict, carefully defined, plodding process the computer would have to follow is very different from your intuitive approach, because computers do not know how to look up phone numbers; they only "know" the few simple operations listed earlier. Their lack of intuition, however, is made up for by the speed with which they can go through the steps of the strict process needed to locate a phone number. One of the manipulations computers can perform, you will remember, is to compare two pieces of information to see if they are equal. If you imagine the computer assigning numerical values to letters so that A is the smallest number and Z is the largest, programming a computer "to look up" a name and give you the phone number involves these steps:

1. First, someone must place all the names with their phone numbers into the computer's "memory" and write a program to do the searching. (INPUT)
2. The computer then stores the names and numbers in a form it can use, converting letters into numerical equivalents. (STORAGE)
3. When the user types in a name, the computer (running the program) converts it into numerical equivalents and goes through the list of names in its memory until it gets a match. (MANIPULATION)
4. It then displays the requested information for the user. (OUTPUT)

Computer "Thinking"/ Computer Teaching

That is how computers can seem to think when doing a very simple data processing task. It is fairly simple, but it is not something you could ask your electric range to do. Conceptually, delivering instruction is a much more difficult task. But as our next example shows, the computer can do it.

Suppose a concerned mother, having dressed her little girl in her new riding hood (red for safety from hunters), is about to send her to grandma's house. The mother wants to make sure that her daughter knows what a wolf is—so that she can avoid wolves in the woods during her trip. She might hold up a picture of a wolf and ask her daughter, "What's this?" If the child answers, "A wolf!" to a few examples, the mother probably will be satisfied. If, however, the child identifies the animal in the picture as a doggy, an animal, or an elephant, the mother will explain the critical differences carefully to her daughter and test her with more examples.

The important point here is that, in teaching, various student responses *mean* different things. To confuse a wolf with a dog is one kind of error; to confuse it with an elephant is a different (but depending on the age of the child, not an impossible) error. In providing instruction to the child, the parent internally processes the nature of the response instantly and delivers the appropriate remediation.

Providing instruction and delivering the appropriate remediation may be pretty straightforward tasks, conceivably within a machine's capability. But surely the nature of the response and doing internal processing are *thought* processes beyond the scope of even the "smartest" computer. Well, they are, but *that* part of the instructional process is done by the human teacher who designs the program. It is well within the computer's capacity to *deliver* that human instruction. Compare the following steps taken by the computer in delivering this instruction to the steps in the earlier telephone directory example. They match perfectly.

1. Instead of placing names and phone numbers into the computer's memory, the CBE specialist puts in a variety of answers to the question, "What's this animal?" with appropriate instruction for each answer, then writes a program to search them. (INPUT)

   For example, the possible answer "elephant" might be paired with a unit that showed a picture of an elephant and the printed information: "No, this picture shows an *elephant*. Look at the elephant. It's very large, and it has a long nose called a trunk."

   Then, when the program returned the student to the picture of the wolf, it might print, "Think hard now. What's *this* animal?"

   A similar unit would exist for other animals with which the student might confuse "wolf," providing discriminatory feedback for each wrong answer.

2. The computer then stores the input in a form it can use, converting letters and pictures into numerical equivalents. (STORAGE)

3. When the student types in the name of an animal, the computer (running the program) converts it into numerical equivalents and goes through the list of names in memory until it gets a match. (MANIPULATION)

4. Then the computer either tells the student she has correctly identified the animal or delivers the feedback described above for wrong answers. (OUTPUT)

These instructional steps are represented schematically in Figure 2.1.

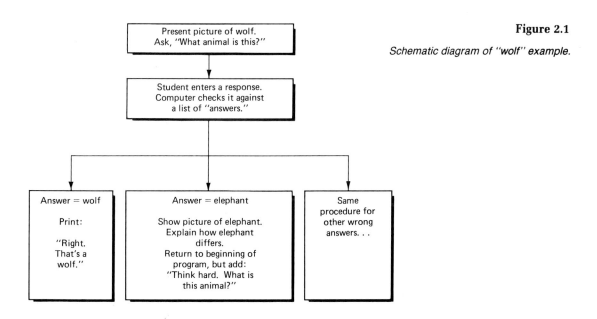

Figure 2.1

Schematic diagram of "wolf" example.

INSTRUCTIONAL STRENGTHS OF THE COMPUTER

In Chapter 1 we said that good computer-based education depends on effective exploitation of the computer's strengths as an instructional medium. The preceding discussion of how the computer works in an instructional environment enables us now to specify the precise nature of those strengths. The examples we have seen show that it is the computer's capacity for *interaction* that sets it apart from other instructional media and defines its unique strengths. Although this is only one of the computer's educational strengths, it is an especially important one for teachers as Third Wave computer users.

On the one hand, the computer is just a machine. Like a punch press or a vacuum cleaner, the computer only does a few simple things in a rigidly prescribed and machinelike fashion. No wonder, as we saw in the last chapter, it was invented and used exclusively for data processing and number crunching for so long! Those are rigidly prescribed and machinelike tasks—Second Wave tasks. Yet internally, when it is delivering instruction, the computer is doing the same things as when it is processing data. In fact, much of the time, when it is delivering text and pictures to students, the instructional computer operates like an even simpler machine—the book. It merely stores information, holding it till the student gets it out.

On the other hand, the computer alone among mechanical instructional media is capable of an instructional subtlety that vastly increases its potential utility to the teacher who employs it. A book, a film, or any other mechanical medium has only one way to deliver the information it has stored: from beginning to end. You read a book "from cover to cover"; a film runs through the projector from beginning to end.

In contrast, although the computer stores information and presents it to students just as books and film do, and although it can only do the four simple tasks of accepting input of information, storing it, manipulating it, and providing output, the computer:

1. Stores its information in a fluid, electronic matrix, so that it can be held in reserve and presented to the student in *any* order—not just from beginning to end.

2. Is interactive, so that the student can put in information as well as receive it.

3. Can combine the potentials of fluid information storage and interactive ability to deliver the information its program contains *contingent* upon the student's input.

These unique abilities comprise its strengths as an instructional medium. They mean that computer-delivered instruction has the capacity *to adapt to* student needs as it delivers instruction. In other words, while books and films contain only *information*, an educational computer program may rightly be said to contain *instruction*—a combination of information and a way to deliver that information to students in a fashion determined by their specific needs.

Range of Adaptivity

As you might expect, not all instructional software is equal in its adaptivity to specific student needs. Not all computer-based lessons exploit the strengths of the medium to the same extent. For reasons we discussed in the last chapter, not all CBE developers have the same degree of computer imagination. In fact, the degree of adaptivity of computer-based lessons varies widely over a continuum bounded by wholly linear programs on one extreme and fully adaptive instruction on the other:

1. Some lessons resemble books, presenting information in an unvarying order to all students from beginning to end. Typically, they limit student "interaction" to pressing a key every now and then to replace information plotted on the screen with new material. Even this might be said to have some small advantage over books, because at least the student controls the rate at which the information is presented. Yet, it can hardly be called a "computer imaginative" use of the medium.

2. Somewhat better are lessons that present information rigidly from beginning to end, administer a little comprehension check at the end, then either "pass" the student (let him or her leave the lesson) or send the student back to redo the lesson and take the test again. Lessons with many practice items ordered like flashcard sets, with missed items moving to the end of the stack for review and further practice, are other variations of this minimally adaptive form of instruction. Again, the strengths of the medium are not being fully exploited—what the lesson does can as easily be done with print media. Such lessons fail because they do not correct problems as they occur the way a teacher would, stopping to correct the student, explaining the error, and providing further practice. They are too mechanical and not computer-imaginative. The student, for example, may well have forgotten an item by the time it returns, something he or she missed and was corrected for early in the lesson.

3. The best computer-based lessons are continuously adaptive. Their design anticipates the errors students can make, classifies them by type, and provides a remedial unit for each. Then, when a student makes an error on an item, he or she is not simply told to "try again" in machinelike fashion. The program checks a response for the type

of error it represents and provides instruction specific to that error. An especially computer-imaginative lesson will also bring that item (or, if appropriate, a similar item) back for review—but not at the end of the lesson. Review items should come at intervals that increase from a single intervening item to several intervening items to shape long-term retention.

The third lesson type shows computer imagination! It exploits the strengths of the computer as a medium—chiefly, its capacity to store information in a fluid environment and deliver it in any order contingent upon the student's particular needs. Yet, it uses only the simple machine procedures we discussed in the "wolf" example. As in all Third Wave uses of the computer, the machine and its capacities are not as significant as the uses to which they are put. Computer imagination is the key in Third Wave computing; machine power is the key in Second Wave computing.

Adaptive Instruction and the Student

Compare each of these cases from a student's point of view. In the worst case the student receives no remediation at all and therefore receives no instruction. If the student gets everything right, it can only be because he or she already knew it—or at least had sufficient clues to be able to pick it up in one pass.

Minimally adaptive instruction gives the student some practice with skills and knowledge that he or she finds difficult, but it forces the student to take all the instruction, whether needed or not. If such instruction is to be effective, it must teach and provide practice on all possible error types, thus running the risk of confusing students or boring them with information they do not need. It risks burying the needed instruction in a tangle of instruction that is not needed. It is inefficient; it wastes the student's time.

A fully adaptive lesson, however, delivers all the instruction a student needs, *but no more than he or she needs*. It utilizes the computer's capacity to hold information invisibly, not even showing it to the student who does not need it. At the same time, it provides a complete and detailed instructional routine, specific to the error the student has made, for each student who needs it. Thus, the fully adaptive lesson, though programmed just one time and in just one way (as a book is written just once and in one order), actually becomes a different lesson for each student who uses it. It provides a quick comprehension check for the student who already knows the information and skills the lesson teaches, and it gives a full, careful explanation of the material with lots of practice to the student who does not know it (just as a good teacher would).

Adaptive Instruction and the Teacher

Now consider each case from a teacher's point of view. Teachers need to have some assurance of what students have accomplished while working on the computer. When teachers administer instruction themselves, they know what students have learned. When the student is remanded to the computer, however, the teacher is not present during instruction and needs to know whether the students have learned what the lesson taught.

The nonadaptive lesson that just takes all students through the lesson in the same order offers no such assurance. The minimally adaptive lesson offers more assurance, but not enough. If students miss many items in a practice set, for example, and receive massed practice on them at the end, did they really *learn* them, or did they just remember over a short period during practice at the end of the lesson?

With fully adaptive instruction, the teacher receives complete assurance that students have learned the lesson's content. The remedial units provided thorough teaching and practice on specific error types, and the lesson shaped long-term retention. The teacher knows that by the time the students finish the lesson, they must know what it taught, because the lesson will have kept each student in instruction until he or she can perform all the tasks it presents.

WHY USE COMPUTERS TO DELIVER INSTRUCTION?

In essence, we have been saying that when the computer is used as a medium to deliver fully adaptive instruction, it does many of the things a good teacher does—not *imitating* the teacher if it is good, but nevertheless addressing the same instructional objectives. That fact, however, raises an important question for the teacher: "If the computer merely does what I already do, why do I need it?"

We pose this question not so much to determine *whether* you should use computers in your instructional environment but literally to ask, "What should you use them *for*?" Just as good computer-based lessons utilize the strengths of the medium to deliver instruction, certain *applications* of computer instruction are particularly appropriate to the medium. Even the best instruction must be used properly if it is to be effective. The best designed screwdriver in the world cannot perform as well at hammering as the worst designed hammer. This part of the chapter, therefore, looks at some of the most important ways to make best use of the best (fully adaptive) computer-based instruction we described in the previous section.

Individualized Instruction

Let us begin by comparing the human teacher to the computer in delivering the "wolf" lesson again. When the mother is administering the instruction, and the little girl points to the picture of the wolf and says, "Doggy!" her mother can use the family's dog to make the discrimination. The computer cannot draw directly upon the student's experience in that way. If, when presented with the picture of the wolf, the student responds, "That's our Spot!" the computer would be lost. If the student's attention falters during the course of instruction, the computer cannot lead the child gently back to the important instructional task at hand. The computer cannot realize that the student is performing poorly today because she is sick and should be sent home. The computer cannot know when the student most needs praise or affection during the course of a lesson and could not provide it if it did.

In other words, in lessons like this one, the educational computer has some disadvantages over the excellent human teacher. If we had an inexhaustible supply of good teachers, and if we did all our teaching in a one-to-one setting, we would not need as much assistance from computers to deliver instruction, although we could still make other effective uses of educational computing.

But we do not teach one-to-one all the time—or even most of the time. Most instruction takes place in classrooms, where one teacher must interact with twenty or more students. In the classroom the teacher cannot give each child the kind of personal attention the mother could in the one-to-one situation described above. The teacher cannot draw on the individual personal experiences of each student in delivering the instruction. In the classroom the best teacher cannot continuously monitor the attention of every student as the mother could, teaching one-to-one. Nor can a single teacher assess and deliver praise and attention to each student in a large class just when he or she needs it most.

In fact, facing twenty students with varying instructional needs, abilities, and preparation for the current lesson, the teacher cannot deliver the fully adaptive instruction described in the preceding section to every student, but instead must teach to the class as a whole.

In other words, while there is no disputing the special advantages of delivering instruction by a caring, insightful, human teacher, the classroom situation often prevents even the best teacher from achieving this potential.

The computer, on the other hand, has a single powerful advantage: It can give its full attention, its best effort to *every* student, at the same time, individually. Compare, for example, the different ways in which a human teacher and a computer might deliver a lesson teaching punctuation rules for forming possessives. The teacher might have the students take out their texts or work-books and follow her as she presented this rule and demonstrated it with a few examples: If the word does not end with s, add an apostrophe and s to make it possessive. If the word already ends with s, just add an apostrophe after the s to make it possessive. Afterward, the teacher would probably use a set of sentences to test the students on the punctuation rules they had stud-ied, using one of the following techniques:

1. Assigning a workbook exercise as homework, collecting and grading it the next day, and returning it to the students the day after that

2. Doing the exercise in class, either by calling on students at random to fix the sentences or by calling on students who raise their hands

Both methods have problems. In the first, students get delayed feedback, often without remediation. They just get a check mark by the words they have punctuated wrong—or possibly just by the sentences in which errors occur. Remediation is up to them. Calling on random students is better in that imme-diate feedback and remediation can be given, but it is inefficient: Students who know which words need an apostrophe to make a possessive get instruc-tion they do not need. Calling only on students who raise their hands is prob-ably least satisfactory, because only students who know the answer are likely to raise their hands. Thus, the only feedback the class ever hears is "Good!" and no remediation is given.

How might a computer teach the same rules? The lesson illustrated in Fig-ures 2.2 through 2.4 is one of a series of computer-based lessons from the

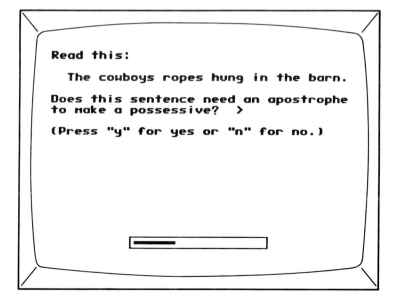

Figure 2.2

Computer-based lesson on pos-sessives. Step one: Student is asked to determine whether the sentence contains a possessive. From R. C. Dixon, M. A. Siegel, and J. M. Felty, "SRA Writing Skills: Punctuation" (Chicago: Science Research Associates, Inc., 1984). Copyright © 1984 by Sci-ence Research Associates, Inc. All rights reserved. Reproduced with the permission of the publisher.

"SRA Writing Skills: Punctuation" program.[2] The lesson shown is the consolidation drill for a sequence of lessons on possessives. The lesson has three steps:

1. The student must determine whether or not the sentence presented needs an apostrophe (Figure 2.2).

Figure 2.3

Computer-based lesson on possessives. Step two: (a) Computer requests the student to underline the possessive, and (b) gives feedback for correct response. From R. C. Dixon, M. A. Siegel, and J. M. Felty, "SRA Writing Skills: Punctuation" (Chicago: Science Research Associates, Inc., 1984). Copyright © 1984 by Science Research Associates, Inc. All rights reserved. Reproduced with the permission of the publisher.

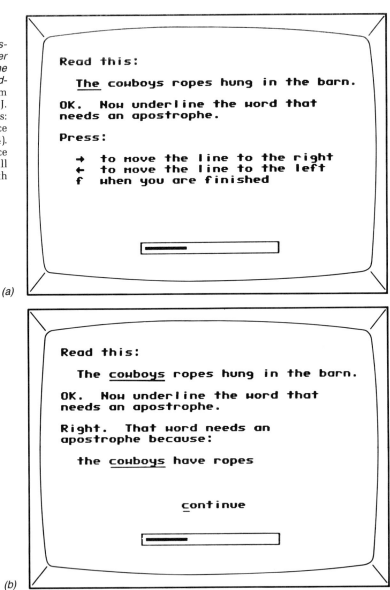

(a)

(b)

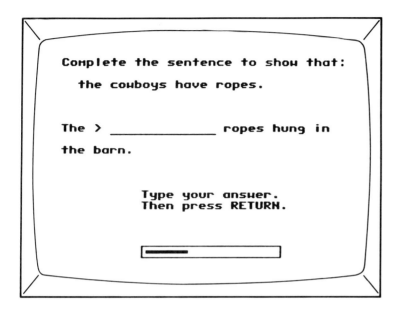

Complete the sentence to show that:

the cowboys have ropes.

The > _____ ropes hung in

the barn.

Type your answer.
Then press RETURN.

Figure 2.4

Computer-based lesson on pos-
sessives. Step three: Student
makes the required change. From
R. C. Dixon, M. A. Siegel, and J.
M. Felty, "SRA Writing Skills:
Punctuation" (Chicago: Science
Research Associates, Inc., 1984).
Copyright © 1984 by Science
Research Associates, Inc. All
rights reserved. Reproduced with
the permission of the publisher.

2. If so, the student indicates which word needs it (Figures 2.3a and
   2.3b).
3. Then the student forms the possessive correctly (Figure 2.4).

If the student gets the item correct, it is retired from the stack of items. A
missed item is returned to the stack for additional practice, recurring with
slight alterations after three intervening items and then again after five more
intervening items. In the first recurrence the lesson presents a different but
similar sentence requiring the same skill. In the second recurrence the original item returns, alternating singular/plural possessive forms. Thus, correct
answers to the three forms of the item might be:

Original Item: The cowboys' ropes hung in the barn.

First Review: The doctors' diplomas hung on the wall.

Second Review: The cowboy's ropes hung in the barn.

When a student who missed the original item and was remediated has performed successfully on the other two forms, the item is retired. If the student
misses an item at any point during the review sequence, however, the process
is begun again.

Getting the Computer's "Best Effort"

The preceding comparison of the two lessons was intended to show that, despite surface differences, both the teacher-delivered and the computer-delivered lessons teach the same content. Yet, in some ways the computer lesson is superior to that of the human teacher delivering the instruction to an entire class. The real difference between the two lessons is not what they teach but how they teach it, and it would quickly become apparent if you were to walk into a classroom in which several students were working on the computer-based lesson at the same time on different computers.

The first thing you would notice is that no two students were working on the same items or getting the same instruction, as they did in the classroom. Not only does the computer lesson automatically change the presentation order of items, it delivers remediation only to students who miss items. If you look at a student who is missing a lot of items, his lesson appears very different from the lesson of the better student who gets no unnecessary remediation (as he does in classroom instruction). The same lesson, programmed only one way, delivers instruction individually to each student according to his or her needs. Students are required to master each punctuation rule before the lesson terminates. If they miss an item, incorrectly applying one of the rules, it is returned to the list and it (or a slight variant of it) comes up in review several times, with an increasing number of intervening items between presentations to shape long-term retention.

Shaping Long-Term Retention

The value of new instructional media—the computer or any new medium—is that when you exploit their strengths and apply them appropriately, they make available something you always wanted but could not get. Textbooks, for example, when they were new, meant that teachers no longer had to memorize every fact students needed to learn. Chalkboards, when they were new, must have opened whole new vistas for the fluid and dynamic treatment of information.

The same holds true for computers. One particular strength of educational computers that stems directly from their original purpose as data processing machines is their "bookkeeping" ability—they are effortlessly able to keep track of several lists of things at the same time. The following example shows how this capacity can be powerfully applied to instructional uses.

A mainstay in the teaching of paired associates—those nasty little rote memorization tasks like spelling lists, math facts, the symbols of the chemical elements, and the names of the bones and muscles of the body, which are so tedious but so necessary—is the trusty flashcard drill. Teachers usually find flashcard drills boring; students do not like them either, for a variety of reasons. One problem is that when the student misses an item, the flashcard is placed on the bottom of the stack. If the stack is large, the student has forgotten the item by the time it recurs. And if the stack is short, the student gets the item correct (and it drops from the queue) even though he does not really know it—it is just that he saw it only one or two items ago.

Suppose, however, that we put the drill in a computer lesson. There are a couple of immediate advantages, often cited on the computer's behalf, that have made computer-based drills one of the earliest and most popular forms of CBE. One is that if the computer does the drill, the teacher does not have to do it. The other is that the computer is a patient and tireless driller that will work with the student as long as he or she can stand it.

Those are fine reasons, but you will notice that neither has much to do with the strengths of the computer as an instructional medium. But suppose that instead of just *imitating* the traditional flashcard drill (we know that is bad!), we come up with a drill technique that *utilizes* the computer's strengths as a medium.[3]

Let the letters in Figure 2.5 stand for a list of n items—each letter representing one item. It shows what happens when a student gets an item right. It goes to the end of the stack for review, because we want the student to get it right twice, just to be sure. But what happens when the student gets an item wrong? Figure 2.6 shows a situation in which a student has missed *two* items (*a* and *c*). If you look carefully at the chart, you will notice that missing an item sets the following set of steps in motion:

1. A missed item comes up for review two items later in the stack.
2. If the student gets it right there, it comes up *four* items later. If he or she gets it wrong again, the procedure starts with step one again.
3. If after four later the student gets it right, the item comes up again *six* later. (Again, missing the item starts the whole procedure over.)
4. Finally, if the student gets it right after six intervening items, the item goes to the end of the stack, because he or she still has to get it "completely right" twice—just as in the case in Figure 2.5.

Meanwhile, of course, the student is likely to miss other items as well, and the same procedure is invoked for each of them. Now, imagine a human

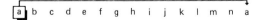

Figure 2.5

Missed item (indicated by the box) in a flashcard drill goes to the end of the stack for review.

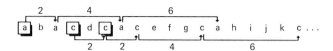

Figure 2.6

Missed items (indicated by the boxes) in a computerized drill are scheduled for increasing ratio review.

teacher keeping track of all that! And that is just for one student. Think what it would be like trying to drill twenty students at once while keeping track of all that for *each* of them! For the computer, however, the task is trivial—*if* you know how to program it to do this task. In fact, we saw it in action in the lesson on possessives just discussed.

The instructional advantage of this format over traditional flashcard drills is that it shapes long-term retention by returning missed items for review after increasing intervals. The point of this *example*, however, is to show how, in addition to utilizing the strengths of the medium, the format provides something teachers always have wanted to deliver but could not.

THE COMPUTER AS AN INSTRUCTIONAL MEDIUM

In Chapter 1 we endeavored to create a perspective that views the educational computer not as a machine but as a new instructional medium. In this chapter we have had occasion to compare it, by means of analogy and anecdote, to *other* instructional media. Before we turn in the next chapter to a consideration of the scope of computer-based instruction—the field whose function it is to create instructional *uses* for this new, exciting medium—it will be helpful to compare the computer to other media in a slightly more formal and much more synoptic fashion.

Computers versus Human Teachers

Shared Features   Computers share three main features with human teachers. Not insignificantly, each feature is related to one of the basic computer operations we discussed at the beginning of this section:

Computer as Instructional Medium	Basic Operations of Computers
• Interactive ability	• Accept user input Display output
• Ability to hold information in reserve in a fluid matrix	• Storage of information
• Ability to deliver information to students contingent on their performance	• Simple calculations

Things Teachers Do Better   Even though computers share all those features with human teachers, they do not interact and provide contingent feedback in the way teachers do. Teachers think, make rational judgments, understand language, and can draw on knowledge of the world and the student's particular experiences. Computers cannot.

Things Computers Do Better   When instruction must be delivered to several students simultaneously, computers offer the advantage of being able to attend to each student individually. At the same time, and partly *because* of their individualizing capability, computers can guarantee achievement, given appropriately designed instruction. In a limited sense, computers may also be regarded as better at storing information. Unlike most teachers, they have total recall; however, they can draw only on information that has been specifically programmed into them for the task at hand. They cannot reach into their "life experience" for additional information and bring it to bear on instruction.

    None of this is surprising; most of these insights have already been implied in this chapter's illustrations. A comparison of the computer to some other instructional media, however, may prove a bit more enlightening.

Computers versus Books

Shared Features   Both computers and books store information. Like computers, books may be said to be interactive to some degree. Textbooks "ask" students questions, and workbooks and similar materials accept student input.

Things Books Do Better   At least at the present time, books are more portable. For delivering long sections of text, books are unbeatable. Who wants to curl up in bed at night with a computer to read *Great Expectations*? (That advantage of books is not offered in jest. The educational advantages of a com-

fortable medium, while perhaps difficult to quantify, are not to be underrated.)

Things Computers Do Better   This is the telling category. For the task of delivering instruction, computers are better than books in almost every way. Their interactive capacity, their ability to withhold and reorder information, and their ability to deliver feedback contingent on student response make them more effective.

That fact may surprise you, but it should not. As educational media (not as repositories for information or devices for personal entertainment and edification), books have always been intended as adjuncts to instruction delivered by humans. By that we do not mean to imply that the computer will obviate human teachers. We mean only that, as an educational medium, the computer's strongest point is that it can work one-to-one with students in an interactive fashion. In fact, because of this quality, we can state that the computer *ought* to deliver individualized instruction to students, and it *ought* to guarantee to teachers that students working by themselves on the computer will return from instruction performing adequately on the skills taught by the computer lesson. As you will see, the same general facts are true of computers in comparison to video media as well.

Computers versus Film

Shared Features   Film (including television and video tapes) and computers share many of the same features as books and computers. Specifically, both media store information, and they are interactive to some extent. However, computers and video media vary in the nature of their interactive and information storage qualities in a different way than books and computers do.

Things Films Do Better   On the surface, the chief advantage of video media is obvious. They present information with a different kind of "fluidity": the continuity of movement and the blending of movement with sound. And they invite a different kind of "interaction" through the vividness of their mode of presentation. It is hardly surprising that significant research is underway to find effective and inexpensive ways to yoke video technology with computers in educational environments.

Things Computers Do Better   These advantages notwithstanding, the same features that distinguish computers from books also make computers a more powerful medium than film or television for delivering instruction. In addition, recent advances in computer graphics and color monitors have made today's computers more competitive with video media. Even though computers still lack the immediacy of impact that characterizes the realism of film and television, computer graphics actually exceed those media in ways that affect the delivery of effective instruction.

The Danger of Imitation

The converse of our statement that good instruction utilizes the strengths of its medium is of equal importance. Good instruction also avoids a medium's weaknesses. It is remarkably easy to violate this "weakness" rule in any instructional medium but particularly in the design of computer-based instruction. One of the most common and most insidious dangers is to try to imitate the strengths of one medium in another. You can see why that is so tempting. It represents the attempt to make a good medium even better by borrowing the instructional or applicational features that make some other medium especially effective. It is extremely well intentioned. Occasionally it works; more often it does not. Even when it does, it takes imagination and insight to make the right kind of translation.

So-called programmed instruction books provide a very good example of the ineffectiveness of imitation. The programmed instruction book seeks to imitate the interactive qualities of a human teacher in the print medium. Books, however, cannot "understand" a student's input the way a teacher can. Books are also limited because they are essentially committed to delivering the information they have stored in a prescribed order—from beginning to end. Programmed instruction books, however, represent attempts to overcome this limitation—to imitate the human teacher's (and the computer's) ability to store information away from the student in a fluid matrix and deliver it in different orders as needed. The results are often ludicrous. The print medium simply does not permit the same fluid and dynamic treatment of information as teachers and computers do.

Unfortunately, a number of CBE programs make similar errors, misjudging or neglecting to exploit the computer's best features. Most computer-based lessons, for example, that accept free-form student answers to questions (with "fill in the blank" items and especially with "short answer" items) fall into this trap. It may be fun for the developer of a CBE lesson to try to imagine in advance all the possible responses a student will make and put them in the computer's memory with appropriate feedback, thereby making the computer *seem* as if it can "understand" language like a human teacher. The technique rarely works. Too often the lesson designer fails to foresee some perfectly reasonable student response and to include it in the program's list of possible correct answers.

Imagine, for example, a computer lesson that describes a famous influenza epidemic and says, at one point, that 22 million people were killed. In the section that tests comprehension, one of the questions then asks, "How many people did the epidemic kill?" The most common answer would be "22 million." Another less common answer might be "twenty-two million." A perfectly correct but infrequently given answer would, of course, be "22,000,000." Suppose, however, that the lesson developer forgot to include it among the possible correct answers. When the student entered the correct but unexpected answer, the computer would haughtily state, "No, 22 million were killed." What would the student think? The computer lesson unsuccessfully attempted to imitate the human teacher's ability to understand a correct answer regardless of the form in which it was stated. No instructional value would have been lost if the lesson instead had used a multiple choice format (much more appropriate to a machine) to check that bit of comprehension.

WHAT YOU HAVE LEARNED IN THIS CHAPTER

1. Computers do not teach; they *deliver* instruction through programs developed by people. They do not think, although they sometimes appear to think because of their capacity to *interact* with the user.

2. In delivering instruction (or performing any other task), computers can perform only four simple operations:
   a. Accept the *input* of information
   b. *Store* information
   c. *Manipulate* information by performing calculations and by processing and comparing pieces of information
   d. Return information *output* to the user

3. The strengths of the computer as an instructional medium stem from the use of these simple operations in ways that enable the computer:
   a. To store information in a fluid, electronic matrix, so that it can be held in reserve and presented to the student in *any* order—not just from beginning to end.
   b. To interact with the student, permitting him or her not just to get information out (like other "mechanical" media) but also to put information in.
   c. To combine the potentials of fluid information storage and interaction to deliver the information its program contains *contingent* upon the student's input.

4. These strengths give the computer the ability to *adapt* to student needs as it delivers instruction. Computer-based instruction varies in its degree of adaptivity from strictly linear programs to continuously adaptive instruction.

5. Fully adaptive instruction gives the *student* all the instruction he or she needs but no more than that. To the *teacher* it offers an assurance of student performance—the teacher can send the student to work on the computer without having to provide constant instructional supervision.

6. We saw that, while good teachers working one-to-one with students have unique and indisputable advantages, computers delivering fully adaptive instruction are better able *to individualize* instruction administered to several students at once.

7. We discussed the dangers of weakening the computer as an instructional medium through attempts to imitate the strengths of other media, including human teachers, on computers. Good instruction, regardless of its medium of delivery, is never imitative.

NOTES

1. Joseph Weizenbaum, *Computer Power and Human Reasoning* (San Francisco: W. H. Freeman & Co., 1976), pp. 1–10.

2. Robert C. Dixon, Martin A. Siegel, and J. Michael Felty, "SRA Writing Skills: Punctuation," Computer-Based Education Lessons (Chicago: Science Research Associates, 1984).

3. Martin A. Siegel and A. Lynn Misselt, "An Adaptive Feedback and Review Paradigm for Computer-Based Drills," *Journal of Educational Psychology* 76, no. 2 (April 1984): 310–317.

3
Approaches to Computer-Based Education I

In this chapter and the next we will present and discuss three different ways in which the field of CBE has been described. Each represents a unique point of view, and each has its own insight to contribute to our perspective. The three classification schemes are:

1. *The Global System.* Its particular strength is to differentiate instructional uses from other educational uses of computers. It serves to introduce the important topics of computer-based testing, computer management of instruction, and "complete teaching."
2. *The Instruction-Oriented System.* This system primarily attempts to differentiate the various types of computer-based lessons. Within the context of complete teaching, it serves to introduce the important notion of restrictive versus nondirective response modes in computer-based lessons and curricula.
3. *The Goal-Oriented System.* This system turns attention away from description of the shared features of individual lesson types and focuses instead on instructional outcomes. It leads to a discussion of the size of instructional computer systems, the particular strengths and weaknesses of microcomputers, large time-sharing systems, and new ways to combine the benefits of both.

MANY POINTS OF VIEW

In the first chapter we referred to the large and confusing quantity of literature directed toward new users of computers, including educational users. This literature on computing and small computers is bewildering, however, not simply because it is so vast but also because no clear perception of the new user has emerged. People seem to disagree about how much and what kind of knowledge teachers should have about computers, and we have suggested that consensus will continue to elude them until the Third Wave user comes to be perceived not just as an amateur programmer—until the notion of people interacting with computers much as drivers interact with cars becomes widely accepted.

Educational users share these problems with all new users, but they have additional problems as well. If you have had an opportunity to compare a number of computer-based educational (CBE) programs, you have probably noticed that choosing among them is even more difficult than choosing among textbooks, and that is certainly difficult enough.

Like textbooks, educational programs differ from one another in the things they teach; in their style, layout, order of presentation of material, and so on. Unlike textbooks, however, CBE programs also differ in ways that are more specifically related to the computer, chiefly in the way their designers expect users to interact with the computer. Most confusing of all, CBE packages not infrequently differ from one another and from traditional classroom instruction in their most basic instructional goals. This lack of consensus about the use of the computer as an educational medium (a concept we hope is becoming familiar), more than anything else, makes approaching CBE lessons difficult.

The purpose of this chapter is to discuss CBE lessons not in specific detail but in general—to survey the field, to sketch the big picture before we examine individual approaches and individual lessons. Because of the kind of confusion new educational users experience when confronting CBE lessons (a much more important concern than the *amount* of confusion), we have given this chapter both a practical and a theoretical thrust. The practical thrust introduces the new educational user of computers to the wide range of approaches to computer-based education, classifying them in ways we hope will supplant bewilderment with order. The theoretical thrust continues to build our overview of the field by analyzing various classification schemes that have been proposed by computer-based educators.

In doing this, we hope to make you aware of the underlying attitudes toward computers in education and toward the goals of instruction, which are represented as much in the classification schemes we shall discuss as in the approaches to (or categories of) computer-based education they articulate. In other words, although we shall present our own organizational view of the

CBE field at the end of the next chapter, we think it important to familiarize you with other views, since our goal is not to present quick answers but to enable you to create your own workable perspective of the field.

DEFINING THE RANGE OF APPROACHES

Perhaps the best way to establish an awareness of the wide variety of approaches taken to instruction in CBE programs and lessons is to compare briefly a pair of lessons that represent the extremes of the range of approaches and the widest divergence of instructional goals.

The Logo Program

Developed at MIT under the direction of Seymour Papert, the Logo program attempts to teach children some important math concepts as well as problem-solving and intellectual modelling (heuristic) skills by teaching them to program computers using the Logo programming language.[1] In the beginning stages of instruction, children write programs that direct the activities on the screen of a cursor, called a Turtle. The computer graphics that the Turtle "draws" on the screen may then be manipulated in various ways. The Logo developers claim that as students learn how to perform the manipulations, they also develop more general principles. The following discussion demonstrates a few steps in the process of learning to manipulate the Turtle.

The small triangle on the screen shown in Figure 3.1 is the Turtle. It responds to simple commands the student types at the computer keyboard. FORWARD 100, for example, moves the Turtle forward "100 Turtle steps," and RIGHT 90 turns the Turtle 90 degress to its own right. The program allows the student to discover that four repetitions of those two commands produce a square on the computer screen like the one in Figure 3.2.

To teach the computer to "remember" how to draw a square, the student describes how "to square" in terms the computer "understands":

TO SQUARE
FORWARD 100
RIGHT 90
FORWARD 100
RIGHT 90
FORWARD 100
RIGHT 90

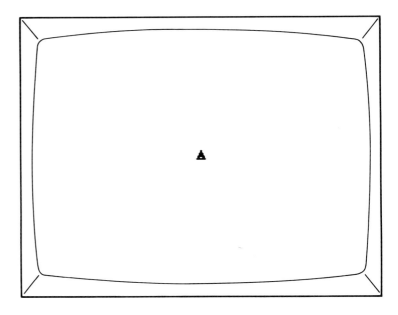

Figure 3.1

Logo Turtle on screen.

FORWARD 100
RIGHT 90
END

Then, whenever a student wants a square, he or she simply types "SQUARE"
and the computer executes the little program above. With more experience,
the student may discover programming shortcuts like this:

TO SQUARE
REPEAT 4 [FORWARD 100 RIGHT 90]
END

The idea of the Logo approach (which is discussed in much more depth in
Chapter 5) is that in discovering such shortcuts and additional manipulations,
the student learns not only computer programming but also what Papert calls
"powerful ideas."

The PLATO Curriculum Project

At the opposite extreme from Logo, the PLATO Curriculum Project (PCP) at
the University of Illinois has developed several computer-based basic skills
curricula for the educationally disadvantaged. The structured, individualized

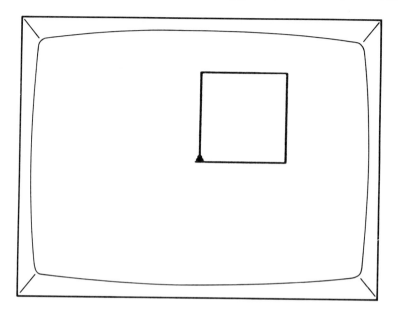

Figure 3.2

Square drawn by Logo Turtle.

approach of these lessons looks very different from the free-form, exploratory atmosphere in the Logo program. The following example briefly discusses a single lesson drawn from the PCP language skills curriculum.[2]

The lesson illustrated in Figure 3.3 is one of a series of lessons that presents and drills the rules for capitalization. The lesson shown is the consolidation

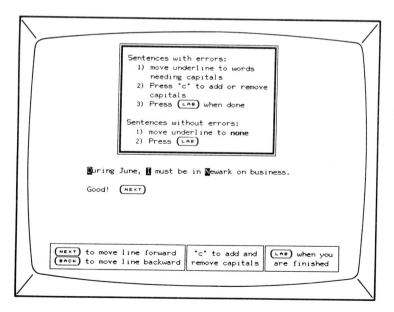

Figure 3.3

PCP capitalization lesson in which student has answered the item correctly. Copyright © 1982 by the Board of Trustees of the University of Illinois. Reprinted by permission.

drill, but the drills for each rule have the same format. In the lesson two kinds of errors are possible. The student may neglect to insert a capital where one is necessary or may insert one where it is not necessary. The lesson handles both kinds of errors.

In using the lesson, students press the keys indicated in Figure 3.3 to move the cursor and underline a word they think needs a capital; then they press *c* to capitalize the first letter of the word. In Figure 3.3, the student has marked the item correctly. (Note that this procedure is very specific to the instructional task; students are not required, for example, to *type* the words that need capital letters.)

Figure 3.4 shows what happens when a student makes a mistake. First, she gets a chance either to look at the rules (which appear on a separate display when the HELP key is pressed), or if she thinks she knows what she did wrong, on the strength of the negative feedback alone, she can try again. If after consulting the HELP page and/or trying again, the student still marks the item incorrectly, she gets instructional feedback similar to that depicted in Figure 3.5. Variants of the items in which a student makes errors recur in the drill after one intervening item until the student gets the item correct. Afterward, variants of the item continue to occur, but the number of intervening items is increased to shape long-term retention. This process continues until the student demonstrates mastery on all the rules of capitalization covered in the drill.

In part, our purpose in presenting and comparing these two very different approaches to CBE has been to provide a concrete demonstration of the broad

Figure 3.4

PCP capitalization lesson in which student has answered the item incorrectly. Copyright © 1982 by the Board of Trustees of the University of Illinois. Reprinted by permission.

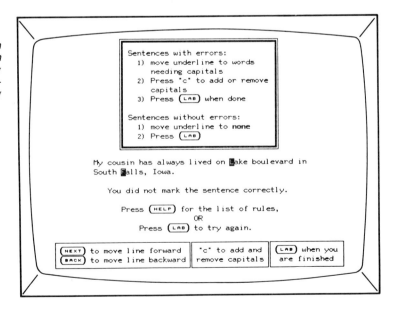

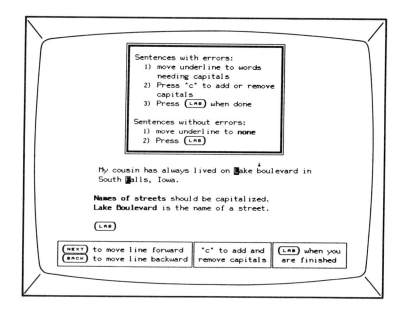

Sentences with errors:
1) move underline to words
   needing capitals
2) Press "c" to add or remove
   capitals
3) Press (LAB) when done

Sentences without errors:
1) move underline to **none**
2) Press (LAB)

My cousin has always lived on Lake boulevard in
South Falls, Iowa.

Names of streets should be capitalized.
Lake Boulevard is the name of a street.

(LAB)

| (NEXT) to move line forward | "c" to add and | (LAB) when you |
| (BACK) to move line backward | remove capitals | are finished |

Figure 3.5

PCP capitalization lesson showing corrective feedback. Copyright © 1982 by the Board of Trustees of the University of Illinois. Reprinted by permission.

range of subject matter, methods of treatment, and instructional perspectives found in CBE lessons and programs. Surely no greater contrast both in content and intent exists than that exemplified in the two lessons discussed. But the comparison also serves a more important function. Recognizing the extremes of the range in approaches to CBE is an important step in coming to grips with the problem of creating a workable perspective within which to view the field.

The next step is to look at various systems of classification of CBE that have been proposed by CBE experts. Each provides valuable insights into the field, and each has the further advantage of pointing up critical issues that affect the uses of computers in education. We begin by examining the global system of classification in this chapter and continue by examining two additional systems of classification in Chapter 4.

THE GLOBAL SYSTEM OF CLASSIFICATION

The focus of the global system of classification is to point out and describe the full range of uses for computers in schools. A typical structure, given in Figure 3.6, depicts the universe of educational computing in the schools (which the figure designates as educational applications of computers, or EAC) divided into two intersecting sets: administrative applications of com-

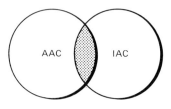

Educational Applications of Computers (EAC)

Figure 3.6

Universe of educational applications of computers (EAC) divided into administrative applications of computers (AAC) and instructional applications of computers (IAC).

puters (AAC) and instructional applications of computers (IAC).[3] Administrative applications include computerized school-wide rosters of enrollment and attendance, records of student schedules, final grades, transcripts, and so on. In the main, instructional applications include computer-based lessons like those described in the examples above.

Because of its wide scope, this system of classification provides no direct help in understanding and comparing individual lessons or computer-based instructional approaches. It is useful because it provides a context within which to introduce and clarify some confusing terminology.

In general, what we have been calling CBE encompasses both strictly instructional applications (lessons and curricula) and that segment of administrative applications represented by the shaded portion of Figure 3.6. (These shared functions include mainly computer-based testing and management, which are discussed more fully below.) Another term sometimes used to describe the same set is computer-assisted instruction (CAI). We do not like that term for two reasons. It is an old-fashioned term that to many people suggests some early, naive, and often unsuccessful computer-based lessons. More important, the term CAI excludes some important new approaches to CBE like the Logo program (see Figures 3.1 and 3.2).

In the first two chapters we talked at length about good CBE as being, in part, defined by the success with which it exploits the strengths of the medium. Well, there is no greater computer strength than data processing. And computer-based testing (CBT) and computer-managed instruction (CMI)—the functions that overlap administrative and instructional applications of computers—fall into this category because of their emphasis on classifying, sorting, comparing, summarizing, and storing large groups of data. In fact, because it exploits the computer in such an obviously traditional way, computer-based testing was one of the earliest of all educational applications of computers—in the scoring, storage, and norming of standardized achievement tests such as the Scholastic Aptitude Test (SAT).

Computer-Based Testing (CBT)

In forms like the SAT, computer-based testing is familiar to all. Testing gains a new dimension, however, when it is delivered on computer and linked *with* instruction. For example, even a simple adaptive testing structure incorporated within a curriculum (wholly or partly delivered on computers) opens up the possibility of criterion-referenced testing that ensures that students will receive necessary instruction and bypass instruction they do not need.

Figure 3.7 demonstrates the principle that might govern the simplest kind of adaptive test. Even though the figure is incomplete, showing the path of only two students through the test, it demonstrates how drastically the linking of testing with instruction changes the nature of testing and increases the power of both the test and the instruction. The figure shows that the test contains a sampling of easy and difficult items. "Student A" represents the path of the student who, because of poor performance, will take the instruction to which the test is linked. "Student B" represents the path of the student who will skip the instruction.

In the figure, *I* stands for items answered incorrectly; *C*, for items answered correctly. The first thing you notice is that the proficient student is given more test items than the less proficient one, which might seem unfair or inefficient. But consider: Since the test is linked to a computerized curriculum, the student who passes the test skips the instruction, whereas the student who fails it must take the instruction. Thus, it makes sense to test a prospective "skipper" more thoroughly, just as it makes sense not to waste the time of the "taker" in testing, when he or she will have to take the instruction in any case.

Such an adaptive testing structure would be used in a curriculum made up

	EASY Items				DIFFICULT Items						
	1	2	3	4	5	6	7	8	9	10	
Student A:	I	I									→ TAKE Instruction
Student B:	C	C			C	C	C	C			→ SKIP Instruction

Figure 3.7

Two students' paths through an adaptive pretest. Student A takes the instruction; Student B skips it.

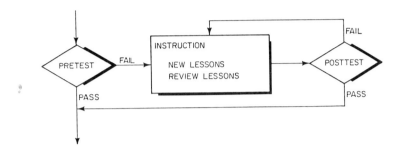

Figure 3.8

Instructional unit using adaptive pretesting algorithm.

of small units of instruction, each of which is formatted as in Figure 3.8. The individual units are linked within the curriculum in a plan shown schematically in Figure 3.9. It is beyond the scope of this chapter to go into the particulars of the structure in more depth. This brief description, nevertheless, suffices to show that testing and instruction—two areas that are often conceptualized separately but that the global system of classification links—are each made more effective by blending them into an integrated unit.

Computer-Managed Instruction (CMI)

Another way in which tasks that have traditionally been labeled administrative can be blended with instructional applications is in computer management of instruction.[4] In CMI, computers may be used not only for traditional classroom management and record keeping but also to develop and administer individual courses of study. The actual instructional units may be computer-delivered or teacher- and textbook-delivered. The term CMI, thus, is loosely used to describe all of the following activities:

1. A computerized gradebook
2. A classroom management program that records information on the topic on which the student is currently working (in an individualized computer-based curriculum): topic assignment date, time in instruction, past history of similar data for previous topics, and other information
3. A combination package with testing, like the one described above, in which the teacher may also use the computer to *prescribe* instruction (both on and off the computer) for students on the basis of diagnostic

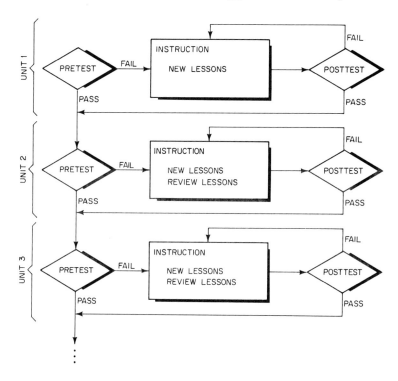

Figure 3.9

Linking of instructional units that use adaptive pretesting algorithm.

tests and may request reports from the computer on student and class performance

4. A fully automated package capable of delivering an entire curriculum or set of curricula on the computer—pretesting, prescribing on the basis of pretest performance, delivering instruction, posttesting, sending students to remedial lessons or advancing them in the curriculum on the basis of posttesting, and keeping full student records as described above—all with minimal human intervention (if desired)

As you can see, each type of computer management is more sophisticated than the preceding one and incorporates all the features of the preceding types. The first two can be easily implemented on microcomputers, and commercial products with these features are beginning to appear.[5] The GEMS system, custom developed in Utah, has many of the features described in the third type of management system.[6] Because of the amount of memory required (for data on students and classes, management system software, and computer-based lessons), only a few examples of the fourth type have been developed, mostly in research environments where large (mainframe) computers are already available. Nevertheless, they give us a glimpse of what schools can generally expect in the near future, and they permit us to specify many of the features computer management systems will eventually deliver to all teachers and students as Third Wave computer users.

Features of a Fully Automated CMI System

Basic Functions The first feature of a fully automated CMI system is its ability to develop an individual course of study for each student and track the student's progress through it, automatically keeping data on student and class performance for the teacher.

CMI systems can manage the delivery of both noncomputerized and computerized instruction, but only the latter can be fully automated. If computer-based lessons were used, the fully automated system would store the lessons as well as the student's individual course of study. A student using the computer could then get access to lessons individually, if he or she knew how to ask the computer for them. The diagram in Figure 3.10 represents this kind of direct access to lessons.

Figure 3.10

Direct student-user access to instructional lessons on computer.

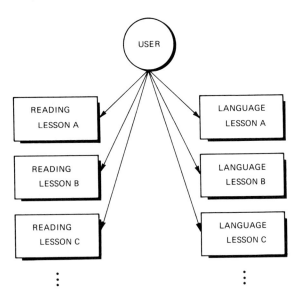

A chief strength of the fully automated CMI system, however, is that the students do not have to ask for lessons themselves. The management system, itself a large and complex computer program, finds the appropriate lesson in the computer's memory and delivers it automatically. So, instead of "entering" a lesson, the student "enters" the management system, which then delivers individual lessons to the student in the appropriate order. Figure 3.11 shows this kind of mediated access schematically. The figure does not, however, make clear the relationship between its curricular units and the individual lessons in Figure 3.10. Figure 3.12 shows that relationship. As you can see, individual lessons are but a small part of the functioning of a fully automated management system.

As it delivers computer-based lessons, the fully automated CMI system keeps track of the student's place in the lesson (so that if he leaves a lesson, he will be returned to the place where he was working when he left). It keeps data on his progress through the various curricula it has prescribed for him. It also provides communication facilities that enable the student and teacher to interact (and enable teachers to interact with one another and with the school administration). Finally, the fully automated CMI system continuously evaluates both student performance and instructional effectiveness (both summative and formative evaluation).

Figure 3.11

Student's path to instruction in a computer-based management system.

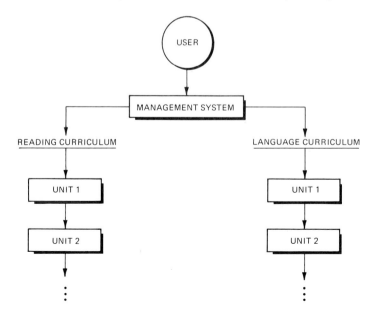

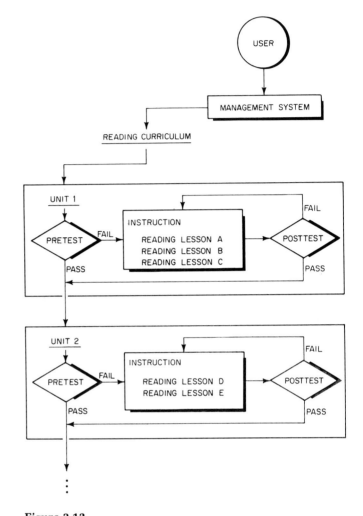

Figure 3.12

Relationship of individual lessons to a CMI curriculum.

Data on Students   The fully automated management system organizes students into groups and keeps the following kinds of data on individuals and groups:

- The student's date of entry into the curriculum
- Which lessons the student has taken (and which he or she was allowed to skip)
- How long the student spent in each lesson

- How the student did on pretests and posttests
- The date on which the student left the curriculum

(The system, by the way, stores all this data "invisibly." The student users see only lessons—just as if they had "entered" them directly.)

In addition, when a student leaves the curricular segment, all data on the student are automatically transferred to a separate storage file, out of the teacher's way but accessible at any time for the teacher to peruse, and for reports and evaluations.

Report Generation   Another part of the master management system consists of a group of programs that sort, tabulate, and analyze the various data by individual student, by lesson, or by group (a particular section, a school, etc.). In other words, in a fully automated CMI system, it should actually be possible to instruct the system to answer a demand like this: "Of all students either currently in the curriculum or who have completed it, tell me the number that, after skipping Units One and Two of the reading curriculum, passed the Unit Three posttest in two tries or less. List their names and print their records."

Teacher Options   So far, we have been looking at the fully automated CMI system mainly from the point of view of the student. The capacity of such a system to provide instant teacher access to student data, automatically tabulated and formatted in a variety of ways, however, can enhance teacher effectiveness remarkably. Thus, the system should permit the teacher to inspect the data and intervene in the instruction in several ways:

- The instructor should be able to inspect the past performance of students in his or her sections individually or by section, requesting the system to tabulate the data in any way that will be useful.
- Student performance on pretests and posttests should be available to the instructor item-by-item with the student's responses to items preserved. The instructor could then override the computer's prescription for instruction based on this information or on the basis of such "outside" information as the student's performance in the classroom.
- At any time, the instructor should be able to view any segment of the entire curriculum delivered by the management system in one of the following modes (listed in order from most general information to most specific):
  - List of all subject areas in which instruction is delivered
  - General prose descriptions of topics within a subject area
  - Specific structure of a topic (a list of the number and sequence of instructional units, consolidation units, tests)
  - All or any part of an individual unit

As a final check, at several points within the curricula a fully automated management system should automatically notify the instructor when problems arise or when human judgment is needed. For example, prescription of instruction on the basis of pretests should be part of such a system. Even though the system automatically administers and scores a pretest whenever a student enters a new unit of instruction, the scoring system is structured in three zones: automatic pass, indeterminate, and automatic fail. When a student scores in the indeterminate range, the system automatically instructs the computer to send a message to the instructor requesting a decision.

Complete Teaching

The preceding discussion of computer-based testing and computer-managed instruction shows that when testing, traditionally conceived as administrative in nature, is linked with instruction by a powerful and sophisticated management system, the power of both the testing and the teaching is enhanced. Doing some testing, some management of instruction, and some delivery of instruction on computers is good. Blending them makes each more effective and represents more comprehensive use of the medium's strengths.

The wide scope of the global system of classification of CBE has thus served to demonstrate that, whether in a fully automated management system or a more modest system deliverable with current microcomputer technology, the basic principle of management and computer-based testing still holds: The efficacy of both is considerably increased when they are delivered *with* instruction in "complete teaching" programs.

Our survey of the field of CBE continues in the next chapter, where we discuss two more systems of classification and explore the insights each contributes to the educational computer user's perspective.

NOTES

1. Seymour Papert, in *Mindstorms: Children, Computers, and Powerful Ideas* (New York: Basic Books, 1980), discusses the Logo program in detail.

2. Elizabeth J. Clapp, Albert Liu, Robert C. Dixon, and Martin A. Siegel, "Capitalization II," Computer-Based Education Lesson (Urbana: University of Illinois, 1982).

3. J. Richard Dennis, *A Teacher's Introduction to Educational Computing*, Illinois Series on Educational Application of Computers, No. 2e (Urbana: University of Illinois, 1979), p. 2.

4. For a thorough discussion of computer management of instruction, see Frank Baker, "Computer-Managed Instruction: A Context for Computer-Based Instruction," in Harold F. O'Neil, Jr., ed., *Computer-Based Instruction: A State-of-the-Art Assessment* (New York: Academic Press, 1981), pp. 23–64.

5. Examples are *K-12 Micromedia Gradebook* by Micromedia (172 Broadway, Wood-cliff Lake, N.J. 07675) and *BURSAR Student Activity and Accounting Software* (Reading, Mass.: Addison-Wesley).

6. See G. Stevenson et al., "Program Statement: GEMS" (Report on the Goal-based Educational Management System adapted by the Jordan School District, Sandy, Utah in 1976. The report was submitted to the Office of Educational Dissemination Review Panel in December 1978.)

4

Approaches to Computer-Based Education II

This chapter continues our survey of the field of CBE. In this chapter, we look at two more systems of classification, the instruction-oriented system and the goal-oriented system, and discuss the insights each can contribute to the educational user's perspective.

THE INSTRUCTION-ORIENTED SYSTEM OF CLASSIFICATION

This taxonomy focuses on the *kinds* of instruction delivered on computers. Like the global system, it has some problems, but it is worth discussing because it is frequently encountered and because, like the global system, it provides certain key insights into the field of CBE. The categories of lessons included in this system vary somewhat from person to person and source to source, but the list below represents a typical grouping.

Drills (often called drill and practice)   In these lessons the computer presents a stimulus to which the student supplies a response that the computer "judges" and for which it provides feedback (sometimes corrective, sometimes qualitative).

Figure 4.1 shows an example of a drill lesson for the Apple computer drawn from "The Elements," by Stanley Smith, Ruth Chabay, and Elizabeth Kean.[1]

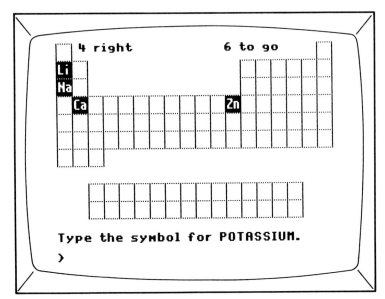

Figure 4.1

Selection from "The Elements." Copyright © 1983 by S. G. Smith, R. Chabay, and E. Kean, Introduction to General Chemistry (Wentworth, N.H.: COMPress, 1983). Reprinted by permission.

The Introduction to General Chemistry series, of which it is a part, was named best microcomputer software of the year by the Learning Periodicals Group in 1983. The lesson presents the names of the chemical elements, asks the student to type in the correct symbol, and then places the symbol in the periodic table when the student gets it right.

Tutorials   These are lessons in which the computer presents information in text (and/or pictures) and then questions the student to check comprehension, to ascertain the student's ability to apply the information, and so on. These lessons are often distinguished by their reliance on "natural language response mode." That is, the student types in a sentence or short answer in response to the computer's questions, and the computer interprets it. Some sophisticated tutorials try to engage the student in interactive dialogues of a Socratic nature.

Figure 4.2 shows a tutorial for the Apple drawn from "Chemical Formulas and Equations (Balancing Equations)."[2] Figure 4.2a shows some of the information presented to the student; Figure 4.2b shows an exercise that requires the student to use what he has learned to balance the equation.

Instructional Games   Many of these lessons aim at providing opportunities for students *to apply* concepts they have learned by creating situations that allow students to manipulate an environment freely. Competition against

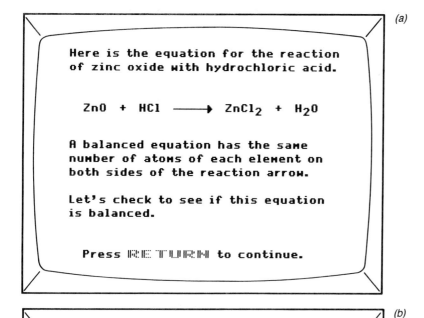

(a)

(b)

Figure 4.2

Two displays from "Balancing Equations": (a) shows the program presenting information, (b) shows the section that requires the student to apply it. Copyright © 1983 by S. G. Smith, R. Chabay, and E. Kean, Introduction to General Chemistry (Wentworth, N.H.: COMPress, 1983). Reprinted by permission.

oneself, an opponent, the computer, or a previous high score record characterizes lessons in this category.

"Chemaze," also from the Introduction to General Chemistry series, is a good example.[3] In this game, shown in Figure 4.3, the player moves a flask of reagent through the maze, removing chemical obstacles (and scoring points)

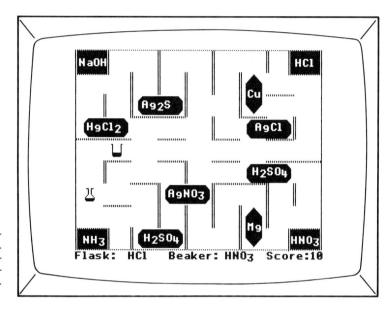

Figure 4.3

"Chemaze," initial display. Copyright © 1983 by S. G. Smith, R. Chabay, and E. Kean, Introduction to General Chemistry (Wentworth, N.H.: COMPress, 1983). Reprinted by permission.

by pouring reagent on them. Meanwhile, a beaker containing a counteractive reagent also moves through the maze to protect the obstacles.

Simulations Simulations are often similar to instructional games, but they usually concentrate on teaching the interrelationship of several factors in an interactive system, while games provide practice in applying just one or a few concepts. Many simulations make extensive use of the graphics capabilities of the computer.

Figure 4.4, for example, shows an early computer-based simulation, "Mouse," by R. A. Avner.[4] This simple, classic design was originally programmed in 1968, but it is still one of the best simulations. The program requires the student to apply operant conditioning principles to condition a rat in the box to press the bar (manipulandum) and get a pellet of food.

Stanley Smith's Introduction to Organic Chemistry series, shown in Figure 4.5, permits the student to simulate a sophisticated set of laboratory experiments on the computer.[5]

Still other simulations model more "conceptual" activities. One such simulation presents many of the decisions that confront a first-year teacher in the public schools—how to handle student behavior, interactions with other teachers and parents, and so on—weighing the decisions of the new teacher as the principal would. As an outcome, the simulation "predicts" whether or not the teacher's contract will be renewed! Still other simulations permit the user to change the weighting or interrelationships among data and instruct the computer to project the effects of the changes—on other data, as a func-

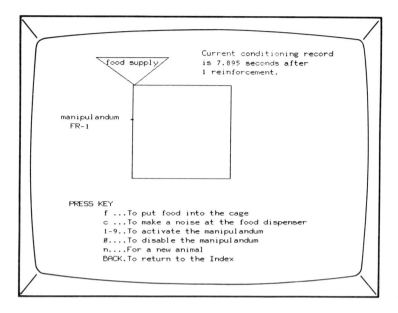

Figure 4.4

The "Mouse" simulation in action.
Copyright © 1968, 1975 by R. A.
Avner. Reprinted by permission.

tion of time, and so on. Such simulations are used to study topics such as population dynamics.

Programming This category does not refer to textbook courses that train computer programmers but to instruction that seeks to use the teaching of programming to develop other skills. "Skywriting and Spider Web," by

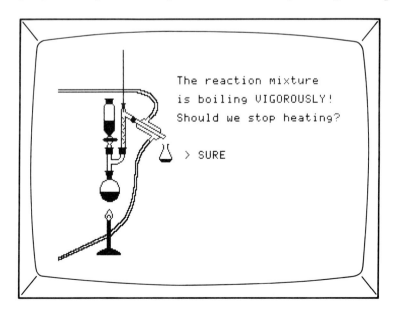

Figure 4.5

A display from "Introduction to Organic Chemistry." Copyright © 1983 by S. G. Smith, Introduction to Organic Chemistry (Wentworth, N.H.: COMPress, 1983.) Reprinted by permission.

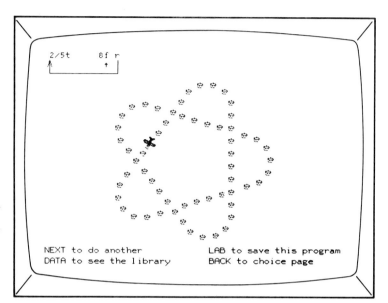

Figure 4.6

"Skywriting" in action. The program that controls the airplane's movements is given in the upper left corner of the screen. It says, in effect, "Turn ⅜ of a circle and move 8 units. Then repeat this procedure continuously." Copyright © 1975 by the Board of Trustees of the University of Illinois. Reprinted by permission.

Sharon Dugdale, David Kibbey, and Barry Cohen[6] (shown in Figure 4.6), lets young students write simple "programs" to move an airplane or spider around on the screen using just three simple commands: "f" to go forward, "t" to turn, and "r" to repeat the program.

As a system of classification, the instruction-oriented system looks better on paper than in practice. CBE lessons frequently overlap their seemingly clear-cut categorical boundaries. For example, it is not unusual to find lessons that combine the explanatory function of tutorials with practice in a drill segment. Instructional games set up a different mode of interaction between student and computer than drills; yet, both provide practice in using skills. The mode of interaction between computer and student in programming lessons such as "Skywriting and Spider Web" is very similar in many respects to a number of instructional game formats. The dividing line between games and simulations is often difficult to define in practice, and the category of simulations itself is so broad and difficult to pin down that one might easily question its utility.

Nevertheless, the list of instructional types provided by this system of classification is important to the user—not for information it provides about *lessons*, but for the insights it allows into the nature of the *field* of CBE. In fact, if you look carefully at a number of these lists in various sources, you will notice that the number of lesson types included varies, as we have said, but the order remains pretty firm, with drills at one end and programming at the other. Why should that be? No criteria for ranking or ordering are given, yet almost the same order emerges in each list.

Implications of the Instruction-Oriented System

Why does this system set up so many different types of instruction, and why do they seem to have designations peculiar to CBE? The notion of *complete teaching* provides part of the answer. A teacher in a classroom using traditional materials teaches "completely" and mixes several instructional types freely. A more common practice among computer lessons, however, is to address only one part of a complete teaching routine. A given lesson, for example, might only

- Present information and check comprehension, as a tutorial does.
- Provide practice examples of concepts taught with instructional games or strict "flashcard" drills.
- Demonstrate relationships within interactive systems with simulations.

Using a single instructional approach is not good, of course, and it limits the effectiveness of what otherwise might be an excellent CBE lesson. The instruction-oriented system designates as separate "instructional types" things that in classroom teaching are just *parts* of a complete teaching presentation. Several factors contribute to this less-than-satisfactory approach to the development of computer-based instruction. Most important among them is the fact that few full-scale computer-based *curricula* have yet been developed. CBE developers have been forced to concentrate on producing small, individual lessons that can be executed on currently available small computers. When choosing or evaluating CBE lessons, therefore, potential teacher/users must pay special attention to the completeness of instruction, or they will often be disappointed in the effectiveness of the lessons they implement.

CBE's concern for naming and differentiating instructional types also reflects the preoccupation of many computer-based educators with response modes in CBE lessons. The educational literature on response modes (true/false, multiple choice, fill in the blank, short answer, essay, etc.) is sizable, but it is mainly centered on testing. In CBE, however, the interactive capacity of the computer means that it does not just *elicit* student responses for testing; the computer *reacts* to student input in important ways, and they must all be programmed. Thus, it is not surprising to find CBE designers and programmers especially concerned with issues involving student response modes.

We have already seen that the list given above does not satisfactorily differentiate "instructional types." We submit that it remains popular among computer-based educators, however, because it divides CBE lessons according to response modes. And it is in this capacity that the *order* of categories on the list becomes important.

The criterion, seldom (if ever) expressed, for ranking CBE lessons in this list, is a continuum that views lessons on the drill end as using *prescriptive* response modes and lessons on the programming end as using nondirective response modes. Drill-end lessons, in this view, are mechanical, while those on the programming end elicit free-form responses—more, one might say, like human responses. In the strictest of paired associate drills on a topic such as the chemical elements, for example, the stimulus "Hydrogen" permits only "H" as its response. Compare that to the Logo example in the previous chapter, in which students can make the Turtle draw anything—and invent their own procedural language to do it!

This restrictive/nondirective criterion for ranking lessons is too simplistic to be of much use. "Appropriate" response conventions cannot be discussed in the abstract; they depend on the nature of the material being taught *and* on the medium that delivers it. To expect a prescriptive answer to a drill item on basic math facts is perfectly legitimate. It is wrong to denigrate lessons of this type just for the mode of response they require. (Actually, what usually happens is just the reverse: Some people praise lessons on the programming end of the continuum simply *because* they use free-form response modes, without taking into account the nature of the material or the medium of instructional delivery.)

Another of our comparative examples explicitly demonstrates the notion of "appropriate" response modes. Figure 4.7 shows the main display of a lesson that is used to help medical, nursing, and human anatomy students learn the names and spellings of the bones of the human skeleton with maximal effi-

Figure 4.7

Computer-based lesson, "Bone," main display. Copyright © 1978 by the Board of Trustees of the University of Illinois. Reprinted by permission.

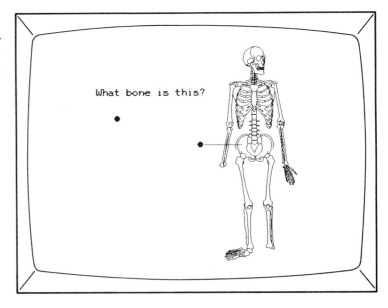

What bone is this?

ciency.[7] Although it may not look like one at first glance, the lesson is a classic flashcard drill. The lesson selects a bone and asks the student to type its name at the marker. A correct response moves the indicator to another bone, chosen at random, and the process is repeated. If the student gets the name of a bone wrong, the correct name is given, and the item is returned to the stack, coming up for review after increasing numbers of intervening items. If the student *confuses* the name of one bone for another, however, the drill behaves as in Figure 4.8. It shows both bones with their correct names and engages the student in discrimination training, both immediately and in subsequent iterations in review.

There is little doubt that the response conventions stipulated by this drill are mechanical in the extreme. There is also little doubt that the students who use the lesson (much of whose mental energy is consumed in striving to master conceptually difficult material in other courses) wholeheartedly applaud this very mechanical approach for its efficiency and effectiveness.

In contrast, consider this old, well-known story William James told. He said that a friend of his once visited a public school and stopped to speak to a class of children. Having ascertained from their teacher that the students were engaged in a physical science lesson on the structure of the earth, the visitor asked the class, "What do you suppose I would find if I were to drill a hole from right here to the center of the earth?" In spite of repeated attempts to elicit a response to that question, she was confronted with stony silence from the children. Finally, the classroom teacher suggested, "You are not asking the right question." Turning to the class, she pronounced in a clear, resonant

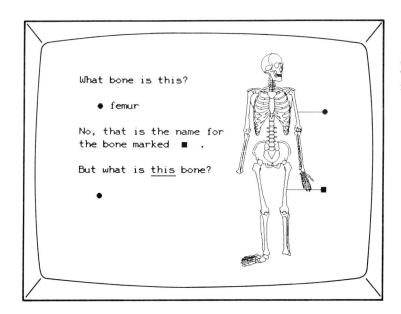

Figure 4.8

Discrimination training in "Bone." Copyright © 1978 by the Board of Trustees of the University of Illinois. Reprinted by permission.

voice, "What is the state of the center of the earth?" to which the entire class as one promptly and vociferously responded: "Igneous fusion!"

Clearly, prescriptive response modes are sometimes inappropriate. Our simple point is this: CBE lessons are neither good nor bad because they require prescriptive or nondirective interactions from students. They are good or bad because the mode of response they require is *appropriate* to the instructional content and to the mode in which the instruction is delivered.

THE GOAL-ORIENTED SYSTEM OF CLASSIFICATION

This taxonomy focuses on the instructional goals of different approaches to CBE. Robert Taylor suggested it in the book he edited, *The Computer in the School: Tutor, Tool, Tutee.*[8] The book is a collection of writings by CBE specialists. Like the instruction-oriented system, Taylor's scheme focuses on lessons and programs, but his change of focus to the goals of instruction makes it at once simpler and more powerful. As the title of the collection suggests, Taylor divides CBE lessons into three categories, which he describes:

THE COMPUTER AS TUTOR

To function as a tutor in some subject, the computer must be programmed by "experts" in programming and in that subject. The student is then tutored by the computer executing the program(s). The computer presents some subject material, the student responds, the computer evaluates the response, and, from the results of the evaluation, determines what to present next. At its best, the computer tutor keeps complete records on each student being tutored; it has at its disposal a wide range of subject detail it can present; and it has an extensive and flexible way to test and then lead the student through the material. With appropriately well-designed software, the computer tutor can easily and swiftly tailor its presentation to accommodate a wide range of student differences.[9]

In Taylor's description of the computer as tutor you will recognize many of the strengths of the computer as an instructional medium that we have discussed in preceding chapters. The example of the computer-based lesson on capitalization, presented in Chapter 3, is an instance of tutor-style CBE.

THE COMPUTER AS TOOL

To function as a tool, the classroom computer need only have some useful capability programmed into it such as statistical analysis, super calculation, or word processing. Students can then use it to help them in a variety of subjects. For example, they might use it as a calculator in math and various science assignments, as a map-making tool in geography, as a facile, tireless performer in music, or as a text editor and copyist in English.[10]

In the instructional process, then, the tool has a special place. Unlike the other two kinds of CBE, tools do not *deliver* instruction; they *facilitate* its delivery in ways we will discuss in depth in another chapter.

THE COMPUTER AS TUTEE

To use the computer as tutee is to tutor the computer; for that, the student or teacher doing the tutoring must learn to program, to talk to the computer in a language it understands. The benefits are several. First, because you can't teach what you don't understand, the human tutor will learn what he or she is trying to teach the computer. Second, by trying to realize broad teaching goals through software constructed from the narrow capabilities of computer logic, the human tutor of the computer will learn something both about how computers work and how his or her own thinking works. Third, because no expensive predesigned tutor software is necessary, no time is lost searching for such software and no money spent acquiring it.[11]

In Taylor's description of tutee-style CBE you will recognize the characteristics of the Logo example from the previous chapter.

Significance of Taylor's System

The best thing about Taylor's system is that it does not try to squeeze CBE lessons into cubbyholes. It is not so much descriptive as intentional. It does not call CBE lessons similar because they share some features, such as a non-directive response mode, as the instruction-oriented system does. Instead, in determining whether two lessons should be called similar, Taylor's system looks at where they are going. It focuses on the instructional outcomes that lessons try to achieve rather than on the means that are employed to get there.

Taylor's is the most useful system we have seen because it demonstrates as well as any other the differences among lessons. But it goes further. It helps make sense of the similarities and differences rather than merely listing them. It does not have to rank-order instructional types. Although Taylor has his personal preferences, his system of classification does not have to state (or, like the instruction-oriented system, *imply*) that some lesson *types* are better than others.

"Which is best: tutor, tool, or tutee?" is a question that you never need ask when looking at the whole panoply of CBE lessons from the perspective of Taylor's system. That kind of question is too abstract. It leads directly into the confusion we mentioned earlier, which many educators face when trying to make sense of the field of CBE. It leads to problems like this: "If tutee is the 'best' form of CBE, then does that mean that the best tool is worse than even the worst tutee lesson? If not, how good does a tool have to be before it is better than *some* tutee lessons?" That is the kind of confusion the instruction-oriented system plunges the user into. Who needs it?

Taylor's system, in contrast, need not be regarded as implying that one goal—one instructional outcome—is inherently superior. It cuts through the confusion, because it allows the user to differentiate lesson groupings meaningfully, and it directs questions of judgment to comparisons of lessons *within* a single category. The question for a user then becomes, "Given that I want the instructional outcomes at which tutor-style lessons aim, which of these two tutor-style lessons will provide them more effectively?" This change in perspective makes making sense of the formerly bewildering array of CBE lessons much easier.

Features of CBE Hardware Systems

Our discussion of the global system of classification introduced the topics of computer-based training and computer management of instruction, and our discussion of the instruction-oriented system introduced the topic of response conventions. In the same way, Taylor's system leads us to a consideration of the hardware features CBE computer systems need in order to be effective tutor, tool, or tutee environments. Especially in his description of tutor-style CBE, Taylor mentions several computer functions that extend beyond simple delivery of instruction:

- Recordkeeping (for management of instruction)
- Large banks of lessons available
- Extensive and flexible testing
- Individualization of instruction

When microcomputers were first introduced into the classroom, some of these functions were difficult to achieve on the hardware. In fact, there was a debate between proponents of microcomputers and proponents of big educational computer systems for development as well as instructional delivery. The former insisted that only big systems could deliver the additional features Taylor mentions, that microcomputers were too small for anything but delivering individual lessons—and even then, the degree of complexity of lessons (and thus, often, their instructional value) was severely restricted. Micro advocates, in turn, argued that big timesharing systems were too expensive for schools, often responded too slowly to students' interactions, were subject to frequent "crashes," and had problems transmitting data over long distances.

Both sides' claims had validity, and recent hardware developments have moved both big systems and microcomputers closer to a middle ground. On the one hand, big systems, like the PLATO system at the University of Illinois, have been working to develop decentralized "clusters" that eliminate many problems that bothered microcomputer proponents. In a cluster, a hub computer sends centrally stored lessons on demand to microcomputers linked to it, using very high-speed methods of transfer. Individual microcomputers store big chunks of lessons in internal memory while the student executes the lesson. Thus, they need "share time" with the hub computer much less frequently. Meanwhile, the cluster's hub computer is linked to the big central computer, so that users are able to communicate with one another and with the central system staff, just as they can on big timesharing systems.

On the other hand, current microcomputer technology has produced machines that have more computing power, faster response time, better and easier graphics generation and display facilities, and *lots* more storage. As a result, the size difference between large systems and micros has already almost ceased to be a significant factor in educational uses. In addition, hardware developments on the immediate horizon will enable microcomputers within a school or group of schools to link together in "networks," making communications possible.

In other words, the CBE hardware debate is being resolved as new hardware configurations incorporate the best of both big system and microcomputer capabilities. As Third Wave users, teachers, of course, are not intrinsically interested in hardware configurations. The debate serves mainly to direct our attention to this user-oriented question: As hardware developers and proponents find the middle ground, what computer features can we expect that affect *educational uses* of computers? Here is a partial list of hardware features that schools can expect to have in the near future:

Communications   The capacity to use educational computers to communicate—teacher to student, teacher to teacher, teacher to administrator, perhaps soon even teacher to parent—may evolve in several forms:

- *Electronic mail* permits users to exchange personal notes. Often, such systems work by depositing notes in a special file to which only the receiver has access. (This feature has many obvious educational uses. A special but not so obvious use: Teachers can use the so-called impersonal computer to personalize their classrooms by sending individual messages to students, commenting on their work, congratulating them, encouraging good performance or discouraging undesirable behaviors in an environment that is both private and special.)
- *Computerized bulletin boards* are often organized by interest areas. They permit users who share that interest to leave notes or respond to the notes of others. (In educational settings, an "interest area"

might be a club or activity, a class or homeroom, general school announcements, etc.)

- *Direct communication* facilities permit pairs of users to communicate instantly. Whereas the exchange of notes always involves delay, in the direct communications mode, users' messages appear on one another's screens as they are being typed. (In educational settings, this feature permits teachers to interact directly with students and facilitates student-to-student sharing of information.)
- Another communications mode available on computers permits any user to make his or her computer *"slave"* to that of another user. Thus, he can see on his screen what the other person sees as he works on a lesson. (In educational settings, especially when yoked with the direct communication feature described above, this feature is powerful. It permits students to share problem solutions and lets students consult with teachers individually from across the room—or across the nation.)
- A feature we could call *"lesson notes"* is still another possible form of communication on computers. These work almost like bulletin boards, except that they are linked to individual CBE lessons. They permit students to record questions or comments on a CBE lesson as they use it. The computer automatically tags the note with the student's name, noting his or her exact location in the lesson, and deposits the note in a special file to which the teacher has access. The teacher sees the student's individual problem and the exact place in the lesson where it occurred. Thus, even when several students are working independently on computers, the teacher can then attend to their problems and questions at any time simply by reading the lesson notes.

Software Maintenance   Just as a few typographical errors escape an editor's notice when a textbook or workbook is in preparation, errors creep into CBE lessons. Software, however, may have not only "typographical" errors (errors in a lesson's information content) but also small programming errors, called "bugs." Bugs are almost certain to occur on occasion, especially in good CBE lessons that permit students to take many different paths through the instruction. No matter how carefully a lesson is tested before publication, not every possible path can be checked. Thus, it is always possible for an undetected bug to be lurking in a program, unnoticed by the majority of students who take the tested paths, but lying in wait for a hapless victim.

Of the two types of possible lesson errors, bugs are worse. Typographical errors can be an annoyance, but bugs may cause the lesson to break down—suddenly the screen goes blank or will not accept user input or commands. Such bugs must be corrected—the software must be at least partly reprogrammed—before the lesson can be used again. When CBE lessons are delivered on cassettes or floppy disks, that process involves returning the faulty disk for exchange. When CBE is stored centrally instead of on floppy disks, however, a bug may be fixed in just one place. Exchanging disks is not necessary. This feature will greatly aid the reliability of CBE in our schools.

Formative Evaluation Educators have long wished for the ability to test and alter instruction systematically and in minimal ways in order to "tune up" its effectiveness, its interest to students, and the clarity and relevance of its explanations. In print media, this goal is impossible in a practical sense. Aspects of instruction can be evaluated, but the evaluation cannot be effected because a new edition of the text would be required each time a change was implemented.

On modern hardware with central lesson storage, however, formative evaluation becomes practical, because a "new edition" is instantly available. You do not have to reprint the whole "book" to incorporate a change; small segments of the program can be changed without affecting the rest of the program. And when lessons are stored centrally, rather than on individual disks, the old version of a lesson can be easily replaced with the new one. Thus, widespread use of CBE delivered by centrally stored lessons will open up new vistas for research on educational effectiveness and the mechanism of learning, and these results will be able to be implemented in existing instruction almost immediately. The impact on school curricula should be dramatic.

Instructional Scale Both the capability of small computers to store large amounts of information and their ability to hold and work on larger program chunks at one time are growing. Both developments have significance for education. Larger processing memory means that computers can run more complex, interesting, and useful educational programs more quickly. Increased storage capacity means that, instead of individual lessons, computers will soon be able to store and access large curricular segments or even entire curricula. The full range of computer-based instructional management and computer-based testing linked to instruction, which was discussed in Chapter 3, then become possible within a single package. Soon, in fact, computers will be available that will permit students to use them for hours at a time without ever having to stop, search for, and load up another disk—and at the same time the computers automatically keep excellent records for teachers.

A Working Perspective

Although each classification scheme we looked at had insights to contribute to the educational user seeking to build a perspective of the field of educational computing, Robert Taylor's system has proven the most useful. Taylor's categories of tutor and tutee represent the two sides of a continuum along which most computer-based lessons are aligned, some falling more toward the tutor end, some more toward tutee. At the same time, Taylor's tool category represents another direction of development in CBE orthogonal to the instructional continuum represented by tutor and tutee.

In the chapters that follow we shall examine in greater detail the goals of Taylor's tutee and tutor instructional approaches by looking closely at a representative of each. Then in Chapter 8 we discuss programs that use the computer as a tool, examining their place in the instructional process.

WHAT YOU HAVE LEARNED IN CHAPTERS 3 AND 4

1. We saw that all nonspecialist computer users face confusion that results from the conflict between the Second and Third Wave computing emphases. But we found that new educational users must also deal with a wide diversity of opinion about suitable goals for computer-based instruction.

2. We looked at a pair of strongly contrasting CBE lessons that demonstrated the range of variation in CBE instructional goals: the Logo program and a PLATO Curriculum Project lesson on capitalization.

3. We looked at the field of CBE from three points of view. First, we examined the global system of classification, which divides educational computing into instructional and administrative applications of computers and shows the relationship of computer-based testing and computer management to instruction.

4. We saw how testing and management can be linked to instruction, augmenting its power in "complete teaching" programs that use adaptive pretesting and sophisticated, automated management systems.

5. We found that the instruction-oriented system of classification, the second point of view we examined, identifies several instructional types, including drills (and practice), tutorials, instructional games, and learning through programming. It places them on a continuum with lesson types that use restrictive response modes at one end and those that use nondirective response modes at the other.

6. We learned that use of a restrictive response mode does not always imply that a lesson is "bad," and a nondirective response mode does not always imply it is "good." In computer-based lessons, as in human teaching or in any other instructional medium, the appropriate response mode varies with the nature of the teaching task.

7. We found that the third view we examined, the goal-oriented system of classification proposed by Robert Taylor, provided the most useful perspective on CBE. It categorizes CBE by instructional outcomes into programs that use the computer as tutor, tool, and tutee.

8. We learned that educational computer systems range in size from individual microcomputers standing alone to large timesharing systems. Each has educational advantages and disadvantages. Micros are currently much less expensive to implement and will, as a consequence, be the practical choice for most schools. The real issue, however, is not system size but whether or not affordable hardware systems can deliver capabilities educational users need.

9. We found that Taylor's categories of tutor and tutee represent a polarity that corresponds in important ways to the Second Wave–Third Wave polarity discussed in previous chapters.

NOTES

1. Stanley G. Smith, Ruth Chabay, and Elizabeth Kean, "Introduction to General Chemistry," Computer-Based Education Lessons (Wentworth, N.H.: COMPress, 1983).

2. Ibid.

3. Ibid.

4. R. A. Avner, "Mouse," Computer-Based Education Lesson (Urbana: University of Illinois, 1968).

5. Stanley G. Smith, "Introduction to Organic Chemistry," Computer-Based Education Lessons (Wentworth, N.H.: COMPress, 1983).

6. Sharon Dugdale, David Kibbey, and Barry Cohen, "Skywriting and Spider Web," Computer-Based Education Lesson (Urbana: University of Illinois, 1975).

7. Martin A. Siegel, J. Michael Felty, and James Mayeda, "Bone," Computer-Based Education Lesson (Urbana: University of Illinois, 1978); adapted from a lesson by Phil Seastrand and Mark Ciskey, "Anatomy and Kinesiology: Human Bones" (Ames: Iowa State University, 1978).

8. Reprinted by permission of the publisher from Robert P. Taylor, ed., *The Computer in the School: Tutor, Tool, Tutee* (New York: Teachers College Press, © 1980 by Teachers College, Columbia University. All rights reserved.). Material quoted from pages 3 and 4.

9. Ibid., p. 3.

10. Ibid.

11. Ibid., p. 4.

5

Logo: A Tutee Approach

The classification system of computer-based education (CBE) with which we ended the previous chapter borrowed concepts suggested by Robert Taylor, but it changed them from categories to poles on a continuum. Many practitioners of CBE would view the poles of tutor and tutee as corresponding to more structured and less structured lessons respectively. We have suggested, instead, that the poles more meaningfully separate CBE programs according to their views of the educational computer user and the instructional outcomes at which they aim:

1. For the educational computer user
   a. *Tutee*-style instruction seeks to make educational users better able to deal with computers on their own terms.
   b. *Tutor*-style instruction treats users as nonspecialists and seeks to make of the computer a transparent medium of delivery.
2. Regarding instructional outcomes
   a. *Tutee*-style programs seek to teach the unique skills of programming and problem solving on computer.
   b. *Tutor*-style lessons deliver instruction in the traditional academic subjects.

In this chapter we examine the tutee side of the CBE instructional continuum, discussing and evaluating the educational goals and emphases of the Logo program.

INTRODUCTION TO LOGO

The representative of the tutee approach we have chosen is the Logo Project, created by Seymour Papert at the Massachusetts Institute of Technology, described in a brief example in Chapter 3. We have chosen Logo for several good reasons. First, it is clearly representative of the tutee approach, perhaps the best example yet developed. Second, the Logo program is easily accessible for your further exploration. Third, Papert is an articulate and interesting educational theorist who espouses exciting ideas about the content and structure of education. Finally, the Logo Project is amply documented.

In addition to the Logo materials, we have relied mainly on Papert's book, *Mindstorms: Children, Computers, and Powerful Ideas*,[1] which explains the project and Papert's ideas about education. In addition, the *Final Report of the Brookline Logo Project*, Parts II and III, provide valuable information on Logo in action with sixteen sixth graders;[2] and the August 1982 issue of *BYTE: The Small Systems Journal*, which is fully dedicated to Logo, contains other valuable information and discussion from various points of view.[3]

THEORY OF LOGO

Logo is the name of a programming language, but it is also the name of a teaching method or program that uses computers and the Logo programming language to teach several things, including geometry and physics as well as computer programming. It is, therefore, instructional content, but it is also a way (Papert suggests a "revolutionary" way) to learn. Logo is, in fact, a whole learning environment composed of floor Turtles, screen Turtles, Dynaturtles, Turtletalk, and Microworlds. In Papert's terms, it seeks to use "syntonic" learning to create "child epistemologists" as it teaches programming, Turtle Geometry, physics, and such diverse applications as "concrete poetry" and juggling. Thus, familiarity with both the *intent* and the *method* of the Logo program is needed to understand Papert's approach to learning. In the sections that follow, therefore, we will first present a summary of Logo's goals, drawn from Papert's writings, and then examine the program as it is presented to students.

Seymour Papert is an avowed educational utopian. There is a great deal about traditional education that he does not like and wants to change. As evidence of the need for change, he cites the advanced state of dissociation of scientific and mathematical knowledge and thought processes from those commonly called humanistic. He fears that the gap between scientists and humanists might well increase as ours becomes a completely computerized culture.

"This great divide is thoroughly built into our language, our worldview, our social organization, our educational system, and, most recently, even our theories of neurophysiology," Papert claims. "It is self-perpetuating: The more the culture is divided, the more each side builds separation into its new growth" (*Mindstorms*, p. 38). He asks "whether personal computers and the cultures in which they are used will continue to be the creatures of 'engineers' alone or whether we can construct intellectual environments in which people who today think of themselves as 'humanists' will feel part of, not alienated from, the process of constructing computational cultures" (p. 5).

He is not trying to lay blame. Traditional approaches to education are both causes and results of the dissociation of humanistic knowledge from mathematical knowledge. Instead, he asserts that "fortunately, it is sufficient to break the self-perpetuating cycle at only one point for it to remain broken forever" (pp. 9–10). He wants to accomplish this goal by creating an approach to education that seeks to break down the "balkanized image of human knowledge" that divides it into "a patchwork of territories separated by impassable iron curtains" (p. 39). He argues:

> My challenge is not to the sovereignty of the intellectual territories but to the restrictions imposed on easy movement among them. I do not wish to reduce mathematics to literature or literature to mathematics. But I do want to argue that their respective ways of thinking are not as separate as is usually supposed. (p. 39)

Viewing the cultural gap from the side of the scientist, Papert calls it by a commonly known name: "mathophobia." The most basic and far-reaching purpose behind the creation of the Logo program may be described as an approach to education that seeks to cure mathophobia.

Curing Mathophobia

Logo teaches children (or anyone) to program computers. Papert's claim is that in learning to program, the student "both acquires a sense of mastery over a piece of the most modern and powerful technology and establishes an intimate contact with some of the deepest ideas from science, from mathematics, and from the art of intellectual model building" (p. 5). That statement is perhaps too modest. It is not merely learning to program that instills these deeper ideas, but the Logo approach to teaching programming. The Logo program is set up to teach programming students "to speak mathematics" and not merely to master a formal body of knowledge and skills Papert calls "school math."

Papert characterizes the difference between the Logo approach and the traditional approach to math in a metaphor. In his view, Logo seeks to teach children to deal with mathematics much as a person would learn to speak

French by going to live in France (p. 6). Another image he suggests is even more vivid:

> *Imagine that children were forced to spend an hour a day drawing dance steps on squared paper and had to pass tests in these "dance facts" before they were allowed to dance physically. Would we not expect the world to be full of "danceophobes?" Would we say that those who made it to the dance floor and music had the greatest "aptitude for dance"? (p. 43)*

Yet, that is just what we do for mathematics, he says. And that is what Logo seeks to remedy, by drawing upon the knowledge children already have as the basis for building further mathematical knowledge, *and* by anchoring formal mathematical principles in concrete applications that have real, immediate, and personal appeal for children.

Logo's Roots

Papert's comparison of Logo to language learning is not a random choice. The acquisition of language by children—untutored and spontaneously—is a central tenet of the learning theory of Jean Piaget, with whom Papert studied and upon whose work Papert's (with some important differences) is based. Especially important to Papert is the distinction between *formal thinking* and *concrete thinking*, which Piaget links to the child's stages of development. Papert, however, believes that "the computer can concretize (and personalize) the formal" (p. 21). In other words, to use the terms we have discussed in Chapters 1 and 2, because of the computer's capacity for interaction, for the dynamic treatment of information, and for contingent feedback, Papert feels that knowledge *content* can be taught in such a way on the computer that the process of acquiring it can also teach what he calls "powerful ideas"—*ways* of thinking and approaches to problem solving that extend beyond the content itself and make a "mathematics speaker" of the child.

The Logo Method

One important way in which the Logo method teaches powerful ideas is through the Turtle, which Papert describes as "a constructed computational 'object-to-think-with'" (p. 11). The Turtle is valuable as an instructional aid, because it can be made "concrete," yet its use embodies *formal mathematical relationships* and imparts mathematical knowledge. The Turtle, Papert suggests, is a "fundamental entity" like the point in Euclidean geometry, but unlike the point, the Turtle "can be related to things people know because . . . it is not stripped so totally of all properties, and instead of being static it is dynamic" (p. 55).

A Euclidean point is at some place—it has a position, and that is all you can say about it. A Turtle is at some place—it, too, has a position—but it also faces some direction—its heading. In this, the Turtle is like a person—I am here and I am facing north—or an animal or a boat. And from these similarities come the Turtle's special ability to serve as a first representative of formal mathematics for a child. Children can identify with the Turtle and are thus able to bring their knowledge about their bodies and how they move into the work of learning formal geometry. (pp. 55–56)

Whether all these properties are actually intrinsic to the Turtle or are in part dependent on the way the child is taught to use the Turtle in the Logo program remains to be seen.

We turn now to a discussion of Logo learning paths in order to see the Turtle in action. "The idea of programming . . . introduced through the metaphor of teaching the Turtle a new word" (p. 12) is an interesting and exciting approach. And so is the following sentiment expressed on page 5 of *Mindstorms*: "It is not true to say that the image of a child's relationship with a computer I shall develop here goes far beyond what is common in today's schools. My image does not go beyond: It goes in the opposite direction."

LEARNING WITH LOGO

This section observes the Logo program at work. It discusses some of the actual programming that students learn. At first glance, the profusion of computer programming may seem threatening, but actually it is not difficult. This section is followed directly by a critical discussion of the Logo program, which concludes the chapter.

Let us begin by looking at four ways to produce a square on the screen using the Logo language:[4]

Drawing

The most straightforward way to make a square is shown in Figure 5.1. The Turtle is the little triangle in Figure 5.1a. It is heading straight up. Instructing it to go FORWARD 100 produces the line shown in Figure 5.1b. The command RIGHT 90 turns the Turtle as shown in Figure 5.1c, and so on.

As you can see, drawing with the computer is easy and fun, even for small children. According to Papert, however, it is a lot more than just fun. One kind of learning that takes place right away, even with such simple drawing procedures, is discussed in *Mindstorms*. The initial commands can make the Turtle move only in a straight line. Suppose you want to make the Turtle

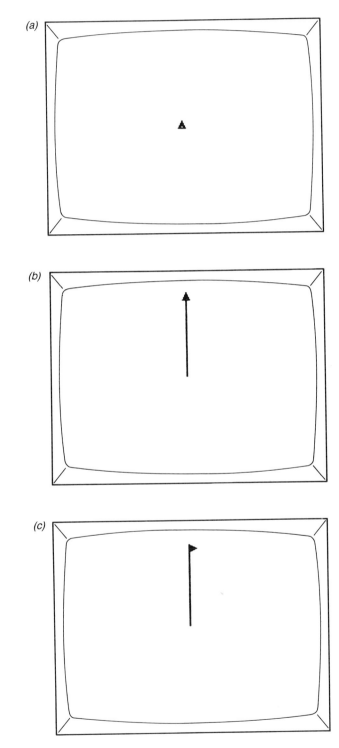

Figure 5.1

The Logo Turtle in action: (a) shows the Turtle's starting position on the screen; (b) shows the Turtle having executed the command FORWARD 100; (c) shows the Turtle having subsequently executed the command RIGHT 90.

move in a circle. The Logo teacher tells the students to "play Turtle"—to move their bodies as the Turtle would, in order to produce a circle, and to describe what is happening. Through the use of this "body syntonicity," students discover that a circle means "go FORWARD a little, then TURN a little," repeating the process many times until the circle is complete. Thus, by figuring out how to program a circle by "playing Turtle," the students not only get insight into the function of the computer language but also learn a mathematically sophisticated way of looking at circles.

In Euclidean geometry a circle is defined with reference to a single point (its center), which is not a part of the circle. In Cartesian (analytic) geometry, circles are also defined with reference to something outside them—the perpendicular coordinate axes—and they are expressed in equations. (The equation for a circle, for example, is $(x - a)^2 + (y - b)^2 = R^2$.) In Turtle geometry, however, the circle is defined without reference to anything outside. Its property of *constant curvature* is highlighted, and the Turtle program itself is "*an intuitive analog of the differential equation, a concept one finds in almost every example of traditional applied mathematics*" (p. 66).

Procedural Approach

Look again at the program for a square that leaves the Turtle in the same position in which it began:

FORWARD 50
RIGHT 90
FORWARD 50
RIGHT 90
FORWARD 50
RIGHT 90
FORWARD 50
RIGHT 90

To make a square this way, the same steps must be repeated four times. That there should be an easier way to do that seems clear. The next step in programming with Logo, then, teaches the concept of a *procedure*—in this case, SQUARE. The program for the procedural approach to drawing a square is given below. It is practically self-explanatory, even for someone who knows nothing about programming:

TO SQUARE
REPEAT 4 [FORWARD 50 RIGHT 90]
END

The most important thing the student learns here is probably contained not just in the procedure itself but in the comparison of the two ways to draw a square. Both do the same thing, so both *say* the same thing. The insight to be learned is in figuring out *why* and just *how* the two methods are equivalent.

Logo procedures have other, more far-reaching importance for programming, as we shall see, but they also have some interesting features that need no further explanation. One is that the student actually names the procedure himself. It might have been called BOX or even SQ. The sense of power over the machine that this process imparts is exhilarating for students and goes a long way toward creating the positive approach to math that is Papert's aim. In addition, once defined, procedures become part of the computer's vocabulary, and whenever the command SQUARE is given, the Turtle will draw a square.

Procedures with Inputs

The next way to draw squares adds a single (and thus easily comprehensible) important element to the previous way. This program:

TO SQUARE :SIZE
REPEAT 4 [FORWARD :SIZE RIGHT 90]
END

differs hardly at all from the last one, so it is easy to understand, but it introduces an important new concept—the *variable*—within the familiar context. The colon (called "dots" by Logoites) indicates that the word following it is a variable and asks the computer to put the value of that variable in this place within the program. You then use SQUARE just like FORWARD or any other Logo command that takes a tag or input. For a square with sides equal to 100 "Turtle steps," you type:

SQUARE 100

For a square with sides equal to 50 "Turtle steps," you type:

SQUARE 50

In the little programs above, SIZE is a variable that was *assigned* a value. That is a nice conceptual introduction to variables. It taught that the *word* SIZE did not change in the program when its *value* changed. Making spirals extends the concept and uses of variables.

To produce the square spiral in Figure 5.2, you *might* use a literal program like this:

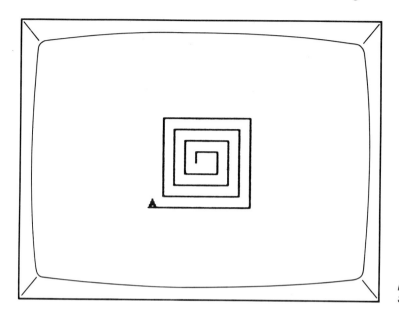

Figure 5.2

Results of executing the program SPI.

FORWARD 10
RIGHT 90
FORWARD 15
RIGHT 90
FORWARD 20
RIGHT 90
FORWARD 25
RIGHT 90
FORWARD 30
RIGHT 90
FORWARD 35
RIGHT 90
FORWARD 40
RIGHT 90
FORWARD 45
RIGHT 90
(etc.)

In *Mindstorms* (pp. 70–71), Papert explains the Logo approach to using *variables* to make a spiral:

In TURTLE TALK, variables are presented as a means of communication. What we want to say to the Turtle is . . . "go forward a certain distance, which will be different each time, and then turn 90." In mathematical language the trick for saying something like this is to invent a name for the "amount I can't tell you." The name could be a letter, such as X, or it could be a whole word, such as ANGLE or DISTANCE. . . . To put the idea of variable to work, TURTLE TALK allows one to create a "procedure with an input." This can be done by typing:

TO SPI :DISTANCE
FORWARD :DISTANCE
RIGHT 90
SPI :DISTANCE + 5
END[5]

In this program, "DISTANCE + 5" takes the place of the increasing increments of 5 Turtle steps in the long, literal version of the spiral square program above. Papert's point is that the student not only learns something valuable about programming, but he learns the concept of variable in a more personal and meaningful context than the way it is typically introduced in "school math," which presents it using equations like: "$5 + X = 8$. What is X?"

Simple Recursive Procedures

The program for the spiral above uses another important feature of programming and of the Logo language. The concept is *recursion*, and it simply means the ability of a procedure to be a subprocedure of itself. Part of the definition of the procedure SPI, in other words, *is* SPI. The program below shows a recursive procedure for drawing a square:

TO SQ :SIZE
FORWARD :SIZE
RIGHT 90
SQ :SIZE
END

The difference between this way to draw a square and the preceding one, which also used the variable SIZE, is that, in this one, the Turtle retraces its steps over and over the same square until you tell it to stop. It is the second to last line in the program that causes this recursion. In effect, the program says, "To make a SQ[UARE] of the SIZE I shall tell you, go FORWARD by the amount of variable SIZE, turn 90, and then keep doing this until I tell you to quit."

Again, the conceptual step taken is small and easy to comprehend, and if the program given above were executed, the results would look almost identical to the previous squares—not a very exciting addition. But when the variable named in the recursive step is increased each time, the program produces the SPIRAL described by Papert just above. (To check, compare the programs for SQ and SPI.)

From this point, it is but a single simple step to declare *two* variables in a recursive program and get an exciting graphic based on squares like that shown in Figure 5.3. The program to make the SPINSQUARE is:

TO SPINSQUARE :SIZE :ANGLE
SQUARE :SIZE
RIGHT :ANGLE
SPINSQUARE :SIZE + 3 :ANGLE
END

It says, in effect, "Make a SQUARE of the SIZE I tell you, then turn the Turtle to the RIGHT by an ANGLE I shall specify. Then (this is the recursive step) keep repeating the process until I tell you to stop, but increase the SIZE of the side of the SQUARE by 3 Turtle steps each time you draw a new one." Then, if you were to execute the program by typing, for example:

SPINSQUARE 1 20

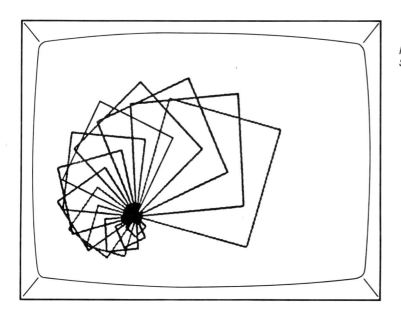

Figure 5.3

Results of executing the program SPINSQUARE.

the first SQUARE the Turtle drew would have sides one Turtle step in length; the second one, sides of 4 Turtle steps (1 + 3); the next, sides of 7 Turtle steps (4 + 3), etc. And each new SQUARE would be rotated 20 degrees to the right of (i.e., clockwise from) the previous one, as in Figure 5.3.

Notice that by this time the student has created a number of procedural cells that work together to produce the graphic.

- To execute the program, he types:

  SPINSQUARE 1 20

- To run that program, the computer has to know what "SPIN-SQUARE" means. The name refers to the recursive procedure with two variables that already has been defined:

  TO SPINSQUARE :SIZE :ANGLE
  SQUARE :SIZE
  RIGHT :ANGLE
  SPINSQUARE :SIZE + 3 :ANGLE
  END

- But to execute *that* procedure, the computer has to know the meaning of procedure "SQUARE." It was defined above, and its program is:

  TO SQUARE :SIZE
  REPEAT 4 [FORWARD :SIZE RIGHT 90]
  END

Thus, the student has learned something about structured programming, about recursion, variables, and procedures, and has done it in the context of creating an exciting computer graphic that is a lot of fun.

Programs with Text

After students have learned quite a bit about programming by using the Turtle, they have the programming expertise and conceptual background to tackle other kinds of problems. As an example, we will discuss a Logo program called POSTCARDS, but to do that we must first briefly examine another feature of the Logo programming language—how it handles collections of data organized in *lists*. Consider this list:

six

4

233.5

11 carrots

independence

The list has five items: some are numbers, some are words, and one of them (11 carrots) could even be viewed as a list within a list. An important feature of the Logo language is that it can handle lists like this, with different kinds of elements, of different lengths, and with internal subgroupings. And the language has a relatively simple way to format lists so that the computer can "understand" them:

[six 4 233.5 [11 carrots] independence]

Once the student has mastered the creation of lists, a program like POST-CARD can be fun. The main program is:

TO POSTCARD
PRINT SENTENCE [DEAR] NAME
PRINT BODY
PRINT (SENTENCE CLOSING [--] NAME)
POSTCARD
END

The language of the program is almost self-explanatory. It says, "To make a POSTCARD, PRINT "Dear" and someone's NAME, then PRINT the BODY of the POSTCARD, then PRINT a CLOSING, add two dashes and sign it with someone's NAME." (Notice that the second-to-last line is a recursive step directing the computer to continue generating postcards until you tell it to stop.) This main program, however, cannot function alone. It uses several procedures that also must be defined. Until you define them, the computer does not understand the procedures NAME, BODY, or CLOSING. So, the following declarations define them:

TO NAME
OUTPUT PICKRANDOM :NAMES
END

TO BODY
OUTPUT PICKRANDOM :PHRASES
END

```
TO CLOSING
OUTPUT PICKRANDOM :CLOSINGS
END
```

Now the whole program is almost complete. The commands OUTPUT PICKRANDOM ask the computer to go to *lists* called NAMES, PHRASES, and CLOSINGS, and randomly pick members of the lists to put into the POST-CARDS. (*Where* they go is specified in the main program.) Thus, for the whole program to work, all we need do is make up those lists. Here are some sample lists—anything similar would do:

MAKE "NAMES [JOHN DOROTHY [AUNT EM] OCCUPANT]

MAKE "PHRASES [[WISH YOU WERE HERE.] [WEATHER'S GREAT!] [SURF'S UP.] [EVERYONE'S FINE!]]

MAKE "CLOSINGS [LOVE [SEE YOU SOON] [WRITE SOON]]

When the student executes the program POSTCARD, the results are then randomly chosen elements of the lists, combined in a PRINTED format like this:

DEAR DOROTHY
WISH YOU WERE HERE.
LOVE--JOHN

DEAR OCCUPANT
EVERYONE'S FINE!
WRITE SOON--AUNT EM

As you can see, even though the Turtle has been abandoned and the student has moved on to working with text, the programming insights first introduced through the use of Turtle graphics are combined and extended in precisely similar ways in the POSTCARD and other text programs.

ANALYSIS AND EVALUATION OF LOGO

Papert's conception of CBE, as he promised, does not merely differ from the one we have articulated in Chapters 1 and 2, it "goes in the opposite direction." Not surprisingly, then, we disagree with the Logo approach in some respects. Nevertheless, we feel that much of the Logo program has unquestionable value.

Turtle Graphics

One of Logo's best features is the idea of introducing programming in the context of graphics and input-intensive programming. Any programming course must teach both the elements of the language and their application. In this respect, learning a programming language is like learning any new language. Students must study to acquire vocabulary and syntax, but they cannot be said really *to know* the language until they can use it *to express ideas*. Similarly, students can study the structure of a programming language in the abstract, but really to know it, they must practice using it to solve programming problems. A typical assignment, thus, would be, "Write a program to solve quadratic equations." This traditional approach to programming lacks the quality of concreteness described by Papert. You may be able to teach kids to write programs that solve quadratic equations, but if they do not understand *why* they are doing it, Papert feels that you have missed out on a valuable component of instruction. There is no good reason why kids cannot program problems that interest them and have concrete meaning for them.

The problems assigned in traditional programming courses lack another kind of concreteness as well. After the student has written the program, the computer "goes away" to execute it internally and out of the student's sight. The student programmer merely sees the *answer* to the problem magically displayed in an output statement. Compare that to Logo and the Turtle. Not only are the programming tasks we saw above more interesting and fun, but Logo's emphasis on input procedures and graphics makes them more concrete. When the student types, "FORWARD 100," the Turtle *does something!* And best of all, what the Turtle does is a *direct visual analog of the program.* Remember, Papert's goal was, in Piaget's terms, to find a way to "concretize the formal." That is precisely what Turtle geometry does. The student moves back and forth between abstract, "formal" procedures (computer programs) and "concrete" representations of the "formal" program in the form of graphics the Turtle draws.

The Logo notion of "playing Turtle" represents still another way to make formal concepts more concrete. Look again at how Papert describes the way in which a student might use the process to teach the Turtle to draw a circle:

> *The child has already learned how to command the Turtle to move forward in the direction that it is facing and to pivot around its axis, that is, to turn the number of degrees right or left that the child has commanded. With these commands the child has written programs which cause the Turtle to draw straight line figures. Sooner or later the child poses the question: "How can I make the Turtle draw a*

*circle?" In Logo we do not provide "answers," but encourage learners to use their
own bodies to find a solution. The child begins to walk in circles and discovers
how to make a circle by going forward a little and turning a little. ... Now the
child knows how to make the Turtle draw a circle: Simply give the Turtle the same
commands one would give oneself. Expressing "go forward a little, turn a little"
comes out in Turtle language as REPEAT [FORWARD 1 RIGHT TURN 1]. Thus
we see a process of geometrical reasoning that is both ego syntonic and body syntonic. (Mindstorms, p. 206)*

Nothing could be more concrete than the use of one's own body to provide
an analogy to an abstract, formal concept like the "computer program for
drawing a circle"! This *principle of body syntonicity* is even more important
in the use of "floor Turtles," which we have not been able to discuss because
of the brevity of our introduction to Logo. The floor Turtle is described by
Papert as a "cybernetic animal." It carries a pen in its belly and may be
directed to draw on paper spread on the floor, or may be taught to do other
things like navigate around obstacles. Like the screen Turtles we discussed,
the floor Turtles are also programmed using the Logo language, but they
embody the principle of body syntonicity even more strongly—they *actually
do what people and animals do when they move!* This added concreteness
makes them especially useful for teaching the principles of programming to
very small children.

Inductive Learning Techniques

The preceding discussion shows how Logo works well as a "tutee" approach
to CBE by teaching a unique content. Another measure of all good CBE,
whether *tutee* or *tutor*, is the success with which it exploits the strengths of
the medium, which include (1) the computer's ability to store information in
a fluid, electronic matrix, so that it can be held in reserve and presented to
the student in *any* order—not just from beginning to end; (2) its interactive
capacity that allows the student to enter information as well as receive it; and
(3) its ability to combine the potentials of fluid information storage and interactive ability to deliver the information its program contains *contingent* upon
the student's input.

The preceding discussion shows how well Logo exploits the first two of
these strengths of the medium, but how about the third? We have said little
in our discussion of Logo about *feedback*. The concept, however, is there—
subtly if not overtly—in the Logo program's inductive approach.

Induction is, of course, the deriving of general principles by reasoning from
the particular to the general—from the concrete to the abstract. The relationship of this definition to the Logo techniques is clear. Much of Logo's thrust
is based on the idea of reasoning to more abstract, formal principles from con-

crete instances of them, of building the unknown or not-yet-known out of the known through many examples. Having seen and done many "drawing" procedures using straight lines, for example, the Logo student induces the way to make the Turtle draw a circle and, Papert hopes, at the same time induces some higher-level concepts about the properties of lines and curves. (In fact, much of what he refers to as "spontaneous" or "untaught" learning seems to be induction at work.)

The inductive power of Logo is enhanced, however, by the Logo emphasis on input-intensive programming within the context of graphics. The children are encouraged *to tinker* with programs that they have written, and to modify, augment, and link them. Because of Turtle graphics, the child can change a program, then run it to see immediately what *effects* the change has. Although the potential for drawing wrong, incomplete, or unhelpful conclusions does exist in this undirected approach, it nevertheless illustrates how effectively inductive processes of teaching work on computers.

As an example, look again at the SPINSQUARE program:

TO SPINSQUARE :SIZE :ANGLE
SQUARE :SIZE
RIGHT :ANGLE
SPINSQUARE :SIZE + 3 :ANGLE
END

(Remember, the command that executes the SPINSQUARE is of this form:

SPINSQUARE 1 20

in which 1 specifies the value for the variable SIZE and 20 specifies the value for the variable ANGLE.)

After the student has written it, he might well ask (in fact, the Logo teacher would make sure he asked) questions like, "I know what SPINSQUARE 1 20 does, but what will SPINSQUARE 5 10 do? And what if I change the increment of SIZE to SIZE + 7 or substitute LEFT for RIGHT in the program? Would the same program work if I did it with a TRIANGLE or a CIRCLE?" Again the child is going from the known to the unknown, and general principles emerge from the manipulation of concrete individual elements in an interactive environment. Within this inductive process the execution of the program—the actual graphic the Turtle draws—is a form of *feedback*! In fact, it is a more useful form than, "Yes, you got that problem right," or "No, try again."

This form of feedback is an important part of Logo, but it is not unique to Logo nor to the use of programming as an instructional vehicle. A simple comparison to another CBE lesson (which also teaches math) makes this point

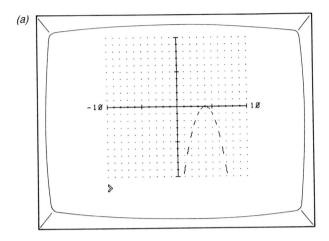

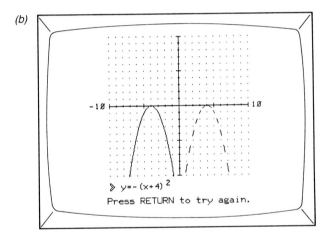

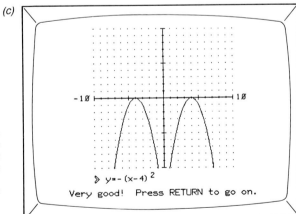

Figure 5.4

Lesson "Exploring Simple Graphs": (a) shows the target curve; (b) shows an unsuccessful attempt to match it; (c) shows final successful match. Copyright © 1979 by the Board of Trustees of the University of Illinois. Reprinted by permission.

clear. Figure 5.4 shows three consecutive screen displays from a math lesson, "Exploring Simple Graphs," by John Gilpin and Sharon Dugdale.[6] The lesson deals with the relationship between equations for curves and their shapes on the Cartesian coordinates. The lesson plots a curve like that in Figure 5.4a; the student supplies an equation at the arrow, and the computer plots the student's equation in another color on the screen. The student's goal is to plot a curve that exactly matches the target curve by entering a correct equation, but, as with Logo, the student's trial answers (Papert calls them "bugs") provide useful information, too. In fact, trial answers are a powerful *means* of learning relationships between curves and equations. Figures 5.4b and 5.4c show a student's first try and a subsequent matching answer.

"Exploring Simple Graphs" and Logo both use graphics. In both, students see the results of small changes instantly in a concrete and direct, visually analogous way. In fact, the only significant difference between the two in the way they teach their respective concepts is that the non-Logo lesson does not require students to know *anything* about programming, whereas in Logo students must master programming and the Logo language before they can use them to discover mathematical concepts inductively. If the goal is to teach programming, that is fine. If it is to teach the concepts themselves, Logo is inefficient. Worse, it is dangerous. Making the learning of mathematical concepts *contingent* on having already mastered the programming language runs the risk of failing to teach the concepts to a student who has not, for whatever reason, mastered the programming—which, in the context of the mathematical concepts being taught, is extraneous.

The point here is not to say that Logo is bad. For teaching programming, it seems to be very good. The salient issue is to recognize that *what* Logo teaches is *programming*. If the instructional goal is to teach concepts of mathematical problem solving, it is neither necessary nor safe to deliver them through the intermediary of a system like Logo that requires previous mastery of computer programming.

Some have challenged Logo as a way to teach programming. There are those who, to use their terms, have claimed that learning to program by the Logo method is like trying to learn economics by playing *Monopoly*. *Does* Logo teach programming effectively? We think it does, and we cite, as just one example, the ease with which the difficult concept of recursion was introduced in the discussion above. Consider the formal, abstract definition of recursion: It is the ability of a programming language to use a procedure as part of its own definition. Imagine that concept being taught in that form and then applied to programming tasks of equal abstractness. The definition itself seems simple enough, but grasping it in a way that leads to its meaningful *use* in actual programming tasks can be very difficult. Not in the Logo graphics, however.

Similarly, Logo introduces the concepts of computer variables, debugging, structured programming, and other programming skills in an exceptionally effective manner. In fact, many features of the Logo *language* itself (like list processing, described briefly above) make it well adapted to the kinds of programming tasks and learning methods the Logo "way of learning" emphasizes. Brian Harvey, in the article "Why Logo?" published in the August 1982 *BYTE: The Small Systems Journal*, discusses the special instructional features of the Logo programming language in clear and comprehensible language for those who may wish to compare it to other programming languages.[7]

Powerful Ideas

Papert has made the claim, however, that Logo teaches more than simply programming. In fact, he suggests (1) that it teaches "powerful ideas," and (2) that it can serve to break down the barriers that divide our intellectual culture into science and humanities. Let us, then, discuss those claims. What are Papert's "powerful ideas," and how do they bridge the cultural gap of which he speaks?

In "Logo—A Cultural Glossary" (also from the August 1982 *BYTE*), E. Paul Goldenberg provides definitions for some of Papert's "powerful ideas":[8]

- *State:* the relevant properties of something. For example, the state of the Turtle includes its position and the direction in which it is pointing, but does not include any of its past history (such as the distance it has traveled). The criterion of relevance here is that the Turtle's future behavior, in response to some Logo program, depends only on its current state and not on its past.
- *Recursion:* a recursive definition defines a procedure or function in terms of itself. (See discussion above.)
- *Subprocedures* (subproceduralization): Logo encourages students to deal with large problems by dividing them into subprocedures. In a "long, featureless set of instructions it is hard to see and trap a bug. By working with small parts, however, bugs can be confined and more easily trapped, figured out" (*Mindstorms*, p. 102).
- *Debugging:* improving the behavior of a program that does not do what you want it to. Logo emphasizes that programs that do not work as desired are merely unfinished, rather than bad finished products. This is in sharp contrast to many school situations in which a task is considered to be over when a particular time has come, rather than when it "works."

Remember, the "power" of powerful ideas depends upon their applicability to other things besides computer programming. Let us look at just one of them—"debugging"—to see how well it applies to nonprogramming tasks. Papert explains the power of debugging in the story of Pamela, who wanted to teach the Turtle to draw a house (*Mindstorms*, pp. 60–62). She began by programming procedures she named SQUARE and TRIANGLE, and put them together in a program called HOUSE:

TO HOUSE
SQUARE
TRIANGLE
END

What the Turtle drew is given in Figure 5.5a. There was a bug in the program. By "playing Turtle" and walking through the steps of the program, Pamela discovered that if she put LEFT 60 between the procedures SQUARE and TRIANGLE, she could get the drawing in Figure 5.5b. That was better, but it still had a bug. The final step in debugging was to begin the program with a RIGHT 90. The final program is given below. The house it drew is shown in Figure 5.5c.

TO HOUSE
RIGHT 90
SQUARE
LEFT 60
TRIANGLE
END

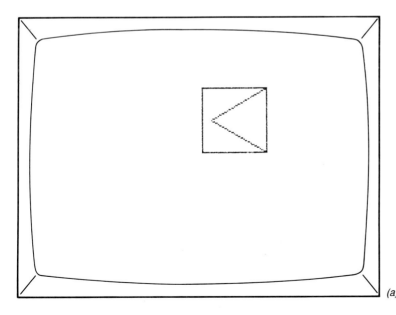

Pamela's "debugging" strategy. (a) shows her first attempt to use the Turtle to draw a house; (b) shows her partially debugged house; (c) shows the fully debugged house.

(a)

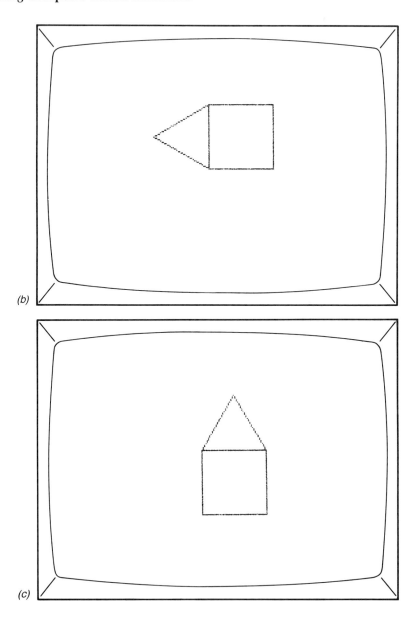

Figure 5.5

(Continued)

        Papert points out: "One does not need a computer to draw a triangle or a
square. Pencil and paper would do. But once these programs have been constructed, they become building blocks that enable a child to create hierar-
chies of knowledge. Powerful intellectual skills are developed in the process
..." (*Mindstorms* p. 60). The power of the debugging process is, then, that it

helps children to overcome the notion, often acquired in school, that "you have either 'got it' or 'got it wrong.'" Papert urges: "The question to ask about the program is not whether it is right or wrong, but if it is fixable. If this way of looking at intellectual products were generalized to how the larger culture thinks about knowledge and its acquisition, we all might be less intimidated by our fears of 'being wrong'" (p. 23).

The question is *how* to apply a concept like debugging to problems other than programming problems. Take, for example, the student who has written a composition in English class and has decided, after finishing it, that it is wrong. He wants to fix it, but he does not know how. If "debugging" in this context can only mean some general notion of "fixing," it will not be much help. If the child were an extremely perceptive Logo student, he might say, "Well, Logo is a language, and English is a language. I write programs in Logo, and I write essays in English. When a program is wrong, I debug it. How can I debug my essay?" In other words, do *techniques* of debugging learned in the context of Logo transfer to noncomputer problem-solving situations? It is hard to see how they might.

Debugging problems in computer programming usually are logical problems. If you say *clearly and unequivocally* what you want a computer to do, it will do it. Problems in writing have many different origins. They could be logical, but they could also be grammatical, stylistic, or conceptual. The student may know, for example, that the middle paragraphs of an essay need "filling out"—that they are too short. He has identified the bug, but he gets no notion from his Logo work about how to fix it.

There is another way to look at this "writing bug," however. The Logo definition of "debugging" we quoted above, in fact, contrasted the idea to that of "many school situations in which a task is considered to be over when a particular time has come, rather than when it 'works.'"[9] The definition goes on to point out that "in school, a written composition tends to be graded as it stands, rather than debugged. (If the teacher does encourage a student to improve a paper, the effort involved can be prohibitive.)"[10]

That is very true, but it is an entirely different point. Of course, it is easy to debug Logo programs. The programming applications are specifically designed to take advantage of the features of the Logo language that make debugging easy. The notion that computers could facilitate the process of fixing and improving students' compositions is certainly valid. It is not, however, the application of "powerful ideas" learned in a course on computer programming that makes the computer so useful in teaching writing. Instead, as the quotation above suggests, it is the fact that the computer can remove a great deal of the effort of recopying or retyping and the difficulty of handling information that has been fixed by being "committed to paper." (Remember, one of the strengths of the computer as an educational medium is its capacity to treat information in a fluid and dynamic fashion.)

Teaching "Applications"

The issue of the transferability of "powerful ideas" to nonprogramming situations (e.g., writing English compositions) brings up the larger question of applications. Specifically, what is the relationship between the things Logo students use the computer to work *on* (the problems they solve using programming, the subjects into which they delve as they learn to use the Logo language), and the primary learning that takes place (the mastery of computer programming and the Logo language itself)?

To highlight this issue, let us consider another Logo student's experience as reported by Papert in *Mindstorms*:

> *Well into a year-long study that put powerful computers in the classrooms of a group of "average" seventh graders, the students were at work on what they called "computer poetry." They were using computer programs to generate sentences. They gave the computer a syntactic structure within which to make random choices from given lists of words. The result is the kind of concrete poetry we see in the illustration that follows [Figure 5.6]. . . . One day Jenny came in very excited. She had made a discovery. "Now I know why we have nouns and verbs," she said. For many years in school Jenny had been drilled in grammatical categories. She had never understood the differences between nouns and verbs and adverbs. But now it was apparent that her difficulty with grammar was not due to an inability to work with logical categories. It was something else. She had simply seen no purpose in the enterprise. She had not been able to make any sense of what grammar was about in the sense of what it might be for. (pp. 48–49)*

At issue in this passage, from our perspective, is what was being taught—not what Jenny learned. There is a potential for confusion, and its source is a paradox associated with the teaching of computer programming. All programming languages, including Logo, are real languages, comparable to French or English in some ways, and this paradox is encountered in teaching any of them. Part of learning a language is mastering its vocabulary and syntax, but part of it, too, is learning *to use* the language.

To use the language, you must talk or write about some content. Even though students' performance in the language is affected by their grasp of the content they seek to express when using the language, that content forms no part of the course that teaches the language. That is the paradox. Every teacher of English composition is familiar with it. When students write essays on the advisability of nuclear energy, or take a stand on the issue of capital punishment, their performance on the skills of writing depends, to some extent, on their insight into, and mastery of, the subject of the essay. Yet, that is not what writing class is about.

On the other hand, on those occasions when students, in preparation for an assignment in English class, think deeply about or research their subject, they

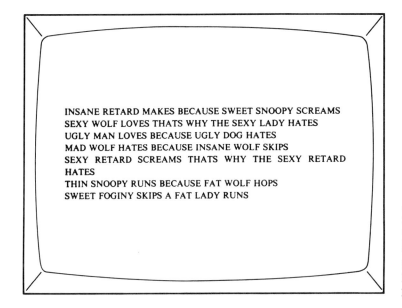

INSANE RETARD MAKES BECAUSE SWEET SNOOPY SCREAMS
SEXY WOLF LOVES THATS WHY THE SEXY LADY HATES
UGLY MAN LOVES BECAUSE UGLY DOG HATES
MAD WOLF HATES BECAUSE INSANE WOLF SKIPS
SEXY RETARD SCREAMS THATS WHY THE SEXY RETARD HATES
THIN SNOOPY RUNS BECAUSE FAT WOLF HOPS
SWEET FOGINY SKIPS A FAT LADY RUNS

Figure 5.6

Jenny's "concrete poetry." From figure, page 49, of Seymour Papert's *Mindstorms: Children, Computers, and Powerful Ideas* (New York: Basic Books, 1980). © 1980 by Basic Books, Inc., Publishers. Reprinted by permission of the publisher.

can (and often do) gain valuable insights about the essay's subject itself. That seems to be what happened to Jenny. In her class, which *taught* computer programming and the Logo language, she *learned* something about grammar. That is wonderful, but we must resist the temptation to conclude that insights into grammar or into other content areas from which applications are drawn (in Logo classes or any other language class) are somehow programmed into the instruction. Instead, they must be viewed as the English teacher views them—as delightful bonuses. It may be that in the story of "computer poetry," Papert has taken too much of the credit for Logo and not given enough to Jenny.

Our claim is not, then, that Jenny's discovery was without value—that somehow it does not count—because she came to it outside English class. We are just calling for a careful discrimination between what is being taught and what students discover on their own. And we do it for some practical reasons. Put it this way: Having found out about Jenny's discovery, can her English teacher confidently drop the study of nouns and verbs from the curriculum, allocating it to the Logo class? Of course not, and it is not only because few students will share Jenny's insight, although that would certainly be reason enough.

An even more important reason for keeping a clear fix on what is actually being taught is something we might call "hook up." It has to do with control of instruction. It is wonderful that Jenny discovered a rule about nouns and verbs. However, her English teacher still needs to control *how* she thinks about those concepts—not out of some desire to coerce her or stifle her creativity, but because the concepts do not, within the study of English, exist in isolation. Mastering them, understanding them—even with the depth of insight Jenny seems to have accomplished—is not all there is to it. If her insight is to be useful, she must think about the concepts in certain *ways*, so that she can build with them as her knowledge about English deepens and intensifies. That is the sense in which "applications" insights like Jenny's must be seen to be gratuitous. The insight she gained in Logo class will certainly help her in English class, but it cannot be a substitute for it.

This does not negate the indictment that Papert is making in the passage about the excess formalism with which concepts like *noun* and *verb* are often traditionally taught. What it indicates, however, is not that we need to teach English via Logo, but that we need English curricula that teach "powerful ideas" (or, as we call them, "big concepts") about *English!* Why, in other words, should students have to learn important things about English secondarily, as a byproduct of their instruction in computer programming? Papert is also right that the computer can be remarkably effective in teaching insights like Jenny's *and* in teaching them with "hook up." It is, in fact, a central tenet of this book that one of the best educational uses of computers is to deliver fully individualized instruction, precisely so that teachers can send students to the computer to work alone on individual topics. Because the educational computer has this capacity, however, it is absolutely necessary that the teacher know in advance *how* the student will return from individualized instruction thinking about the content delivered, and that this assurance be built into the instruction. (And again, the necessity of learning to program in order to gain the benefits called for by Papert seems questionable to us.)

The Dictum

> In many schools today, the phrase "computer-aided instruction" means making the computer teach the child. One might say the computer is being used to program the child. In my vision, the child programs the computer. (Mindstorms, p. 5)

This dictum is perhaps the most famous and widely quoted of Papert's many aphorisms. The notion of creating a computer-based educational environment, in which the child programs the computer to replace one in which computers program children, is attractive enough to serve as the basis for a Madison Avenue advertising campaign. With the preceding introduction to Logo and the critical discussion presented so far, we have a sufficient basis for examining it more closely.

First, we should make it clear that the two varieties of CBE to which the dictum refers are what we have called the "tutor" and "tutee" approaches. In terms of the dictum, the tutor approach is the "bad guys." But the central issue stated in the dictum is one of control: *Who is in charge?* Papert's claim is that in "bad" CBE, computers control children, drilling them and putting them through their paces, while in Logo, the children are in control. In Logo, the computer does whatever the student tells it to do. That is Papert's claim, but is it true?

We have stated that in the best CBE of what we now know to be the *tutor approach*, the computer functions as a *transparent medium* for delivering instruction in some subject area. We explained the concept of transparency by analogy to television, in which the viewer concentrates not on the TV set as machine, but on the programs it delivers. The medium is good if it stays out of the way and lets the programming flow through it to the viewer. In CBE for which that is true, the teaching is obviously done not by the *computer* but by the human teachers who have created the lessons or curricula that the computer delivers interactively as a transparent educational medium. Thus, using the computer to deliver tutor-style instruction "programs" students no more than tutor-style instruction delivered by teachers, books, or any other medium. Papert is a Second Wave computer person and places too much emphasis on the computer as a machine. As Third Wave users we understand that it is not the machine itself but the instruction it delivers that matters in educational computing.

So tutor-style CBE does not program students, but let us examine Logo on the same issue. Logo teaches students to program computers. At the surface level Logo thus presents no restrictions to the student whatever: Having learned the programming language, the student can use it to do whatever he or she wants. But programming languages are themselves restricted, artificial, severely limited, and constrained phenomena. It takes professional programmers years to develop skill sufficient to make the machine do what they want. And even then, they have to do it "the computer's way"—they have to work around the limitations of the machine and its programming language.

By forcing students to interact with the computer only in terms of a programming language, therefore, Logo frees students at the surface level to make anything they want, but it imposes the strongest kind of machinelike restraints (those of the programming language's limited vocabulary and syntax) on *how* they make it. Tutor-style CBE, however, which interacts with the student in English (not in a programming language), imposes no such intrinsic mechanical restrictions on how students think about what they learn (although *bad* tutor instruction can certainly make this mistake).

The difference, quite simply, is between concentrating on the machine and concentrating on the instruction the machine transparently delivers. It is the former, not the latter, that in a subtle, deeper, more enduring way "programs" children—by forcing them to interact with the machine on machine terms.

Logo and Complete Teaching

Our final criticism of Logo is based not on anything it *does*, but on something it fails to do: deliver complete teaching. Many of the things Logo does are excellent; a few seem to us to have problems. The failure to exploit the medium to the fullest in delivering complete teaching, however, is a problem shared among all the representatives of the *tutee approach* we have seen, not just of Logo.

In the story of Jenny and her concrete poetry, we saw a Logo-specific instance of the problem. Jenny learned something valuable about nouns and verbs, but the instruction in which she learned it did not *guarantee* that she had learned it. She might not have learned it, and many students going through the same programming lesson probably would not have learned it. Thus, the computer's utility to the teacher fell short of what it might have been if Jenny's teacher could have known in advance that the instruction that taught Jenny's insight to her would have taught the same insight to all students who underwent the instruction. Teachers need that assurance. Maximally effective CBE must permit students to pursue their own paths, but in such a way that the teacher knows what they have learned without actually having to be there watching.

In fact, in spite of the many excellent instructional insights it provides and the power of its "big concepts" (or "powerful ideas"), Logo seems to make no progress in individualization of instruction. That is unfortunate, since the computer's potential for individualization is so strong. Logo instruction seems to us to require, if anything, *more* teacher input, more time, and more specialized teacher training than traditional instruction. Even if the quality of the final instructional outcome is higher, that kind of labor intensification (on the part of both teachers and students) seems to miss the point about the kind of contribution computers can best make and will make to education in the future. If teachers *that* well trained could spend *that* much time with *that* few students, we truly would not need CBE!

We do not mean to claim that Logo does not permit students to work on their own, to pursue their own projects, create their own applications—in fact, enhance their creativity. Of course it does. Nevertheless, an instructional system that requires more intensive and specialized teacher training and more personal, intensive attention to students than traditional instruction can still not be called "individualized" in any meaningful sense. Too many demands are already made on teachers' time and attention to permit them sufficient high-quality personal interaction with students. We do not need to use computers to make *more* work for them. "Individualization" in the sense in which we use the term helps liberate teachers and students. Such individualization represents the best use of computers in education, and the best examples of the tutor approach create that kind of individualized instruction.

WHAT YOU HAVE LEARNED IN THIS CHAPTER

1. Logo's main goal is to teach children to program computers, and the program seems to accomplish the objective quite effectively. Its creator, Seymour Papert, claims that the program teaches much more than "just programming," and we have seen some examples that justify his claim as well as some problems with it. Our main objection to Logo centers on some educational objectives that it and other tutee approaches ignore.

2. We have suggested that the best features of Logo are:
   a. The teaching of computer programming through the use of direct visual analogs in an interactive graphics environment.
   b. The idea of using "syntonic" learning to "concretize" formal concepts.
   c. An inductive approach to instruction that utilizes the computer's capacity for fluid, dynamic treatment of information for immediate feedback.
   d. An instructional approach that deemphasizes abstract, excessively formal treatment of content in favor of building generalizations from known facts and situations.
   e. Instruction that aims at the teaching of "big concepts" or "powerful ideas" rather than merely the inculcation of facts and skills.

3. The main problems we find with the Logo approach are:
   a. For most of the goals mentioned above, the prior mastery of computer programming should not be necessary.
   b. Further, making instruction on some academic or problem-solving content contingent upon prior mastery of programming is dangerous; students who fail to achieve mastery on programming will consequently miss the content instruction as well.
   c. Insights into "powerful ideas" learned in the context of computer programming may not effectively transfer to nonprogramming situations, and even if they do, "hook up" may be ineffective.
   d. Some confusion seems to exist between the main content Logo teaches (programming) and "applications" knowledge that is incidentally imparted. Specifically, Papert sometimes seems to allocate students' "applications" insights to Logo without sufficient justification.
   e. In requiring *more* teacher training and input into instruction than is required in the traditional classroom setting, Logo fails to capitalize on the computer's special capacity for individualized instruction.

NOTES

1. Seymour Papert, in *Mindstorms: Children, Computers, and Powerful Ideas* (New York: Basic Books, 1980), discusses the Logo program in detail. Copyright © 1980

by Basic Books, Inc., Publishers. Quoted material reprinted by permission of the publisher.

2. Seymour Papert, Daniel Watt, Andrea di Sessa, and Sylvia Weir, *Final Report of the Brookline Logo Project. Part II: Project Summary and Data Analysis*, Artificial Intelligence Laboratory Memo No. 545 (Cambridge: Massachusetts Institute of Technology, September 1979); and Daniel Watt, *Final Report of the Brookline Logo Project, Part III: Profiles of Individual Students' Work* (Cambridge: Massachusetts Institute of Technology, September 1979).

3. *BYTE: The Small Systems Journal* 7 (August 1982).

4. This discussion and its examples are patterned closely after Harold Abelson, "A Beginner's Guide to Logo," *BYTE: The Small Systems Journal* 7 (August 1982): 88–112.

5. The colons were added to Papert's text to make this program consistent with the other Logo programs discussed.

6. John Gilpin and Sharon Dugdale, "Exploring Simple Graphs," Computer-Based Education Program (Urbana: Computer-Based Education Research Laboratory, 1979). A published version of this program, which provides a more structured learning sequence and adjusts difficulty to the student's performance, is found in Sharon Dugdale and David Kibbey, "Graphing Equations," Computer-Based Education Program (Iowa City, Iowa: Conduit, 1983).

7. Brian Harvey, "Why Logo?" *BYTE: The Small Systems Journal* 7 (August 1982): 163–93.

8. These definitions are quoted nearly verbatim from E. Paul Goldenberg, "Logo—A Cultural Glossary," *BYTE: The Small Systems Journal* 7 (August 1982): 210–28. Material quoted from pages 214 and 226. Copyright © 1982 Byte Publications, Inc. Used with permission of Byte Publications, Inc.

9. Ibid., p. 214.

10. Ibid.

6

Tutee to Tutor: Bridging the Gap

This chapter is devoted to making the conceptual journey along the instructional continuum from the tutee-style CBE of Chapter 5 to the tutor-style lessons and curricula that will be discussed in Chapter 7. In order to do that, we shall adopt a different perspective. "Tutor" and "tutee" are useful for differentiating computer-based instruction chiefly because they reflect the general educational concerns of two main branches of learning theory and instructional theory. The tutor approach corresponds to what Robert F. Biehler and Jack Snowman call the behavioral approach.[1] The tutee approach corresponds to what is commonly called *discovery* learning.

This is not an educational psychology text, so it is neither necessary nor appropriate to compare these two theories in depth here. In order to compare tutor and tutee meaningfully, however, some critical issues raised by proponents of these two instructional theories should be examined. Thus, we shall devote this chapter to a brief comparative discussion of the learning theories underlying these CBE instructional approaches, with the aim of facilitating the conceptual transition from the tutee to the tutor perspective.

A consideration of teacher-centered, learner-centered, and content-centered instruction provides the framework for our discussion. This will serve to introduce the important issues of instructional efficiency, learning transfer, problem solving, and instructional individualization in computer-based lessons and curricula aimed at maximizing the computer's strengths as a medium to deliver complete teaching.

THE THIRD WAVE AND CHILD-CENTERED EDUCATION

We have already encountered Alvin Toffler's book, *The Third Wave*, a study comparing our present industrial culture (called the Second Wave) with the postindustrial (or Third Wave) culture that is emerging.[2] Our discussion of this book in Chapter 1 stressed the changing role of the computer in our culture, but Toffler's treatment of the conflict between Second and Third Wave cultures also has many interesting implications for education. A list, presented in Chapter 4 of his book, enumerates the prime motive and organizational forces in Second Wave culture, *viewed from the perspective of the emerging Third Wave*. The list of key concepts offers powerful ways to compare Second Wave to Third Wave culture and helps us to understand how and why things are changing so rapidly.

One of these key concepts is *standardization*. A good concrete symbol of industrial standardization is the notion of interchangeable parts. It is common knowledge that our industrial lifestyle depends on our being able to replace a spark plug or tire or faucet washer with a new part and count on it to fit, but it is easy to forget that this was a new idea at the beginning of the century. Toffler points out, however, that the idea of standardization runs far deeper in Second Wave culture than that. From the very beginning of industrialism, the standardization of "hardware" (interchangeable parts) was accompanied by the standardization of "software"—the way things were done, particularly in business and manufacturing.

The assembly line provides perhaps the most powerful symbol of this phase of standardization, but Second Wave culture also has standardized wages, work days, lunch hours, holidays, and grievance procedures in the factory. And outside the factory we have standardized weights and measures, currency, grammar, usage, and spelling; standardized images disseminated by television; and even a standardized landscape, as identical gas stations, chain restaurants, and prefab housing have come into being.[3]

Most important of all, standardization affected people. On the First Wave (or preindustrial) farm, people made their own schedules, rose with the chickens, and did things their own way. In the Second Wave factories of the cities to which so many Americans fled for better pay, people had to work the same hours and do things the same way. They had to be punctual, work at the same rate, even hold the same values and want the same things in order to make the whole cultural process work.

In short, the Second Wave is the natural exponent of the machine culture we described in our brief social history of computers in Chapter 1. Standardization—particularly the standardization of people—was a desideratum of the Second Wave; it is a scourge of the Third. Now it is fashionable to emphasize the routine nature of work on the assembly line, to fault its monotony and characterize it as dehumanizing. We seem to have lost our creativity and individuality, even as Second Wave culture has increased our personal liberty by freeing us from the drudgery of dawn-to-dusk labor on the farm, from the ravages of disease, from famine, starvation, and want. The Third Wave perspective reveals that, while the standardization of Second Wave culture brought many benefits, it also took its toll in the nonmaterial quality of our lives and personalities.

This clash between the Second Wave emphasis on standardization and the Third Wave's concern for individuality naturally has strong impact on education—in part on what is taught, but even more on how we think about the social or cultural functions of education. To put it succinctly, Second Wave education aims at "human standardization"; it attempts to produce people who are the human equivalents of interchangeable machine parts, a point Toffler's lucid discussion of the "covert curriculum" demonstrates.

Toffler points out that as people left the farms for the factories, patterns of education had to change. Children had to be trained to become good factory workers at an early age, because the values required by the industrial workplace were very different from those needed on the farm. The mass education to which this need gave rise approached education almost as a manufacturing process. On the surface schools taught the three Rs, but there also was a "covert curriculum" that Toffler says taught three other things that were even more important to keeping the factories running smoothly: punctuality, obedience, and rote, repetitive work.[4]

Industrial culture had scarcely reached full swing when far-seeing educators throughout the industrial world began to question the notion of Second Wave educational standardization and to urge the schools to respect the individuality of students. By the beginning of this century A. S. Neill (of the Summerhill School) in England, Maria Montessori on the Continent, and John Dewey in the United States—to name only some of the better known and most influential educational thinkers—had all begun educational reforms. They concentrated on replacing the standardization of education in industrial culture with a recognition of students' individuality as persons—what is often called "child-centered" education with its emphasis on learning differences or individual styles of learning among children.[5]

Since then a wide variety of educational approaches and experiments devoted to fostering students' individuality has arisen in this country, including the "open classrooms" of the 1960s and 1970s. A currently popular approach (the one, for example, on which Logo is based) is the so-called discovery method, which has as central tenets both increasing learner-centeredness and moving away from an emphasis on memorization of facts and rules by rote.[6] Learning by discovery was, in fact, first conceived as a *reaction* against learning by the standardizing "expository," "didactic," or "teacher-centered" methods of the Second Wave, with their emphasis on rote memorization and disregard for the individuality of students that the Third Wave values so highly.

Keeping the Balance: Education as Communication

Given our preoccupation with individual rights—even individual whimsy!—it is certainly understandable that our educational system would place ever-increasing emphasis on the learner. The learner is, after all, an individual—with individual strengths, differences, and preferences. Respecting the individuality of persons, including students, is a very important part of the Third Wave perspective, whether in education or outside it. Within our educational process, however, the question arises of whether we have gone too far in our emphasis on the student's individuality.

But the educational process has two other important components besides learners: the teacher and the instructional content being taught. The familiar comparison of education to a communications process points out the importance of each of these components and their relationship to one another. Teachers correspond to senders of communications, students to receivers, and instructional content to the message being sent. In the Second Wave view of education, the teacher was viewed as the exclusive sender and students mainly as passive receivers of the educational message—which itself was often conceived mostly as strictly factual content of the old-fashioned kind described above. No wonder that in this form the communications analogy is out of favor among Third Wave educators!

The aspect of the analogy we want to stress, however, is its power to point out the importance of *interaction* in the educational process. Suppose Receiver is a visitor in a strange town and has asked Sender for directions. The goal of their communication process is for Receiver to find his way. How is that goal best achieved? Sender may rattle on without interruption, but the longer he goes on, the greater the chance that Receiver may miss some vital piece of information or may be getting more direction than he needs. However, Sender does not realize it until too late (if at all), because he has failed to *interact* sufficiently with Receiver. Sender took too dominant a role in the communication process. That is what happens in the too exclusively teacher-centered educational approach of the Second Wave, and it is why educators have rejected it.

But it does not serve communication any better for Sender to say to Receiver, "You tell me which way *you* think you ought to go, and I'll correct you when you're wrong." Receiver might, in fact, come up with a novel approach to reaching his destination, an approach that Sender never thought of, but even if he did, the communication process is likely to waste too much time for both parties. It is an inefficient way to communicate, and it is inefficient because Sender and Receiver have not *interacted* enough. Sender put all the burden of communication on Receiver. All too frequently that is what happens in learner-centered approaches to education.

Clearly, the key to successful interaction is to maintain a *balance* of interaction among senders and receivers—among teachers and students. Focusing too exclusively on *either* element leads to problems with the "communication." (We do not mean to imply that teachers and students have difficulty *talking* to one another; rather, it is the "message" part of the educational communication process—the *content* of learning—that suffers when balance is lost.) Anytime the focus shifts away from the communication process itself—whether to a too exclusively teacher-centered or learner-centered point of view—the effectiveness of instruction is jeopardized. Communication is impaired, and students do not learn as well as they should.

We already know, from bitter past experience of classrooms in which teachers did all the sending and students all the passive receiving, how a predominantly teacher-centered approach impairs educational effectiveness. Despite their popularity, reinforced by the cultural changes we have discussed, approaches that unbalance the communication process in favor of learners run into difficulties as well. Attending to students individually, testing them to determine their aptitudes and individual learning styles, developing and administering individual programs and materials according to the individual differences measured, supervising students as they work at their own rate and in their own way, guiding them in their individual odysseys of discovery—all these take a great deal of time on the part of both teachers and students. A single teacher faced with a class of twenty to thirty students has enough problems keeping educational effectiveness high, even when little or no attempt is made to accommodate the individuality of each learner. As always, in other words, when balance is destroyed, educational ineffectiveness is the result.

Both the advantages and disadvantages of centering the instructional process on learners can be illustrated concretely in this anecdote reported by Jerome Bruner:

> We hit upon the happy idea of presenting this chunk of geography not as a set of knowns, but as a set of unknowns. One class was presented blank maps, containing only tracings of the rivers and lakes of the area as well as the natural resources. They were asked as a first exercise to indicate where the principal cities would be located, where the railroads, and where the main highways. Books and maps were not permitted and "looking up the facts" was cast in a sinful light. Upon completing this exercise, a class discussion was begun in which the children attempted to justify why the major city would be here, a large city there, a railroad on this line, etc. . . .
>
> The children in another class taught conventionally got their facts all right, sitting down, benchbound. And that was that. We will see in six months which group remembers more. But whichever one does, one thing I will predict. One group learned geography as a set of rational acts of induction—that cities spring up where there is water, where there are natural resources, where there are things to be processed and shipped. The other group learned passively that there were arbitrary cities at arbitrary places by arbitrary bodies of water and arbitrary sources

of supply. One learned geography as a form of activity. The other stored some names and positions as a passive form of registration.[7]

This description of discovery in action sounds exciting and challenging. It certainly did much more to accommodate the individuality of students than the traditional, passive classroom approach with which Bruner compares it in the second paragraph. It also raises some provocative questions, all ultimately having to do with instructional effectiveness, either directly or as a function of classroom time efficiency:

- Did *all* the students learn the material? Those who got caught up in the activity seemed to enjoy themselves. Did all the students participate actively? What happened to those who did not?
- What exactly was it that students learned? Many students seemed very definitely to learn things—perhaps even *many* things. But exactly what, after the unit was completed, does the teacher know for sure that the class as a whole learned? If it is true, for example, that different students learned widely different things depending on what part of the discovery process they were involved in or attended to most actively, then what can the teacher, in planning the next unit or some subsequent unit, count on all the children to have learned in such a way that the knowledge can be used as a foundation upon which to build subsequent instruction?
- If on a comprehension or mastery posttest, students show some marked differences in what they learned, whose fault is it? Can the teacher conclude that some students are just "poor discoverers"? If so, what does that mean? How can knowing it be useful to the teacher? In other words, where does the discovery process allow the teacher *to intervene* to make sure some knowledge "gets across" to students? Is it unfair to say that, while students have more individual *freedom* in this discovery approach (that is, that their individuality is more fully accommodated), they are also forced to accept almost complete individual *responsibility* for learning?
- What about this method of learning makes the facts and principles of geography easier to learn or makes students better able to apply them successfully in subsequent lessons? Was the lesson just "more fun" for students who enjoyed it, or did it really ensure that learning took place more successfully? What might the effect be, for example, on comprehension and internalization of principles, if students found out that some large cities are located in places the principles say they should not be—or if some excellent locations for big cities turned out not to have them? Can we say for certain that this kind of "challenge" helps rather than hinders comprehension of the basic principles being taught? Might not a large amount of such extraneous facts,

encounters with exceptions to rules not yet mastered, and false hypotheses on which students spend a good deal of time as likely create interference to learning as aid it?

- If, in teaching tennis, for example, we let pupils get on the court and bat balls around at random, attempting to "discover" a good form, would we not have a very justifiable fear that they would waste a lot of time learning bad habits that later instruction would have to correct? Would we not, in fact, call such behavior in a tennis teacher "irresponsible"? What makes us think it will work better in geography class?

- Finally, what good teacher, textbook, or method *advocates* the approach to instruction Bruner describes in the "other classroom?" Are we really to believe that the nondiscovery children sat completely bored and "benchbound," suffering patiently through rigorous, dehumanizing, authoritarian teaching? Perhaps they did—but only if they had a bad teacher. Adopting the discovery method is no sure safeguard against bad teaching. Why does Bruner insist on making the situation seem so grim—as if our choice were the bright sunshine of discovery versus sending our children to toil in the mines of bad, uninspired, didactic instruction? Are those really the only two choices?

There is a "theme" to these questions. Together, they stress both the importance of, and the relationship between, educational efficiency and effectiveness. Bruner points out that "the word teaching is not very fashionable anymore."[8] Neither is the concept of efficiency. It conjures up visions of "getting through the material" no matter the cost to students as individuals. Yet, the association of efficiency with the Second Wave, teacher-centered approach to education is unfortunate, because good use of time is important in *any* instructional approach, particularly in relation to instructional effectiveness.

Instruction can be ineffective in two ways. Bad instruction is inefficient because students who take it simply do not learn what they were supposed to learn. But of equal importance in classrooms, textbooks, and instructional programs is the sort of ineffectiveness that is related to efficiency. If students in two different instructional programs learn the same things, but one program takes significantly less time (that is, it is more efficient), it is better. If we had all the time in the school day and the school year that we needed, perhaps this would not be the case. But students have a lot to learn and no surplus of learning time. In fact, many recent, high-level studies paint a bleak picture of educational effectiveness in this country.[9] Given this situation, the more efficient instructional program is the more effective, because, in saving time in one segment of the curriculum, it creates time in another.

It is to this notion of effectiveness as a function of efficiency that the preceding questions about the two geography classes were directed. Specifically, the problem is this: The process of "discovering" the geography of the Midwest took these fifth graders considerably more time and required more teacher (and experimenter) input than a traditional unit covering the same material would ordinarily take. Unless the students stayed after school to do the discovery unit, however, the extra time came from one of only two possible places. Either some other material in their geography class got short shrift, or the extra time came from time that would otherwise have been devoted to one of their other subjects.

On the positive side Bruner makes the claim that, although he lacks data to confirm it, he feels certain that discovery students would retain the knowledge they discovered longer than the students who acquired the same knowledge passively. He could also have pointed out that they had a much better opportunity *to apply* facts and principles they learned in the discovery unit, that they were much better able to bring knowledge they had acquired in other subjects to bear on instruction in the discovery unit, and that they almost certainly learned some additional things by engaging in discovery that the "benchbound" students did not.

We can summarize this comparison of the two learning approaches in the following way:

- The "other" (Second Wave, standardizing) classroom's instructional method was very *efficient* in teaching the facts and skills at which it aimed. But it was not very *effective*, because, according to Bruner, it did not teach students to apply what they had learned—or probably even to remember it for long.
- The discovery classroom's instructional program increased *effectiveness* by incorporating the skills lacking in the "other" classroom. But by centering on the individuality of the learners, it did so only at the cost of decreasing *efficiency*, because it took more time.

This comparison of Second Wave and discovery educational approaches illustrates the importance of maintaining the educational "communication" balance. Both teacher-centered and learner-centered instructional methods upset the balance, and each creates problems with effectiveness and efficiency. What we need, instead, is an instructional approach that avoids this dilemma—one that increases effectiveness *without* losing efficiency.

RESOLVING THE DILEMMA: CONTENT-CENTERED EDUCATION

Let us look again at Bruner's example and focus our attention on the *content* of instruction. Although it may seem at first to contrast two contents, the geography anecdote actually sidesteps the issue of content. In describing the lesson, Bruner discusses a learning *activity* in which students engaged as they *applied* some principles of geography. But he does not talk about how they learned the facts and principles—the *content* they applied in this new, interesting, and engaging activity. How did students even know where to begin considering placing cities and railroads on the map? Did they know some principles before they began the lesson? Did the experimenters and their teacher instruct them as they went along? When and how did the educational "communication" process take place—what was taught, and how? These are the relevant questions, though Bruner's anecdote ignores them.

He does not, for example, discuss how they learned that cities must have a water supply, that railroads exist to connect cities, that the paths of railroads are constrained by topography—the content they needed in order to be able to engage in the discovery activity with meaningfulness. In fact, it is almost as if he were somehow relegating the teaching and learning of content to the "other classroom"—to the sphere of passive fact acquisition and rote memorization—thereby suggesting that it is inimical to learner-centeredness, a threat to the student's individuality.

The critical point is that, *regardless of how they do it, students must still learn some content*. It need not be passively acquired facts and rote tasks, but it must be some body of knowledge. Communicating some content—whether defined as facts or skills—is the *sine qua non* of any effective educational process. No amount of attention to students' learning differences and individual learning styles, no amount of accommodation of their individualities as persons will help them learn, if our instructional method neglects *what they learn*. In our solution to the dilemma, therefore, we must pay close attention to content as the key to educational effectiveness.

We might, for example, say, "Brian is an affective kid. Therefore, he needs a different instructional approach than Jane, who is a cognitive type." We can notice, very accurately, that, in fact, *all* students differ significantly in very many ways: in their rate of learning, style of learning, background, and a host of other factors. Taking such observations in sum, the inevitable conclusion of the learner-centered approach to education is that each child ought to have a completely individualized educational program tailored just for him or her.

Think about that! In what ideal educational utopia of the future is such a possibility remotely practical in the "real life" classroom—even a fully computerized classroom? How could it ever be feasible to have twenty or thirty students each on a different learning path, thinking about things in terms that bear little relationship to the thought processes of other students? How could teachers ever administer such a program? What would it cost in time and money to devise a completely different learner-centered curriculum for each child based on his or her individual strengths, differences, and preferences? How much time would it take simply to find out what kind of completely individualized curriculum each child needed, and how much time would be left over in the school year for instruction after it was determined? We have trouble enough teaching even a single curriculum effectively; twenty to thirty simultaneous curricula seem, very practically speaking, utterly impossible!

But now consider what happens if we shift the emphasis onto content—that is, onto instruction. We might begin instead by saying, "Brian and Jane are fifth graders. When they spell, both have trouble deciding when to drop the final e before adding a suffix. That is the content they need. The skills required of both students—regardless of their many and real individual differences as young students—are the *same.*" Unlike the learner-centered approach, this "content-centered" point of view provides a fixed referent in the educational process: It holds constant the *content* all students need to learn. It allows us to shift the focus of attempts to individualize and destandardize the educational process away from students' individual learning styles and differences—away, in other words, from an unproductive preoccupation with their individuality—and to concentrate instead on remediating their individual problems in mastering the content they need to learn.

Holding content constant does not mean that learning must be passive and standardizing like the old-fashioned teacher-centered approach. That much is clear. But neither must it require all students to get the same instruction. In terms of the example above, all students who need this content might enter the same *lesson* or series of lessons that teaches it. Within that instructional program, however, students will make different kinds of mistakes on the road to learning the "final e" generalization. The content-centered approach differs from the learner-centered approach by making these differences in *performance on the skills being taught* the "individual differences" according to which instruction is varied for different students.

Many different paths through the same instruction, thus, are possible and to be expected, even when the content being taught is a basic skill *all* students need to learn. Later on, as students' interests and aptitudes diverge, they will not even take the same *lessons.* But, wherever their individual learning paths may lead, the criterion upon which instruction is varied from student to student is determined by the nature of the content they have chosen to learn. Therefore, the content-centered approach preserves the balance of the educational communication process. Unlike learner-centered approaches, it does not imply a methodological instructional diversity that is impossible to achieve. Its goal is effectiveness, and it suggests a maximally efficient means for achieving this effectiveness. It is, in other words, *both* individualizable *and* efficient.

In summary, the advantages of a content-centered educational approach include:

- It teaches *effectively* because it preserves the interactive "communications" balance. It overemphasizes neither the role of the teacher (thus turning students into passive recipients of standardized, mass instruction) nor that of the student (becoming so bogged down in students' differences as individuals that effective instruction of many students at once becomes difficult or impossible).

- Rather than focusing attempts to individualize and destandardize education on the *learner*, it concentrates on the *content*. It recognizes that, however much students may differ as individuals, the content needed by students who are learning the same skills does not vary.
- It is *efficient* because it ensures that each student receives the instruction he or she needs with remediation specific to his or her individual errors.

INDIVIDUALIZING INSTRUCTION

So far in this chapter we have discussed the old-fashioned, teacher-centered education of the Second Wave, which is disagreeable to all because it seeks to standardize students. We have discussed learner-centered educational approaches, viewing them as a laudable reaction to the stultifying effects of teacher-centered instruction. But we found they have a drawback: They accommodate the individuality of students only at the cost of efficiency. In the immediately preceding section we discussed content-centered education as a means to increase instructional efficiency, but we have not yet discussed how it can be delivered on computers in such a way as to accommodate the Third Wave concern with students as individuals. That will be our task in the remainder of the chapter.

Learner-centered approaches focus the individualization process on efforts to accommodate the *individuality* of learners. In the content-centered approach the focus is on instruction, which is held constant, because the facts and skills students need remain the same regardless of their individual differences. Thus, from our perspective it is on *the delivery of instruction* that the process of educational individualization must be centered. In essence, individualized delivery of instruction means (1) that each student must get every bit of instruction he or she needs to master content effectively, and (2) that no student should get one bit more instruction than he or she needs.

At this point we are *defining* individualization from the content-centered perspective. In the next chapter we will examine specific techniques for *achieving* it. In specific terms, individualization means:

1. In delivering instruction, we must devise some means for determining whether a student already knows the content taught in a lesson and, if he or she does, individualizing the lesson by permitting the student to skip it.
2. For students who do not already know the facts and/or skills the lesson teaches, and who thus enter instruction, we must:

   a. Teach them only the skills they do not know. Delivery is not fully individualized if the lesson is "all or nothing"—if students who enter it must take all the instruction, even though they make only a subset of possible errors in performing on the content.
   b. Give them immediate corrective feedback on their performance. Most instruction includes some form of feedback, usually delayed. For fully individualized delivery, students must get *immediate* feedback, and it must be specific to the learning errors they have made.
   c. Provide some efficient means for extended practice on the skills they have learned in the lesson. Again, most instructional programs include practice, but individualized delivery means that practice focuses on the specific skills with which a student is having difficulty.

There is another important reason for holding instruction constant and individualizing its delivery. In Chapter 5 we called it "hook up." Effective instruction at the *curricular* level requires control not just over *what* students know, but over *how they think about things.* How students think about the skills of adding columns of numbers and carrying when they are studying addition, for example, "hooks up" to instruction in multiplication of multidigit numbers. Thus, when a curriculum seeks to control the way all students think about adding columns of figures and carrying numbers, its goal is not to constrain the individuality of the student. It merely controls thinking, because later things in the curriculum build on earlier things; later things have to be explained *in terms of* earlier things. If each individual student "discovers" his or her own way of conceptualizing early skills in a curriculum, the instruction has no efficient way to build on that thought process later on, as we pointed out in the last chapter's analysis of Logo.

Role of the Computer

If you think carefully about the program for individualizing instruction that we have described, you will see that it has a problem. It does avoid confusing the need to individualize education with respect for student individuality. It does keep the educational communication process balanced by focusing individualization on delivery of instructional content rather than on a teacher-centered or learner-centered imbalance. But it is just as hard in the classroom to individualize instruction in the way we have suggested as it is to deliver a learner-centered program tailored to the individuality of every student.

   There is, however, a critical difference between the learner-centered approaches and our content-centered approach. Learner-centered approaches are inefficient. Regardless of the means employed to deliver them, they require significantly more time and effort from students and teachers than the "ordinary" classroom instructional methods. The problem of getting all the content delivered to all the students is already too large a task for the time available. Our content-centered approach, however, is deliverable on *computers* with a high degree of both efficiency and effectiveness, thus freeing teachers' time as it individualizes students' instructional experiences.

Keeping content constant means that a single excellent lesson to teach a skill can be developed, written one time and in just a single way. It becomes individualized by delivering instructional feedback to different students *contingent upon* the kinds of errors they make. In this way a single lesson is able to provide several different learning paths and to accommodate a wide variety of individual differences: All of the instruction needed by any student is written into the lesson, but only that part an individual student needs is delivered to that student. The criterion that "decides" how much and what kind of instruction the student receives is determined by the student—by his or her performance on the skill.

Translated to the computer medium, then, content-centered instruction *is* using the computer as a tutor. (Learner-centered CBE is mainly of the tutee approach.) And content-centered instruction that does the things described in the preceding paragraph *is* complete teaching, as we presented it in Chapters 3 and 4. Computers are extremely well suited to this kind of individualized delivery of instruction. It is a major "strength of the medium"—something they do very well and very easily. In effect, then, every student who needs the instruction enters the *same* lesson, but you would never realize it by looking at the computer screen. The lesson *behaves differently* depending on the mistakes the individual student makes. In other words, a single lesson, programmed just one way, is built *to adapt* to the performance of each student, giving just the instruction he or she needs—no more and no less. We will examine several example lessons in the next chapter.

Tutor-style lessons and curricula of this kind are not easy to develop. Once in place, however, they not only teach their content very efficiently from the student's point of view, they also increase instructional efficiency by freeing the classroom teacher for other kinds of high-quality student interactions. This second, derivative form of classroom efficiency is especially important in CBE. We have faulted many learner-centered educational programs not for the value of what they do, but because they *add* to the workload and the timeload of both teachers and students. If the computer is to win a place of significance in the educational process, it must not only deliver excellent instruction but also *save* time and effort for both teachers and students. We do not need CBE that makes things even harder and more complicated than they already are. Tutor-style, content-centered CBE, of the kind we have suggested here, increases instructional effectiveness and efficiency while meaningfully individualizing the instructional process, and that is what it takes to justify the expense in time, money, and effort needed to implement CBE in the schools.

WHAT YOU HAVE LEARNED IN THIS CHAPTER

1. In this century, Third Wave concern for the prerogatives of individuals and the failure of Second Wave educational methods to accommodate them have led to an increased emphasis on learner-centeredness, which has created an imbalance in the educational process.

2. In terms of the communications analogy, too much emphasis on receivers (the learner-centered approach) is as bad as too much emphasis on senders (the Second Wave approach). Both reduce the effectiveness with which the message (instructional content) is conveyed.

3. Second Wave education was very *efficient* in teaching facts and skills, but it was not very *effective*, because it did not teach students to apply what they had learned. Third Wave learner-centeredness increased *effectiveness* by providing opportunities for application of principles and concepts, but only by decreasing *efficiency*. An individualized content-centered approach can maximize both *efficiency* and *effectiveness*.

4. The content-centered learning approach makes it possible to individualize instruction effectively while keeping efficiency high through the use of complete teaching in a computerized instructional environment.

NOTES

1. Robert F. Biehler and Jack Snowman, *Psychology Applied to Teaching* (Boston: Houghton Mifflin, 1982), p. 254.

2. Alvin Toffler, *The Third Wave* (New York: William Morrow & Company, 1980).

3. Ibid, pp. 62–65.

4. Ibid, p. 45.

5. For further information on the history of American education and the conditions giving rise to the child-centered approach, see Larry Cuban, *How Teachers Taught: Constancy and Change in American Classrooms 1890–1980* (New York: Longman, 1984), pp. 17–40; for a contemporary account, see Vivian T. Thayer, *The Passing of the Recitation* (Boston: D. C. Heath, 1928).

6. The educational literature on discovery learning is extensive. One of the best summary treatments of the approach (and one to which this chapter makes frequent reference) is a collection of thoughtful papers edited by Lee S. Shulman and Evan Keislar entitled *Learning by Discovery: A Critical Appraisal* (Chicago: Rand McNally, 1966); for a thorough critique of discovery learning, see David P. Ausubel, *Educational Psychology: A Cognitive View* (New York: Holt, Rinehart & Winston, 1968), pp. 467–504.

7. Jerome Bruner, "Learning and Thinking," *Harvard Educational Review* 29 (1959): 187–188. Material quoted from pages 187 and 188. Copyright © 1959 by President and Fellows of Harvard College.

8. Jerome S. Bruner, "Some Elements of Discovery," in Shulman and Keislar, *Learning by Discovery*, p. 103.

9. For one well-known study, see The National Commission on Excellence in Education, *A Nation at Risk: The Imperative for Educational Reform* (Washington, D.C.: U.S. Department of Education, April 1983).

7

The Tutor Approach: Computer Delivery of Instruction

This chapter is the last in a group that began with Chapter 5. Here we continue the investigation of educational individualization undertaken in the previous chapter, moving from the theoretical to the practical level, as we examine in depth some lesson formats and instructional techniques of tutor-style CBE.

In the last chapter we discussed two divergent views of educational individualization:

1. The learner-centered view (reflected in tutee-style CBE) attends most to the *individuality* of students—to their individual differences, learning styles, prerogatives, and so on.
2. The content-centered view (reflected in the tutor-style CBE illustrated in this chapter) emphasizes individualized *instruction*. By making sure each student gets all the instruction but no more than he or she needs, content-centered, tutor-style CBE maximizes efficiency while keeping the effectiveness of instruction as high as possible.

Our goal in this chapter is to enumerate and discuss the components of content-centered, tutor-style CBE, which include accurate placement, variable lesson content, and instructional feedback contingent upon performance, distributed practice, and sequencing of instruction. We shall see how these features combine to enhance instructional individualization while maintaining high levels of instructional efficiency and effectiveness.

A BASIC TECHNIQUE FOR INDIVIDUALIZING INSTRUCTION

Suppose you wanted to teach a class of students the rule for doubling the final consonant of a monosyllabic word. The rule states that if the root word ends "consonant-vowel-consonant" (abbreviated "cvc" in the following discussion), the final consonant is doubled when a suffix beginning with a vowel is appended (e.g., stop + ed = stopped).

First, you might analyze the task and discover that there are really only four types of mistakes students could make on this task:

1. Root word ends "cvc" and suffix begins with vowel, but student does not double the final consonant:

    shop + ing: shoping

2. Root word ends "cvc" and suffix begins with consonant, but student doubles final consonant:

    hot + ly: hottly

3. Root word does *not* end "cvc," but student doubles final consonant anyhow:

    farm + ing: farmming
    warm + ly: warmmly

4. Misspellings:

    snap + ing: slapping

Having done this task analysis (or having adopted a textbook that employed it), you would present the basic rule to the class, illustrate the error categories with examples, show how the rule tells the student what to do to avoid each kind of error, practice some on the skills together, and so on. After you had finished this teaching segment, you would test it somehow to find out whether the students understood the rule and how to apply it.

Some students, of course, would catch on quickly, generalizing from the basic rule to the instances represented in the error types on their own, even before you explained it. Those students might become bored while you patiently went through each application and practiced it with examples. At worst, they might even become confused by too much explanation. How much time did *you* have to spend studying the chart above before it made complete sense—and you know the rule perfectly!

Another group of students would probably have some trouble mastering the rule and considerably more trouble applying it in the instances. They probably would not *tell* you they did not understand it, of course. In fact, they would probably try to hide out. You are a good teacher, so you would probably find most of them out, spot check their comprehension, and stall the rest of the class while you spent some time remediating them. You might not find *every* student with problems, however. You might spot check a particular student on an application she knew but not on one that was causing problems for her—especially if she raised her hand on the one she knew but slunk down in her seat for the ones she did not!

It seems a shame, does it not, that some students should have to be bogged down and possibly confused by instructional overkill in a lesson like this? Yet even the best teacher, faced with twenty students to teach at the same time, has no choice but to present *all* the material to *every* student—straight through from beginning to end. It is either that or risk omitting something crucial for some other students who need it. And this is not a "smart kids/ dumb kids" kind of problem. The student who happens to catch on quickly to this skill may be the one who stumbles on the next.

It seems a shame that a learning task as regular and specifiable as this should not be able to be taught to a normal classroom of twenty children with 100 percent reliability. Yet, try as we might, some students always seem to slip through the net of even the most careful teacher.

You see where this discussion is leading. The computer can present this instruction to all twenty students one at a time, not all together as the teacher and textbook must. A computer-based lesson that utilizes the strengths of the medium can hold instruction in reserve and deliver it only to those students who need it, not to every student as the teacher and textbook have to. The computer's interactive capacity can let the student's performance on a skill dictate the amount and kind of instruction he or she needs and deliver them contingent upon the student's performance.

If a computer lesson is to accomplish this instructional goal, it cannot imitate the way a teacher or a textbook would deliver the same instruction. We would expect the computer lesson somehow to vary the order of the teacher-delivered or textbook-delivered lesson that went: "Teach, then test." If you teach first, you *have* to teach everything—all the lesson content—because you have not permitted the student to tell you, by his or her performance, what part of the instruction it is safe to omit and what part must certainly be included. A computer-imaginative computer lesson, however, might invert the order, turning the main part of the instruction that all students get into a *test*like format and putting the *instruction* for each type of error into feedback delivered only to students who fail to perform on an item in the testlike segment. Such an inverted lesson structure is possible, because the computer is delivering *individualized* instruction to each student who uses the lesson.

Here is how an individualizing tutor-style lesson that teaches this content might look:[1]

1. Some students in a basic skills curriculum may not know the difference between a vowel and a consonant, but most students will. Thus, the lesson opens with a very short quiz testing vowel/consonant recognition (just one item each). Students who "pass it" go right on to the next step. Those who do not receive a remedial lesson to teach the skill.

2. The lesson presents the following rule briefly, to explain that "cvc" stands for the "consonant-vowel-consonant" pattern, but it does *not* teach the applications of the rule in specific instances:

   If the word ends "cvc" and the suffix begins with a vowel, double the final consonant.

3. Then, all students move quickly into the testlike section of the lesson in which they practice *applying* the rule.

   For students who catch on to the rule right away and make no mistakes applying it, this section merely functions as a quick, painless verification of mastery. They get no instruction, because they need none.

   For the student who makes errors, the adaptive quality of the lesson comes into play. The lesson checks the student's answer against possible error types and delivers instruction specific to that error type in corrective feedback. The student gets all the instruction he or she needs, but only that instruction. A wrong answer does not send the student to a unit that explains *all* the error types; it merely delivers instruction on the error type he or she missed in this item.

A sample item of each error type with its corrective feedback is presented in Figures 7.1a through 7.1d. Figure 7.1e shows the hint students get if they press the key marked HELP.

The lesson is also programmed to insert any item missed into the test automatically after increasing numbers of intervening items in order (1) to provide distributed practice in the application, and (2) to shape long-term retention of the skill. This review feature means that even the student who performs poorly will come to criterion on all the skills taught in the lesson before he or she finishes it. Thus, the teacher receives the same guarantee of mastery for this student as for the top performer, and the slower students get a "tutor" with infinite patience that does not care how many mistakes they make.

This "test/teach" lesson format, thus, takes advantage of the computer's interactive capacities to store information invisibly and to deliver it contingent upon students' performance. In addition, the lesson changes—or *adapts*—for each student, to make sure that each student gets all the instruction he or she needs, and no student gets more than he or she needs. Most important, all these features are contained in a single lesson programmed just one way. In other words, you do not need separate lessons for students who perform at different levels in order to achieve individualization. A single lesson, exploiting the strengths of the medium, adapts itself to the needs of each particular student to deliver fully individualized instruction.

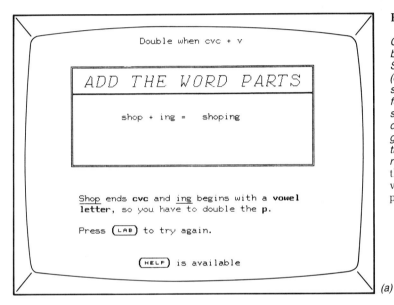

(a)

(b)

Figure 7.1

Computer-based lesson, "Doubling," from the PCP Language Skills Curriculum. Parts (a) through (d) show four possible types of student errors, with the corrective feedback specific to each. Part (e) shows what happens when a student presses the HELP key: The general rule is displayed to help the student figure out his or her response. Copyright © 1982 by the Board of Trustees of the University of Illinois. Reprinted by permission.

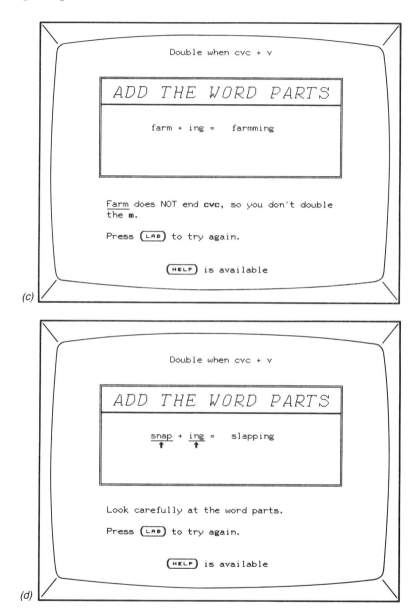

Figure 7.1

(Continued)

COMPONENTS OF
INDIVIDUALIZED CBE

The "test/teach" lesson format used in the preceding example demonstrates several components that any CBE lesson must include to deliver fully individualized instruction that guarantees mastery. Taken together, these fea-

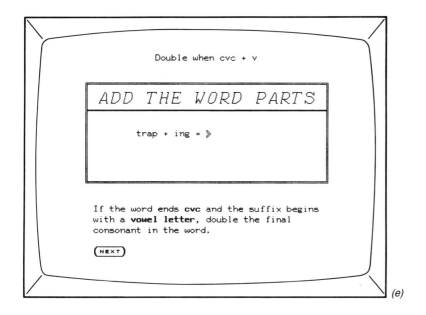

Figure 7.1

(e)

(Continued)

tures make up what we have called "complete teaching" in previous chapters:

- Accurate placement
- Immediate, instructional feedback contingent upon performance
- Variable lesson content, contingent upon performance
- Distributed practice
- Sequencing of instruction

Our discussion in the preceding example concentrated on *instructional feedback*, so important to the "test/teach" lesson format. Each of the features in the list above, however, contributes to the individualization process. We examine each one individually below.

Accurate Placement

Placing students accurately in instruction is important for increasing instructional efficiency and thus for maximizing effectiveness. The goal of delivering to every student neither more nor less instruction than he or she needs depends on accurate placement—but not the common notion of placement as "determining students' grade levels." Accurate placement should enhance the process of instructional individualization; placing students in "grade levels" does the reverse. It is standardizing and constraining to students, because it is based on a fundamental misconception.

The notion of grade levels implies that learning is *linear*. After students' appropriate grade levels have been established, they are placed in that grade, and all begin to move along the same well-worn path together. The problem is that, even though all students must master the same content, which means that they all need the same preskills, different students have different preskill gaps. The problem with grade levels, in other words, is that we know learning is *not* linear.

Students often, for example, test at different "grade levels" in different subjects. If learning were linear, we would not expect that. If we say that Michael is "at the fifth-grade level" in math, "at the sixth-grade level" in science, and "at the seventh-grade level" in reading, in what sense is the term "grade level" meaningful? At which "grade level" should the single, actual, real-life Michael be placed?

More important, by testing, reporting, and using the measure of "grade levels" in different skill areas individually, we are asserting that performance in each area is *independent*, when we know they are, in fact, interrelated. We know, for example, that Michael's performance in math must be affected by his skill in reading, since he has to read the math book to acquire the math skills. In this sense reading is a *preskill* for math. In turn, his performance in science is affected directly by his mastery of both reading and math skills. In what sense, then, is it meaningful *within the instructional process* to consider these skill areas separately from one another? For purposes of evaluation, they may have some value; for placement, they have none.

The reason we have placement by grade level is, of course, the same reason that we have grade levels. It was simply the best individualizing technique available in a classroom with twenty students and one teacher. But now we have educational computers and tutor-style CBE. Students no longer need be herded into groups by such rough measures of their level of performance as the grade level. Each student can make his or her way through the content with maximum efficiency, because each student can practice just the preskills he or she needs to ensure mastery. In other words, a student can use tutor-style "test/teach" lessons with instructional feedback to learn both the content that is needed and the preskills that are lacking. This is the way placement and instructional feedback work together to individualize instruction.

The Individualized Approach to Placement   The real answer to the problem of placement, then, is to supplant it with the fully integrated curricula that tutor-style CBE makes possible. Attempting to fix up the old linear, standardizing approach to grade-level placement by shifting to a learner-centered placement that stresses individual learning paths and differences is well-intentioned, but it is neither sufficient nor particularly effective, because it still accepts the basic classroom situation of one teacher and many students that makes placement a problem in the first place. When the educational computer is used to deliver fully individualized instruction that guarantees mastery, the problem of placement disappears.

Imagine a complete, computerized basic skills curriculum in language arts, containing lessons on synonyms and antonyms, formation of verb tenses, possessives, prefixes and suffixes, and so on—all of them like the lesson on doubling that we discussed. Each lesson is delivered by a sophisticated management system, so students can easily get from one lesson to another. The entire curriculum is integrated and mastery based. That is, it is made up of small units of instruction that are not organized into grade levels but rather sequenced according to skills. When a student masters a skill, he or she moves on to the next. Lessons are put "later" in the curriculum if they require skills that are taught in "earlier" ones, and students can get immediate access to any lesson in the curriculum they need, whenever their performance indicates that they lack a needed preskill for the current instruction. The computer is programmed to assess the needed preskill and to branch the student automatically to the lesson that teaches it.

This solution to the vexing problem of accurate placement is no dream of the future. It will soon become available to schools generally, as powerful but inexpensive hardware systems and sufficiently full, integrated computer-based curricula become available.

Variable Instruction Content

Astute observers will notice that the example lesson on the doubling rule that embeds instruction in a set of testlike items behaves very much like a drill. Those who know something about research on drills will also know that they are considered an inappropriate instructional technique for teaching many kinds of content. They are considered to be effective for teaching only what we have earlier called "nongeneralizable" content. As we said, paired associates and fact systems are very important kinds of learning, and if the lesson format were restricted only to teaching them, it would still be valuable. Actually, the lesson format is different from drills precisely because it is *not* so limited. In fact, the lesson on doubling discussed above teaches a generalizable skill. One does not memorize a list of words with suffixes; one learns (that is, generalizes) a *rule* by which even words not directly taught in the lesson can be treated appropriately.

Nevertheless, the doubling rule is a very simple and straightforward kind of generalization. To teach more complex generalizations in a fully individualized lesson that guarantees mastery, the lesson must be able to vary the *content* of missed items when they come up in review. A student who responds "S" (instead of "Ag") to the stimulus "silver" in a simple drill on the chemical elements merely needs more practice *on that item*. But what happens if a student, having read a passage in a lesson on *WH questions* from a reading comprehension curriculum, responds to a question about *when* something happened with an answer that tells *where*? It is insufficient merely to remediate the error and then bring back *the same* item in review, because the object of the lesson is not to teach a specific answer to a specific question, but to teach a generalization about WH questions.

Here is a specific example from a reading comprehension lesson that teaches this more complex generalization.[2] The student first reads a passage like this one:

> *The knitting machine was invented in England in 1589, and the cotton gin was invented in America in 1793.*

When the student signifies that he has finished reading, the lesson presents a WH question. Figure 7.2a shows how the student moves a cursor to underline the part of the sentence that answers the question and then reports his or her choice. Two kinds of errors are possible. If the student chose, for example, "was invented" as the answer to the question about "*when* the knitting machine was invented," he or she would get feedback like that in Figure 7.2b. If, however, the student confused one kind of WH question for another, by underlining, for example, "in America," he or she would receive feedback like that shown in Figure 7.2c. For either kind of error, the passage on which the student made the mistake is brought back for review several times during the lesson.

Remember, though, the goal is not to teach the item itself, as in a drill, but the generalized skill of finding the parts that answer WH questions in *any*

Figure 7.2

An item from the PCP Reading Comprehension Curriculum. Part (a) shows how the student moves an underlining cursor to select a response. Part (b) shows a "regular" error in comprehension, with the feedback specific to it. Part (c) shows an error in discriminating different kinds of WH questions, with the feedback specific to it.

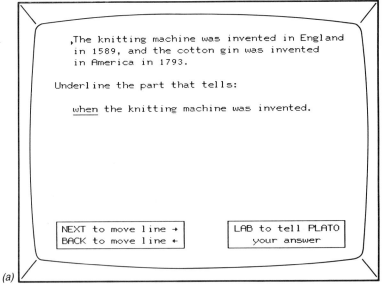

```
,The knitting machine was invented in England
in 1589, and the cotton gin was invented
in America in 1793.

Underline the part that tells:

    when the knitting machine was invented.




    NEXT to move line →        LAB to tell PLATO
    BACK to move line ←           your answer
```

(a)

```
      The knitting machine was invented in England
      in 1589, and the cotton gin was invented
      in America in 1793.

  Underline the part that tells:

      when the knitting machine was invented.

  Look:

      The knitting machine was invented in England
      [ when ], and the cotton gin was invented
      in America in 1793.

      The knitting machine was invented in England
      in 1589, and the cotton gin was invented
      in America in 1793.

      [NEXT]
```

(b)

```
      The knitting machine was invented in England
      in 1589, and the cotton gin was invented
      in America in 1793.

  Underline the part that tells:

      when the knitting machine was invented.

  No.   That answer tells:

      where the cotton gin was invented.

      [NEXT]
```

(c)

Figure 7.2

(Continued)

sentence. What would happen, then, if the lesson brought back the item for review just as it was presented above? Would it not be likely that the student would learn this misrule: "The answer to this sentence is 'in 1589.' That's what I should underline each time"? In other words, no generalization to the skill of finding *any* "when" question would have taken place. That is the limitation of normal drills.

This lesson, however, *modifies* the original passage when it comes up for review. If the student failed to answer the "when" question in the item correctly the first time, review presentation will change the original item in three increasingly generalized ways:

1. *By changing the original "when" part:* "in 1589" is replaced by one of these phrases:

   in the sixteenth century
   in the fifteen hundreds
   almost 400 years ago
   in the 1580s

2. Later *by changing the other "when" part:* "in 1793" is replaced by one of these phrases:

   soon after the Revolutionary War
   in the late 1700s
   in the eighteenth century
   shortly before 1800

3. Finally, *by varying the sentence structure* along with the "when" parts: For example, the order of parts within the clauses might be changed like this:

   Almost 400 years ago the knitting machine was invented in England, and shortly before 1800 the cotton gin was invented in America.

   Or, the order of clauses might be reversed:

   The cotton gin was invented soon after the Revolutionary War in America, but the knitting machine was invented in England in the sixteenth century.

This reading comprehension lesson also demonstrates another small but important feature related to the issue of variable instructional content. Look again at Figure 7.2b. This lesson teaches a basic skill in reading. Unless the student's computer can deliver oral instructions, the lesson has available only written feedback that the student must *read*. Whatever instruction the lesson provides in feedback is thus likely to be *more* difficult to read than the passage on which the student made the error.

Thus, the lesson replaces verbal with *graphic* feedback that is also *dynamic*—the student actually watches the box and arrow being drawn. The lesson, in other words, draws on the strengths of the medium to deliver instruction in a way that looks different from other media but accomplishes the desired objective. A teacher, for example, would be able to use speech and pointing to make this remediation. (But the teacher, of course, could not do that for all twenty students in the class individually according to their performance errors.) Lacking those capabilities, the computer must be made to accomplish the same instructional goal, but in a way that is appropriate to the medium and that offers the advantage of increased individualization.

The main point we are making here, however, is that of variable instructional content. It is easy to see how the "flipbook" parts of sentences in the passages, which we demonstrated and discussed above, are variable content. The fact that the lesson is programmed in such a way as to be able to draw boxes and arrows like those in Figure 7.2b around *any* part of the passage that is tested is, however, also an important part of lesson content variability. We have seen several other examples in lessons discussed elsewhere in this book. Each one differs in its particulars, but the underlying notion of providing variable content is common to all.

Although it may not be immediately apparent, the doubling lesson discussed earlier in this chapter, for example, uses a technique very similar to the "flipbook" parts in the reading comprehension example just discussed. Look again at Figure 7.1, and you will see that the instructional feedback is particular to the item. In Figure 7.1a, for example, it would be much easier to make the instructional feedback for each item say,

> *This word ends with cvc and the suffix begins with a vowel, so you have to double the final consonant.*

To say instead,

> *Shop* ends *cvc* and *ing* begins with a vowel, so you have to double the *p,*

is far more difficult to program, but the added instructional value of this variable content is apparent. Like the features of accurate placement (discussed above) and instructional feedback contingent upon performance (illustrated in the discussion of the doubling lesson), the feature of variable instructional content is more than just a special feature of the lesson format. It is a requisite to all CBE of the tutor style intended to provide fully individualized instruction that guarantees mastery.

Distributed Practice

Effective learning has two important parts. Students must understand the content being taught, in the sense that they can apply the skill in new situations; and they must *remember* what they have learned until they have an opportunity to put their skill into practice. We have already discussed the first of these components in the preceding chapter. Here, we focus on the problem of teaching content in such a way that students remember it long enough to get a chance to apply it.

We know from psychological research on memory that skills must be practiced, not in massive doses, but in small doses distributed over time, in order to be retained. Yet, little attention is given to this well-known fact in the design of instruction. An occasional review or consolidation lesson is about all that most textbooks or curricula provide to help shape long-term retention. That flaw of instructional design is not fatal in the classroom of a good teacher, because the teacher can detect retention problems and insert additional practice when necessary. If, however, we plan to create CBE curricula in which students learn and practice skills on their own, apart from the teacher's constant monitoring and supervision—in other words, fully individualized instruction—we must take the issue of long-term retention much more seriously in the design of instruction. Let us, then, discuss a means for achieving distributed practice in CBE lessons.

Increasing Ratio Review   The doubling lesson example utilized a drill-like structure both to provide review of missed items and to achieve distributed practice. The means by which this was accomplished is a programming technique we call increasing ratio review. In the explanation of this technique in the section below, notice both its functional similarities to and differences from traditional "flashcard"-type drills:

- Think of all the items in the practice section of a lesson as a stack or queue.
- When a student gets an item right, it drops from the queue. He or she has demonstrated mastery by getting it right and needs no further practice on this item. (Of course, the queue also contains other items *like* this one, so there is little chance of the student's missing instruction by a fluke.)
- When a student gets an item wrong, it does *not* go to the *end* of the stack. Instead, the queue is reformed on the spot, and the missed item (or a variant of it, if the concept being taught is a generalization) is inserted at several review positions, with increasing numbers of intervening items between each review iteration.
- This same procedure is followed for *each* missed item. If a student makes another mistake on an item at some point during review, the entire process starts over for that item. (If a student misses items near the end of the stack, items he or she previously got correct are "resurrected," so that the student's long-term retention still gets shaped.)

We first encountered this technique in Chapter 2, in the context of a discussion of the strengths of the computer as an instructional medium. There we learned that the technique of increasing ratio review is but one of a number of instructional techniques combined in an instructional design approach called the corrective feedback paradigm (CFP).[3] In all, the CFP blends three programming techniques to achieve fully individualized CBE that guarantees mastery:

1. The "test/teach" lesson format seen in this chapter
2. The use of instructional feedback
3. Increasing ratio review

It is the last component feature of CFP, the increasing ratio review, that shapes long-term retention.

Sequencing of Instruction

In simplest terms instructional sequencing is answering the question, "What should the student do *next?*" That question may not at first seem to be closely related to the topic we are discussing—components of individualization. After all, the "proper" sequence of instruction is commonly believed to be intrinsic to, or dictated by, the subject matter being taught. And to a certain extent, of course, it is. It makes very little sense to attempt to teach multiplication to students who cannot add, or complex sentences to students who have not mastered simple sentences. The problem of sequencing comes in when such clear-cut reasons cannot be found.

If we know, for example, that performance in mathematics depends to a large extent on students' being able to read and understand their text, the directions for problems and tests, and the content of word problems, we face the sequencing problem of *how much* reading students ought to get before they begin some level of math instruction.

The word "level" is a clue, of course. Like the notion of placement, to which it is related, the notion of sequencing has roots in our old-fashioned conception of learning as a basically linear phenomenon. In the case of sequencing, the problem of linearity is exacerbated by the belief that there is, in fact, one optimal way in which the content of a subject matter ought to be presented. It is precisely this latter notion that Papert questions in the Logo rationale. There is not a *right* order in which to teach math, he reminds us. There is a *conventional* way, but it has been determined by considerations that have nothing to do with a determination of instructional efficacy.

In *Mindstorms*, Papert explains how our approach to organizing math for instruction is in large part determined by "accidents"—by the restrictions imposed by old instructional media.[4] (We might add that another organizational impulse in math has been what mathematicians perceive as the field's intrinsic logic. That makes a fine criterion for organizing it, if one's goals are to discuss or to summarize the field for mathematicians. Again, however, it has only an accidental relationship to the order in which *students* who are not mathematicians might best be able to understand it.) In the last analysis, when you press most advocates of a particular organizational plan for instruction for their reason, the answer will usually boil down to, "Because that's the way we've always done it."

As with placement, before we had computers, we had little practical choice but to come up with a single way in which to sequence instruction, whether or not we believed there was "one true way." We could not conceive of individualizing an instructional sequence because, even if we had invented a plan to do so, we would have had no way to effect it. Educational computing makes it possible to tailor the presentation of instruction, as well as review and remediation, to the individual student. But, as with placement, this capability requires new approaches to both the design and management of instruction—both instructional and technological issues are involved.

Among instructional components that make possible individualized sequencing of instruction are the elements of complete teaching that we have discussed earlier. Constructing an individual sequence for each student on the basis of his or her particular needs becomes possible:

- When instruction is broken into small units that teach just one skill or a very few closely interrelated skills.
- When the unit is preceded by an efficient (perhaps an adaptive) pretest that quickly determines whether the student has already mastered the skills the unit teaches.
- When instructional units are delivered within a sophisticated management system that keeps accurate and easily accessible data on student performance and has the capability to route students semiautomatically to units containing instruction on preskills they may lack on an individualized basis, contingent on their performance in testing and lessons.

When a sophisticated management system is available, planning the sequence of lessons becomes an empirical question. The instructional designer need not, for example, decide where in the curriculum a group of instructional units on interpreting maps and charts should go. The answer to that question is, "Students get them when they need them," and if you have a management system that can diagnose the need and route students to the lessons, that answer is viable. A flexible approach to the sequencing of instruction, in other words, is another instructional "strength of the medium." The designer of a textbook that will incorporate instruction on the interpretation of maps, charts, and graphs must find some single defensible place in the book in which to place the unit, because books lack the computer's ability to withhold information until needed and then to present it in a fluid and dynamic fashion. As we saw with placement, then, the advent of the computer changes our traditional thinking about the sequencing of instruction at the same time that it increases our ability to deliver truly individualized instruction that guarantees mastery.

Another important consideration in sequencing is review. How often should reviews occur? What content should they stress? The answers, considered without regard to instructional limitations, are that each student should get reviews as often as his or her performance dictates, and the review should stress those skills and concepts that the student had most difficulty mastering. Without computers, our ability to devise a system for accomplishing this admirable goal simply does not exist. No book could *ever* do it. Even the best of teachers could not do it very effectively—even if they had only one student to teach! A computer, however, which can *easily* be made to keep track of a student's performance, even on an item-by-item basis if necessary, can do it very effectively.

Imagine a computerized foreign language curriculum—to teach, for example, the first-year college course in French. Such a computerized course would have many components, but one component might be a vocabulary module that presented and tested the students on all the vocabulary in the course—perhaps a thousand words total. All the vocabulary would not be presented at once, of course. Each lesson might present about twenty vocabulary words—not a random sample from the entire vocabulary, but the words most appropriate to that lesson (perhaps those used in a dialogue). So far, the computerized sequencing of vocabulary instruction looks very much like what we would find in a textbook.

The special features of the computerized treatment of vocabulary drill (with CFP, by the way) surface when you look at how the computer lesson handles review for each individual student. Suppose the vocabulary module kept records on each item for each student, automatically computing an index of difficulty (for example, the number of times the item was missed divided by the number of times it was presented). The drill for the first unit would contain twenty new words, but the drill for all subsequent units would contain fifteen new words and the five words from the previous unit that had the highest index of difficulty. The effect would be a review sequence specifically tailored to the individual student's performance so as to maximize mastery—in effect, a separate sequence for each student. The corrective feedback paradigm actually has this feature built in. The process is represented schematically in Figure 7.3.

Consolidation units would work according to the same principles. They would include the items in previous lessons with the highest index of difficulty along with a random selection of nondifficult words from the previous lessons. The frequency of consolidation units could be determined by a parameter that specified a consolidation drill after the unit in which the nth item occurred that had a difficulty index over some specified amount. Thus, students who missed few items would need (and would get) few consolidation drills. Those for whom memorizing vocabulary was difficult would get many. Again, the net result is sequencing of instruction specifically tailored to the individual student, structured according to his or her performance, and designed to maximize both the efficiency and effectiveness of the student's mastery of the course's vocabulary.

Finally, the computer could be programmed to administer periodic tests of vocabulary mastery and report the results to the teacher. Although the tests

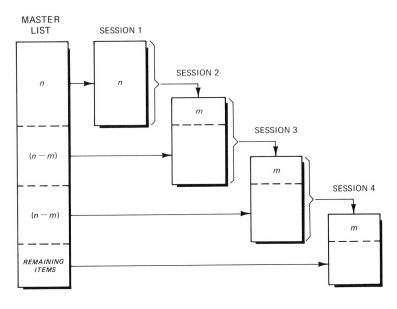

Figure 7.3

How the PCP corrective feedback paradigm constructs review sequences for individual students. In the figure, n represents the number of items in a sublist (the number of items in a drill session); m represents the number of most difficult items from the preceding session.

would be evaluational in nature, they, like the rest of the instruction, could also be mastery based. The computer could automatically construct review drills from missed items on the test, just as it did for the consolidation units. It is easy to see that these review and sequencing techniques, combined with the other features of complete teaching that we have discussed, not only increase instructional efficiency by individualizing instruction for each student, but they also have a dramatic effect on the ultimate effectiveness of instruction. The techniques for review discussed above *alone* represent an individualized instructional intensity that is wholly impossible to achieve in the classroom. In combination with the other components of complete teaching, the net results in increased effectiveness can be astounding.

CRITICAL REMARKS AND EVALUATION

Critical concerns with tutor-style CBE can be grouped into three categories: courseware problems, issues of computer imagination, and limitations of the lesson format and instructional techniques presented in this chapter.

Courseware Problems

Much tutor-style CBE (often called "traditional" computer-assisted instruction (CAI); its lessons called "courseware") is *not* of a caliber of instructional or design excellence equal to that described in this chapter. Part of the reason is historical. Courseware of what is now called the "tutor style" was first developed for computers twenty-five years ago, while most examples of the tutee approach (such as Logo) are much more recent developments. Thus, some tutor-style courseware is old, unsophisticated, and out-of-date in its approach both to education and to the medium. These pioneering efforts form the foundation on which all more recent approaches to courseware are built, and we should be grateful for that contribution. Nevertheless, they will not suffice for the present.

A worse problem is that all bad tutor courseware is not old. With the advent of the microcomputer, the market for educational software is beginning to explode. Meanwhile, the computer industry is selling the idea of hobbyism to new, naive educational users. Yet the public schools and even university departments of education are doing little about it, for the simple reason that they have almost nobody to prepare qualified CBE designers, and nobody to educate educational users as consumers. Thus, growth in computer imagination is slow in coming among new users and just as slow among developers of educational software. The result is that, while we have a marked increase in the number of courseware packages available, a large number of them are almost wholly derivative in nature, based either on approaches to the computer as a medium now twenty-five years old, or conceived as blatant (and thus almost wholly ineffective) imitations of other media—usually teachers and books.

Whatever the reason, a justifiable criticism of the CBE picture we have painted in this chapter is that we may have given the impression that CBE capable of delivering fully individualized instruction with the guarantee of mastery is "ready to go"—that we might have included an order blank at the end of the chapter. It is not, of course. Some of the big conceptual and delivery problems have been tackled with some success, but many problems remain. Even if they were all resolved, we would have a mammoth task of producing the whole, huge curricula we need to implement CBE in public schools nationwide. (We shall discuss this "courseware" problem and some means for addressing it more fully in Chapter 10.)

Computer Imagination

We cannot deliver CBE on a national scale because of bad and insufficient courseware; moreover, we do not have a really good and workable means for educating the people to develop the good courseware we need. The reason is one we have discussed at some length before. Much courseware will inevitably be imitative in nature—modelling on teachers, books, other instructional media, or earlier, outmoded courseware rather than effectively exploiting the strengths of the *computer* as a medium—at least until we find a way to educate enough people who are able to combine instructional design and subject area expertise with knowledge of the computer's possibilities. In other words, we will not have good courseware in abundance until educational users and designers of CBE develop computer imagination.

However, even if the problem of computer imagination were completely solved—in the sense that educational users were perspicacious and critical, and several universities in the country were supporting productive research and training excellent, imaginative CBE designers and programmers—the excellent courseware would not be immediately available. We would still need some years of full-scale production of courseware, management systems, testing packages, and other "service" software (for example, online dictionaries and reference books of other kinds) before CBE could become a powerful tool in the hands of teachers, fully capable of delivering individualized instruction on whatever subject the teacher wanted, for whatever student, at whatever level. Computer-based educators are beginning to solve some of the problems of design and delivery of CBE, but even if we could devote full time to production of excellent courseware, even if we knew *exactly* how to do all of it just right, it would take quite a while to get all of it into operation.

Limitations of the Lesson Format and Instructional Techniques Discussed in This Chapter

This chapter has focused on content-centered CBE of the tutor style using the corrective feedback paradigm and a content-centered instructional approach. For the reasons given above, we know this format to be powerful and effective for many kinds of teaching. It belongs to the class of "good CBE" as we have defined it in Chapter 2, because it effectively exploits the strengths of the computer as an instructional medium.

Summative evaluational studies have shown that the instructional techniques we have discussed in this chapter—variable items, item-specific corrective feedback, instructional use of graphics, increasing ratio review, and discrimination training techniques—increase instructional efficiency and effectiveness.[5] And ten years of implementation have yielded a wealth of informal verification of the formal studies.

Nevertheless, the format we have discussed is just one approach among many. It is no panacea. It cannot be used to teach everything, and even if it could, it would not be *best* at teaching everything. Other design insights, equally powerful, exist, and more are needed. Our concentration on a single lesson format and group of instructional techniques was intended:

1. As an example of CBE that does not imitate other instructional media and that does exploit the strengths of the computer as a medium.
2. As an example of a content-centered approach to CBE that can deliver fully individualized instruction.
3. As a means of illustrating both the components of individualized instruction and the relationship between individualization and instructional efficiency and effectiveness.

One limitation of the lessons we have seen, for example, is that they do not take as much advantage of the graphics capability of the computer to teach formal abstractions by permitting students to manipulate concrete individual instances of generalizations, as do Logo and the Gilpin and Dugdale lesson on "Exploring Simple Graphs" (both discussed in Chapter 5). Those lessons are good because they do not limit the range or kind of student responses. Students may make any kind of change they want in the formal statement, and they see the effects of the change no matter what its nature (i.e., even if the response is "wrong" it *does* something).

It is possible to argue, of course, that such open-endedness is useful only after students have mastered the range of the concept being taught. Nevertheless, the uses of induction seen in Logo and the graph lesson are "good CBE" according to our criterion of exploitation of the strengths of the medium, and any computer-based instructional format would benefit from them.

WHAT YOU HAVE LEARNED IN THIS CHAPTER

1. We opened the chapter with a discussion of a sample lesson that used the computer's strengths as a medium:
   a. to hold instruction in reserve for delivery only to students that need it, and
   b. to deliver that instruction interactively, contingent on student performance.

2. The lesson inverted the typical "teach/test" format of textbooks and teachers facing a whole class, substituting a "test/teach" format that individualized instruction and provided a guarantee of mastery.

3. The sample lesson served as a basis for discussing the several components of fully individualized, tutor-style CBE lessons:

a. *Accurate placement.* Placement by "grade level" is inadequate for two reasons:
   (1) Learning is not strictly linear—students have various preskill gaps.
   (2) Subjects are interdependent—performance in one subject area often affects another.
   Full tutor-style curricula managed by computer make it possible to sequence instruction according to skill level in a mastery-based curriculum rather than *placing* students by grade level.

b. *Variable lesson content.* Flipbook parts and similar computer-based techniques, which permit instruction specific to the individual item in corrective feedback, enable a tutor-style lesson to teach generalizations using the "test/teach" format.

c. *Distributed practice.* Effective learning demands that students (1) be able to apply a skill in new situations, and (2) be able to *remember* what they have learned until they have the opportunity to apply it. Remembering is a function of distributed practice, and increased ratio review is one way in which tutor-style lessons can provide it.

d. *Sequencing instruction.* The "right" order to teach a subject should be not a logical but an empirical matter determined by an individual student's preskill gaps. Treating it that way requires a very flexible curriculum and delivery system. Tutor-style lessons, which break instruction into small units with diagnostic pretesting and deliver them via a sophisticated management system, provide that flexibility.

4. Tutor-style CBE has its problems and limitations: bad courseware, an insufficient amount of courseware, and a lack of computer imagination in courseware design.

5. The lesson format on which this chapter concentrated also has limitations. One limitation is its failure to utilize the computer's ability to teach formal abstractions by permitting students to manipulate concrete instances as Logo and the "Exploring Simple Graphs" lesson do.

NOTES

1. Robert C. Dixon, Albert Liu, and Martin A. Siegel, "Doubling," Computer-Based Education Lesson from the *PCP Language Skills Curriculum* (Urbana: University of Illinois, 1982).

2. Martin A. Siegel, Louis V. DiBello, Elaine C. Bruner, and J. Michael Felty, "PCP Reading Comprehension I–IV," Computer-Based Education Lessons (Urbana: University of Illinois, 1977).

3. Martin A. Siegel and A. Lynn Misselt, "An Adaptive Feedback and Review Paradigm for Computer-Based Drills," *Journal of Educational Psychology* 76, no. 2 (April 1984):310–317.

4. See Seymour Papert, *Mindstorms: Children, Computers, and Powerful Ideas* (New York: Basic Books, 1980), pp. 51–53.

5. Stephen M. Alessi, Martin A. Siegel, Dorothy Silver, and Hank Barnes, "Effectiveness of a Computer-Based Reading Comprehension Program for Adults," *Journal of Educational Technology Systems*, 11, no. 1 (1982–83): 43–57; Robert J. Stevens, *Strategies for Identifying the Main Idea of Expository Passages: An Experimental Study* (Unpublished doctoral dissertation, University of Illinois, 1983); see also Siegel and Misselt, "Adaptive Feedback and Review Paradigm," pp. 312–315.

8

Educational
Software Tools

In Chapter 4 we presented Robert Taylor's goal-oriented system of classification for the field of CBE, concluding that it was the most useful system for our perspective, which seeks to disentangle Third Wave from Second Wave computing concerns in education. Taylor's system has three categories: tool, tutor, and tutee. (You may wish to look at Chapter 4 again, to compare his discussions of all three categories of educational computer use.) Chapters 5 through 7 of this book have been devoted to a discussion of tutor and tutee software. In this chapter, we shall discuss educational software tools.

A CONTEXT FOR TOOLS

Our remarks in Chapter 4 indicated that, while tutor and tutee are organically related to one another as two sides of a continuum describing the range of instructional goals, tools were different—not part of that continuum. Indeed, we said, they might be viewed as orthogonal to the *instructional* continuum implied by tutor–tutee. In order to be more precise and to show how tools fit into the larger picture sketched in this book, we must examine that relationship. We must define a context for tools by answering these important questions:

- What is a software "tool"?
- What do tools do?
- What is the relationship between educational software *tools* and the tutee–tutor *instruction* discussed in previous chapters?

What Is a Software Tool?

A tool is a computer program or group of programs that performs a specific task or group of tasks such as word processing or calculation. Tools accept some form of information input from the user and then perform a preprogrammed operation or set of operations on the information according to the user's instructions. Robert Taylor points out that most noneducational computer use falls into this category.[1] Most business computer applications, for example, and even the educational uses we discussed in Chapter 3 under the classification "Educational Applications of Computers" (automated student scheduling, grade reports, transcripts, etc.) employ the computer as a tool.

Taylor also has something to say about the *way* software tools are used— about where their value lies:

> *Because of their immediate and practical utility, many . . . tools have been developed for business, science, industry, government, and other application areas, such as higher education. Their use can pay off handsomely in saving time and preserving intellectual energy by transferring necessary but routine clerical tasks of a tedious, mechanical kind to the computer.*[2]

Second and Third Wave Tools

As Taylor describes them, software tools are what we would call a Second Wave use of computers. Taylor's tool is a software *machine*. A machine is a tool that repeats a small number of steps over and over again in a cycle. Its advantage is that it can repeat the cycle tirelessly, doing a job faster than people can, thus saving them labor and time. A construction carpenter, for example, must cut many boards a day when building a house. To do that, he uses a tool: a saw. Suppose that someone invents a machine to do this task: an electric saw. The new tool enables the carpenter to cut many more boards a day, expending much less effort and saving a great deal of time. The new tool, the machine, greatly benefits the carpenter.

As Taylor describes them, software tools operate much the same way. Instead of cutting wood, however, the computer as a machine-tool operates on information. From the Second Wave perspective, the computer is in fact a "data processing machine" and is often described using that exact term.

As we pointed out in Chapter 1, however, that benefit is coupled with a danger. Wide-scale use of Second Wave machines inevitably mechanizes and standardizes the culture that depends on them. Because machines must always do things exactly the same way, a culture that depends on them experiences an overwhelming, though covert, pressure to become machinelike itself. The dynamic goes like this: The more people become standardized—

want the same things and function in society like interchangeable parts—the more machines can do for them.

But there is another way to look at tools, and that is from the Third Wave perspective. Suppose a carpenter is not working in a Second Wave, "industrial" environment. Suppose he is a craftsman, interested in making fine furniture. Like the construction carpenter, he could benefit from a new machine-tool such as an electric saw. But instead of using it to increase his output while decreasing his expenditure of energy, the craftsman could use it to create a variety of new, imaginative things. Instead of changing his output *quantitatively*, it would affect his work *qualitatively*.

The same is true for software tools. One of the best and most obvious examples of a Third Wave software tool is the computer used for medical diagnosis. Its primary goal is not to process more patients in a shorter time but to provide more and better information about the state of patients' health and internal functioning than ever was possible. Moreover, such computers often eliminate the need for exploratory surgery or other procedures that traumatize an already sick patient's body, further endangering health. In short, their chief value lies in the new possibilities they open to users.

Our point in extending the Second Wave–Third Wave comparison to the area of computer-based tools is not to dispute Taylor's definition, which is useful, as are the kinds of tools he discusses. Education has some Second Wave tasks to perform, especially in the administrative and management areas, and Second Wave tools are perfect for those tasks. Our goal is rather to extend Taylor's discussion to Third Wave tools, which derive their utility not so much from the way they cut time and save labor, but from the exciting educational possibilities they create. Our discussion in this chapter will, in fact, focus exclusively on Third Wave educational software tools.

Relationship of Tools to Instruction

If we were talking about Second Wave software tools, the nature of their relationship to instruction would be easy to describe. As Taylor points out, a Second Wave tool does not teach, it just does better and faster some task that users already perform.[3]

In Third Wave educational computing, however, the separation between tools and instruction is not so well defined. Clearly, tools are not the same as computer-based instructional lessons, but they must somehow be incorporated into the instructional process in order to be maximally useful to teachers and students. In fact, there are four important considerations that affect the employment of educational software tools in the instructional process. We list them below and then devote a section of the chapter to each, in order to provide a more complete explanation and as a context within which to present and discuss the use of specific educational tools:

1. *Product versus process:* We have said that tools are programmed to do a specific job—they are *product oriented.* The user merely supplies the input. The computer then takes over, processing it and returning the "answer"—the result—to the user. That makes it very handy in business, where results are just what the user wants.

   Education, however, is often *process oriented.* The goal is not necessarily to get results in the fastest, most labor-saving way. Doing the task—going through the process—is often more important. In fact, obtaining the "correct answer" is often significant only as an indication that the student has done the task correctly.

   When using software tools in education, therefore, we must decide when product orientation is useful.

2. *Machine tasks versus people tasks:* One of the central themes of this book is the principle of exploiting the strengths of the computer (and its converse, avoiding imitative software). Like computer-based instruction, software tools can be imitative, as when they are programmed to do a job that can only be done effectively by people.

   There is nothing immoral or threatening about attempting to use a machine to do tasks that are better done by people. The only problem is that, while computers are extraordinarily useful for many things, they are never as good at being a person as a person is. Thus, imitative tools are merely useless.

   When using software tools in education, therefore, we must be sure that the task they are programmed to do is one best done by a machine.

3. *Tools and computer imagination:* Recently, the University of Illinois Library implemented a computer-based circulation system that doubles as an online catalog of the library's holdings. Some users have complained that this tool makes available to library users only the same information as the old card catalog. They have pointed out that, were the system more computer imaginative from the library patron's perspective, it might have changed the way that library research is conducted.

   In the opinion of the critics, in other words, the developers of the system failed to see how the new tool could do more than simply permit an old task to be done more quickly and easily. Computerizing a task may change the way it is done—and computer-imaginative software can make the new way more powerful than the old.

   When using software tools in education, therefore, we must be aware of how the tool affects the nature of the task it is programmed to perform, and we should be prepared to make fullest computer-imaginative use of its possibilities.

4. *Integrating software tools:* A friend of ours owns a company that produces a computer-based data and office management system designed for churches. The system is modular, comprising several software tools, each dedicated to an individual task such as accounting or processing membership lists. Alone, each module is a tool that helps the church to do a specific job faster and easier than before. The system, however, is *integrated:* When information is changed in one module, it is automatically updated everywhere in the system.

The degree to which an individual software tool is integrated with the larger job context in which its specific function is performed, the more useful it will be.

When using software tools in education, therefore, we must be aware of possibilities for integration. An educational tool will be maximally useful only if it is smoothly and organically integrated with the instructional process.

Let us now discuss each of these basic tool considerations more fully in the educational context, bringing in discussion of specific educational software tools where appropriate.

PRODUCT VERSUS PROCESS

Perhaps you remember the controversy that arose when hand-held calculators became popular among young students. The pocket calculator is not a real computer, but it is a tool, and the controversy it caused was one of product versus process. Like many tools, calculators were originally developed for scientists and engineers—people who need quick results. Some parents and teachers felt that children who used them would not learn basic math skills. "Let children, like scientists, learn the process first," these critics said. "Afterward, they can use the tool to get quick and easy results."

Computer-based educational tools raise similar issues. For example, consider a very computer-imaginative tool, the word processor. Many nonspecialists think of word processors as something like the next generation of the self-correcting or memory typewriters, and indeed, Lillian Bridwell, Paula Nancarrow, and Donald Ross point out that they were originally developed for typists in a business environment.[4] The standard, commercially available word processor is not, however, a glorified typewriter; it is a software tool. Like other tools, it accepts input of user information—in the form of text—

and then manipulates it as requested by the user. It is different from a type-writer, then, because it does not really start *its* job until the information has already been entered.

Once text has been entered, the word processor permits these kinds of manipulations:

1. Editing
    a. Add, change, or delete words, lines, or paragraphs.
    b. Move blocks of text (sentences or paragraphs) within the text.
    c. Global search and replace. Suppose, for example, you used the word "vernacular" throughout a text and later decided to change it in every instance to "demotic." This feature would allow you to do it in one operation.
2. Formatting
    a. Center lines.
    b. Add underlines, boldface, change typefaces.
    c. Indent blocks of text (as in a block quotation).
    d. Construct stepped lists (as in an outline format).
    e. Change the number of characters in a line of text.
    f. Justify the right margin.
    g. Change the spacing between lines (single, double, triple, etc.).

In each case, the user merely uses some command to specify the operation he or she wants, and the computer does the work automatically, reshuffling the input (the text), redistributing words on different lines, turning boldface on and off, and so forth. Thus, word processors are not concerned with typing; they edit and format text after it has been typed into the computer. Like other software tools, once the computer has performed the required operations, the tool delivers the results to the user—in this case, in the form of a flawless, printed document, error-free and attractively formatted.

Thus, by its design and the way it functions, such a word processor is obviously product oriented. The operations it permits users to perform on text are clearly intended to facilitate the production of a clean, attractive, finished product. Take another look at the list of word processor editing and formatting options presented above. You will notice that all are directed toward producing a finished document; none directs a student user's attention in any way to the process of writing itself. As a tool, most of the word processor's functions are focused on the stage of writing that occurs after a text has been composed but before it has been committed to paper in finished form.

The true strengths of the standard word processor are revealed if you imagine a word processor used, for example, in a law office. Lawyers have many contracts, leases, official letters, and other documents to produce. Each is unique in what it says, but the uniqueness comes from small changes of wording in standard paragraphs, the substitution of one clause or paragraph for another, the reordering of paragraphs, and so on. Thus, when lawyers "write" a contract, they often merely assemble an assortment of previously composed elements, making small changes.

The word processor described above is the perfect tool for such operations. It permits the user to select paragraphs from storage files in the computer's memory, dump them into the word processor, make the required changes, and when the "new" document is ready, automatically format it and print a flawless copy.

Such a tool is not without value in education. College students and professors, for example, find word processors excellent for editing and formatting papers, articles, and books. (This book was, of course, produced on a powerful word processor.) The question that arises about young students using word processors, however, is similar to that which arose when the pocket calculator became popular: What does the tool do for students trying to master the *process* of writing?

If you think of the writing process as divided into three main phases—prewriting (or planning and organization), writing, and revision—educators have found standard word processors to be especially valuable for the last phase. Robert Shostack points out that getting students to revise their writing is a perennial problem that word processors can help to solve.[5] They make it easier for students to revise, so that they will be more willing to do it; they eliminate the need to retype the revised theme, so students need not waste time recopying; and they permit the student to focus attention exclusively on the elements of a theme that need revision, thus maximizing the educational value of time spent in revision.

But revision is editing—the job for which, as we have seen, standard word processors have been designed. What of the other stages in the writing process? Up to now, there has been minimal exploration of the potential contributions of word processors to the prewriting process. Most educators working with prewriting in a computer-based learning environment have chosen another approach to deal with the issues of invention, planning, and organization. We shall discuss their efforts in another section.

Bridwell and her colleagues point out some potential problems in using standard word processors in the writing stage of the writing process.[6] For example, the word processor's mechanical capacity to move blocks of text around within a composition will not necessarily lead to more coherent compositions. The reverse seems equally likely.

In addition, while word processors permit students to make changes easily, that very capability may cause problems for student writers. For example, when using a word processor, the student often cannot see the entire composition on the computer screen at one time and as a result may find it hard to attend to the composition as a whole. And because the standard word processor greatly facilitates attention to details (directing the student's attention *away* from the whole theme), the tool may operate to narrow the student's focus too much when writing. The result is that students spend too much time fretting over small details while ignoring the composition as a whole.

Finally, even if the word processor succeeds completely, stimulating students' desire and willingness to write and revise more than ever, the problem of feedback still exists. Teachers have enough trouble now dealing with the mass of student papers they receive. Word processors could worsen the problem. It seems likely that, if students produce a larger amount of carefully revised writing but nobody has the time to read it, their motivation soon will decline.

None of these criticisms should be viewed as diminishing the value of word processors. It would be unfair to expect a tool invented for one group of tasks (which it performs admirably) to perform well on another simply because the need exists. These criticisms are therefore merely indications of problems we have yet to resolve as we incorporate this powerful tool into the educational process. We need—and are beginning to get—word processors specifically designed for student use, and we shall discuss them later in the chapter. For the present, however, our focus is on the issue of product versus process. We must understand that issue in order to discover the qualities needed to adapt this tool to educational use.

MACHINE TASKS VERSUS PEOPLE TASKS

Many software tools are conceived, designed, and used to do Second Wave tasks, even in education. Since Second Wave tasks are always mechanical in nature, computer-based tools often perform admirably. Take educational statistics packages, for example. A good package will permit the user to come to it with either raw data to be analyzed or a statistic or value to be evaluated. The user can enter the raw data directly at the keyboard or load in preformatted data. At any point as data is entered, the user may request an instant analysis of data so far, including the mean (with confidence intervals), median, dispersion estimates (including range, standard deviation, and average deviation), get the value for Σx or Σx^2, or see a graphical representation of the data.

After data are entered, the user may request t-tests, correlation and regression, analysis of variance, partial or multiple correlation, confidence intervals, tolerance levels, and other measurements. Any and all of these operations are instantly available on data entered and stored by the computer. The task of manipulating these data and reporting the results of operations is a tedious and time-consuming task for people, but one that a computer can do instantly and effortlessly. Statistics packages are a good example of a powerful software tool of great value to the Third Wave computer user.

The word processing capability of computers may also be applied to appropriate machine tasks in the school environment. As part of a computer-based management system, for example, teachers may employ word processing to prepare personal assignments for students and to send them messages. If students' computers are linked, they may use word processing operations for electronic mail and notes files (discussed in Chapter 4). Teachers also may use word processors to prepare partly individualized report cards for students (including both general comments and comments directed to each student on his or her performance).

When we attempt to extend software tools beyond these machine tasks, however, problems may arise. We have seen, for example, how the word processor stimulates the writing process by eliminating useless recopying of themes during revision, thus increasing the instructional quality of student time and effort spent on this important task. However, the effectiveness and value (measured as useful results as a function of time and effort expended) of some other software tools designed to facilitate the revision phase of the composition process are not so easy to establish.

To see why, let us examine Bell Laboratories' *Writer's Workbench*,[7] a collection of software tools designed to aid the revision process. Having produced a draft, the writer subjects it to the various tools in the *Writer's Workbench*, each of which provides a different kind of analysis.

The *Writer's Workbench* "Style" package, for example, performs such tasks as measuring readability; counting word and sentence lengths; and ascertaining the number of simple, compound, and complex sentences in a document. The "Org" package extracts the first and last sentences of each paragraph in a text, displaying them for the writer, who can use them to check coherence. "Diction" identifies potential problem phrases in a text, and "Suggest" supplies alternatives for them. "Rewrite" checks for dangling prepositions, empty phrases, and forms of the verb "to be" (to assist in eliminating passive constructions). "Abst" identifies abstractions in the text, and so forth.

Each of these checks is one that a good writer (or the teacher of a novice writer) would want to perform on a draft. From the standpoint of instruction, however, these packages have some problems. First, tasks that can only be done by people have been given over to a machine. Unlike the teacher, the software tool doing the checking is not smart enough to find all the errors. For example, Bridwell and her associates point out that the "Style" package cannot identify sentence fragments or run-on sentences.[8] Sometimes good, coherent writing does not have a direct link between last and first sentences of paragraphs. Passive voice, dangling prepositions, and the use of abstractions are not always bad. Stated generally, the instructional problem is that, being mechanical, a software tool is just not a good enough judge of style to correct student essays. That is a task for people, not machines.

Another instructional problem with *Writer's Workbench* is that it is not remediative. Beginning writers need more than merely a knowledge of their errors or of possible alternatives. They are learning the process of writing, and they need to know *why* the choices they have made are unacceptable. They need to form generalizations. The *Writer's Workbench* is thus too product oriented to be of maximal value in instruction. Assuming that the writer will know how to correct his or her mistakes once they are pointed out, the program merely identifies potential problems (and, in one case, provides some alternatives). It does not explain why a choice is ineffective, let alone hook up to instruction that will teach the generalization involved or provide additional practice on the skill in question. Indeed, as Bridwell and her colleagues point out, the formula-based approach taken by the *Writer's Workbench* packages easily could be detrimental to beginning writers.[9]

Finally, as Bridwell and her colleagues point out, the approach to editing embodied in the *Writer's Workbench* packages is more appropriate for some kinds of business or technical writing in which important stylistic and organizational criteria can be defined independently of content.[10] The "Prose" package, for example, compares the draft being examined to exemplars of the genre to which it belongs. Thus, its goal is to minimize the number of ways individual instances of a literary genre differ from one another in style, diction, word and sentence length, and so on. It seeks, in other words, to standardize individual efforts within a genre. While such rigid conformity may be desirable in some Second Wave writing applications (such as business letters, training manuals, and technical reports), it is hardly appropriate for most student writing, in which content dictates form. From the instructional perspective, therefore, "Prose" appropriates to a machine a task that properly belongs only to people.

The *Writer's Workbench* tools were not, of course, designed as instruction. They were designed for a product-oriented, technical writing environment and not for the process-oriented environment of the school. They were designed for writers with sufficient experience to recognize what they want when they see it, and for whom the question of *why* it should be that way is less important than producing an acceptable final document.

We have cited the *Writer's Workbench* solely as a context within which to discuss the issue of machine tasks and human tasks in software tools. Within a product-oriented environment like professional technical writing, the tasks performed by the *Writer's Workbench* tools are performed adequately by machines. In the process-oriented environment of the school, many or all of the same tasks may have to be done by people. Besides understanding the difference between the two, the important conclusion to draw is that it is often impossible to ask in the abstract, "Is this a good tool?" The answer depends on whether, in the context of its proposed use, the job it does is best done by a machine or a person.

TOOLS AND COMPUTER
IMAGINATION

In a product-oriented, Second Wave environment, a software tool merely does a machine task faster and easier than people can do it without a computer. Imagine, for example, a simple software tool that is programmed with the formulas lenders use to compute loan payments. That is a machine task, and a software tool can do it faster and more flexibly than a loan officer using a calculator. The tool might simply present a list of the variable loan factors (loan amount, amount of payment, total number of payments, interest rate, and number of payments per year), request the user to fill in amounts for all but one of them, and press a key. The tool would compute the missing factor instantly.

Such a tool permits the user to ask the standard question: What are the monthly payments on a loan of a certain amount for a certain interest and a certain length? But the software tool is capable of computing just as quickly and easily questions such as: "How much do I still owe on the principal of a loan at 10 percent with twenty-six remaining monthly payments of $160?" or "After how many months will I have paid half the principal of a 10 percent loan of $3,000, when my monthly payments are $145?" Further, since all of the calculation is done essentially instantaneously, the user of such a tool could play around with different payment amounts, different term lengths or different interest rates and get comparisons instantly.

In a process-oriented, Third Wave environment, however, using a software tool to do a task has effects—often important ones—on the nature of the task itself. For example, using a word processor can change the way people (including students) go about the process of writing. This is computer imagination territory—it calls on us to find ways to exploit the computer's particular strengths in new ways appropriate to the new tool.

Perhaps the most important way in which word processors can affect the writing process is by freeing the writer from the *linear* approach demanded by traditional composition media (typewriters and paper and pencil). Composition is not a linear process, but the media in which writers must compose impose linearity on the process. Experienced writers have learned to surmount this constraint; student writers have a great deal of trouble with it because they must master it simultaneously with all the other skills of writing.

Teaching writing on a word processor is comparable to fitting a child who wants to learn to walk a tightrope with combat boots, saying, "When you master the skill with this impediment, you may take off the boots." There is little danger of the child's reaching that stage, however. With the extra impediment, most will never learn the skill.

Let's look at an example. Using traditional media, a writer must first generate ideas, then copy them over in an organized list. If she gets the list right the first time, she is lucky; usually, the list must be reorganized, perhaps several times, and each requires a new "pass"—a new document that supersedes the former. Fleshing out ideas into an outline requires yet more passes—more documents—and so does each draft version of the composition itself. The "combat boots" aspect is this: To the inexperienced writer each pass *looks* like a separate document. But the individual passes are *not* separate, they have an organic, developmental relationship—a relationship that traditional composition media *obscure* rather than clarify.

In contrast, the way a word processor works can actually be analogous to the composition process itself. The writer can "jot down" ideas in a fluid electronic environment, rearrange them, and add, change, and delete them easily—not by producing additional documents in additional passes but by performing operations on the original list. Satisfied with the number and order of ideas, the writer can then expand each into a topic sentence; the result is a sentence outline produced not as a separate document but by minimal transformation of the original list of ideas. Using the insertion function, the writer can then expand each topic sentence into a full paragraph to produce what would have been (using paper and pencil) the first draft. The difference is that on a word processor the *outline itself* will have been transformed into the draft. It may then be edited and refined into a final draft just as it is, without having to make another "copy." In short, when using a word processor, the organic relationship of the various steps in the composition process are not merely shown to the student, they become part of the instructional process.

Let us look at another example of computer-imaginative use of software tools. Two important problems incurred in teaching writing are stimulating students to generate ideas and giving them sufficient feedback at each stage of the writing process. All too often, students must either generate ideas by themselves or make individual appointments with their teacher, who simply does not have time to interact with every student on each theme. Later, students often receive feedback only on final compositions, rather than on several steps of the writing process, for the same reason. Various software tools have been developed in an effort to solve the general underlying problem of high-quality interaction with students as they develop a theme.

Both Hugh Burns of the Air Force Academy[11] and Helen Schwartz of Oakland University[12] have developed software tools to "stand in" for the teacher, helping students to generate and develop ideas. Both use a tutorial format in which the program draws on information students have provided, encouraging them to refine and expand their ideas in response to a set of general questions applicable to many different topics. When students have worked all the way through the program, the tool provides a print of the ideas each student has generated, which the student may use to develop a composition.

The question that immediately arises is whether this is truly a machine task—whether being queried by a machine that cannot understand the information students supply can be all that helpful. More precisely, one could ask

whether the same set of questions printed in a book might not be just as effective. In other words, does the software tool adapt its questions in any significant way to the individual student and topic? If not, a printed list of questions
would seem to do just as well, and these tools would not be a computer-imaginative use of the medium.

Schwartz's program, however, takes the process one step further and in
doing so (1) corrects in part for the limitation of the machine, and (2) provides
students with additional needed feedback at this early stage of writing. In her
program, the ideas a student has generated in response to the program's questions may be copied automatically to a notes file (under a pen name), so that
other students may read, comment on, and critique them, or offer additional
ideas. This process helps not only the student whose ideas are being critiqued
but the students who comment on them.

The general conclusion to be drawn from this section is that neither software tools nor their use by teachers and students is automatically computer
imaginative. We need more study of the ways in which software tools affect
the nature of tasks they help users perform. We need to incorporate those
insights into instruction that uses the tools. And we need to attend to the
training of educational users—teachers and students—to point out the use of
software tools in ways that promote computer imagination.

INTEGRATING SOFTWARE TOOLS

At the beginning of the chapter, we cited Taylor's statement that Second
Wave tools do faster and more easily some task with which the user is already
familiar. Fruitful use, therefore, depends only on having the tool available
and making sure you know how to use it.

Third Wave tools, however, affect the nature of the tasks they are designed
to do. Therefore, if a Third Wave tool is to be maximally useful, potential
users must learn not only how to operate it but how to make creative use of
it.

To see this difference more clearly, and to understand what we mean by
creative (that is, computer imaginative) use, compare Third Wave software
tools to an erector set. Children interact with erector sets with varying
degrees of success. Some of them seem to be "mechanically inclined."
Whether the skill is inborn or, as behaviorists would say, one they learned or
generalized from some other situation, they seem to know what to do with a
set from the moment they receive it; they begin immediately to plan and execute elaborate and interesting projects. Other children are able to read the
complicated directions and from them figure out things to do with the set.
Many, however, will tinker with it for awhile, not discover anything particularly interesting or engaging, and soon abandon the tool.

In other words, to use a tool like an erector set creatively, just *having* one is not enough. The tool itself contains the same potential in each case, but some users fail to realize its full potential. Learning to use such a tool effectively is only partly a question of learning the purpose of its components and how to assemble them. To get the most out of an erector set, the user must also develop insight into the range of things the tool can do and the exciting things he or she can build.

When the tool involved is not a toy but an educational software tool, this distinction becomes more critical. In an educational setting, the difference between using a tool well or poorly has an impact on how well the student using it learns. Thus, in educational settings, the degree to which a software tool is integrated with instruction is extremely important.

As a comparative example, consider two educational software tools that perform exactly the same task: On the computer's screen, they automatically plot the graph of a mathematical equation supplied by the user. The first is a typical Function Plotter tool, useful to students and teachers in mathematics and physics courses. Its function is quite simple. Figure 8.1 shows the basic screen display. At the arrow, the user types in a function and presses a key. The computer automatically draws a graph of the requested function, as shown in Figure 8.2. Now, compare that tool to "Graphing Equations," developed for microcomputer by Sharon Dugdale and David Kibbey.[13] As you can see in Figure 8.3, the basic display of this tool is quite similar to that of the Function Plotter. In Graphing Equations, however, the graph is already drawn, and the student must type in the expression that describes the graph. The computer then plots the graph of the expression the student has entered.

Figure 8.1

Function Plotter, initial display.

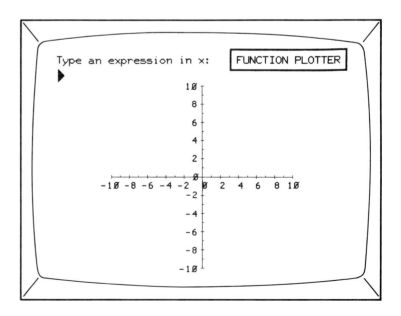

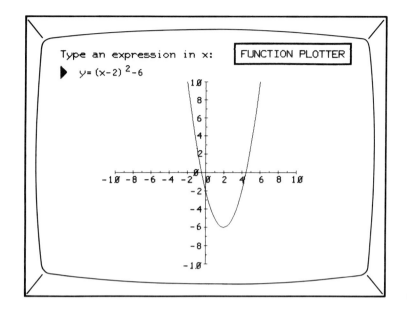

Figure 8.2

Function Plotter, function plotted.

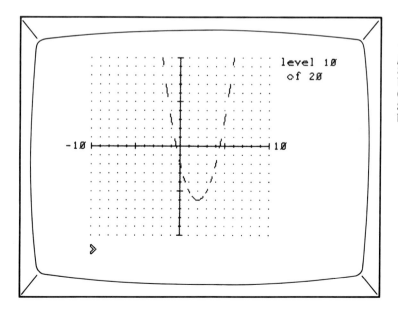

Figure 8.3

"Graphing Equations," initial display. Based on Fig. 1, page 3, of Sharon Dugdale and David Kibbey, Graphing Equations (Iowa City, Iowa: Conduit, 1983). © 1983 Sharon Dugdale and David Kibbey, University of Illinois.

If it matches, the student knows he has typed the correct expression. If it does not match, the student can see how his graph differs from the target graph. He can keep trying until he gets a match, varying the equation in small ways and checking how each alteration of the equation affects the plotted graph.

Graphing Equations is organized into many different levels according to difficulty. Thus, the graph a student is required to match is only minimally different from one he or she previously matched successfully. In addition, by leading students systematically through various minimally different graphs and equations as it moves from level to level, Graphing Equations permits them to learn many subtle relationships between equations and their graphs.

As you have seen, the basic tool operation in both Function Plotter and Graphing Equations is the same. The big difference is the way in which Graphing Equations integrates the tool function with instruction. In terms of our analogy, it is an "erector set" that guarantees student success by ensuring not only that the student knows how to operate it, but that he or she explores the full range of its possibilities. In fact, you could say that it is not really a tool at all; it is computer-imaginative and powerful *instruction* with a *built-in* tool.

Let us examine how integration can increase the educational effectiveness of a tool used in the classroom in one more example. Many word processors come with (or have the capability of adding on) a tool often called a dictionary program. Actually, such tools should more properly be, and often are, called spelling checkers. A spelling checker is a tool that contains a list of several thousand correctly spelled words. At the user's request, it compares a text entered in the word processor word-by-word to a stored list of correctly spelled words, identifying any words in the text that do not occur in its list.

In educational settings, this product-oriented tool has some limitations. For example, it cannot detect homonyms incorrectly used. "To," "too," and "two" probably appear in its list, but the tool cannot ascertain if they are used appropriately in the text. Further, such a tool provides no remediation other than suggesting alternative spellings for words that do not match. To use it confidently, a teacher might expect the tool to do something like saving incorrectly spelled words in a list for further practice. Even better, the tool might be integrated into instruction, perhaps by automatically transferring misspelled words to a computer-based spelling *lesson* that provides spelling practice for the student. At the very least, it might save a list of words students misspelled and give that information to the teacher to be incorporated into instruction elsewhere in the curriculum.

Again, it is not really fair to criticize spelling checkers for being difficult to integrate with instruction. Very few currently available word-processing packages were developed for use in schools, and the few that were seem to differ minimally from the run-of-the-mill packages. Up to now, word processing has been a product-oriented undertaking for professional writers—mostly business and technical writers—an affluent market prepared to pay for a slick product. Spelling checkers, as an offshoot of the word processor, are intended for the same audience.

When the emphasis is not on the process but on the product, when the aim is not to make sure students who use the tool learn something at the same time, even our homonym criticism hardly applies. If, when used by a business executive to write a letter, the spelling checker is applied to a text and it catches eight spelling errors but misses two homonyms, that represents an 80 percent efficiency record with just one quick and effortless pass over the text—a wholly acceptable cost-effectiveness figure in a business environment.

But we are, of course, speaking about applying tools in a process-oriented, educational environment. Let us compare the spelling checker with a similar but educationally oriented tool to further illustrate the importance of integrating educational tools with instruction to increase their power.

One feature, in a series of computer-based lessons that teaches general science, is a glossary function.[14] As the student reads a lesson passage and encounters an unfamiliar word, she may press the HELP key. When she does, the lesson asks what word she wishes to inquire about (see Figure 8.4), and the student types a word at the arrow. Figure 8.5 shows what happens when the student misspells the word. When she spells it correctly, the tool provides the pronunciation, a definition, and sometimes a sentence using the word, as shown in Figure 8.6. When the student follows the directions, pressing BACK to return to reading the passage, the information about the word remains on the screen, so that she may refer to it as she continues reading.

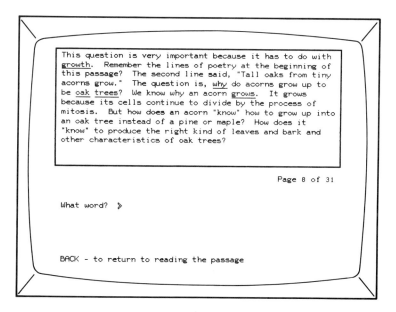

Figure 8.4

"GED Curriculum: Science," Glossary, initial display. Copyright © 1983 by the Board of Trustees of the University of Illinois. Reprinted by permission.

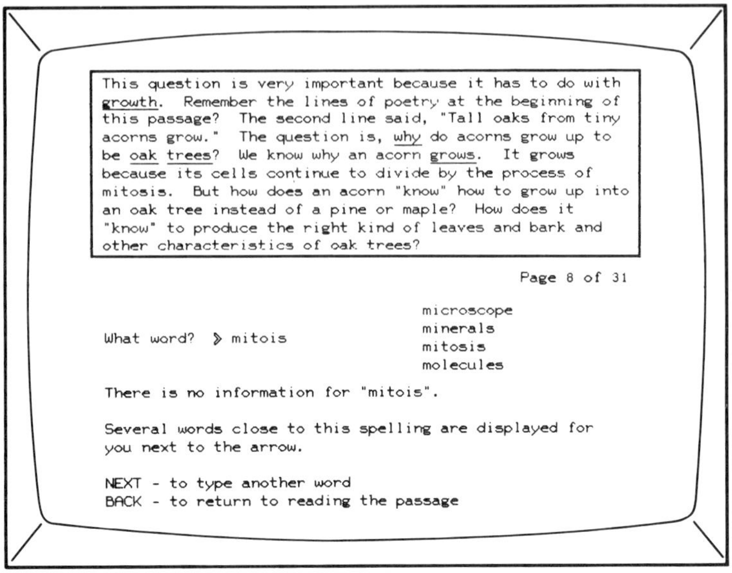

Figure 8.5

"GED Curriculum: Science," Glossary with word misspelled. Copyright © 1983 by the Board of Trustees of the University of Illinois. Reprinted by permission.

Figure 8.6

"GED Curriculum: Science," Glossary with correct spelling. Copyright © 1983 by the Board of Trustees of the University of Illinois. Reprinted by permission.

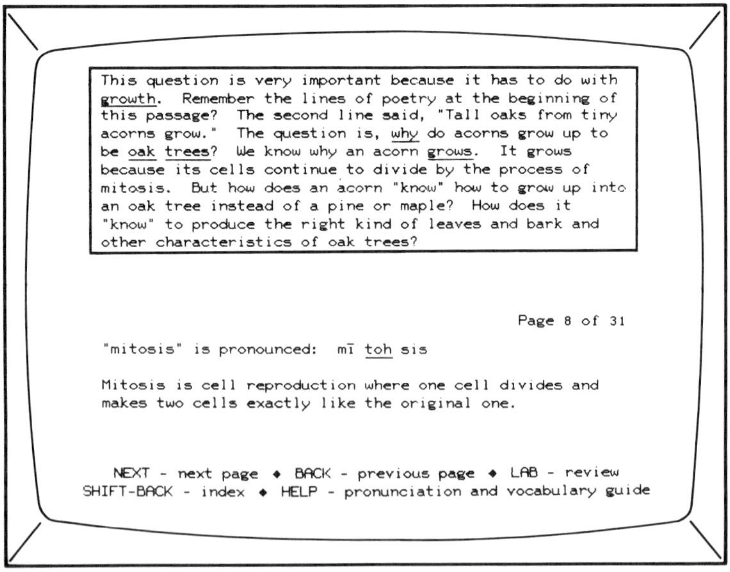

As you can see, this glossary tool is fully integrated with instruction. Like Graphing Equations, it is actually an integral part of a computer-based lesson. In its design and implementation, it also corresponds more closely to what we ordinarily mean by a dictionary, yet still exploits the strengths of the computer to compare the word typed to a list stored in the computer; when it does not get a match, it provides alternatives—just as the product-oriented spelling checkers do.

THE TIP OF THE ICEBERG

The idea of using computers to deliver instruction, which we have discussed in the preceding chapters, is still quite new and in an early conceptual stage. The idea of applying software tools like word processors in the classroom is even newer. The idea of conceiving and developing software tools *specifically* for process-oriented, educational uses is just beginning to capture the imagination of teachers and software developers on a large scale. Yet, tools represent a branch of CBE that is exciting and promising. There is much room for creativity in designing computer-based instructional lessons of the future, but instructional lessons are, after all, constrained in many ways—by the content they teach, by the need to present new material, provide practice, sequence material, review it, and test it. Tools, on the other hand, are limited only by the mind of the inventor and the ever-increasing flexibility and power of the computer. The old cliche describes the state of educational tools perfectly: We have seen just the tip of the iceberg.

Although we cannot know what the software tools of the future will look like or do, in this chapter, we have discussed the basic principles that the design of specifically educational tools must embody to be maximally useful for teachers and students. Let us, then, examine a representative of what we might call the "next generation" of educational software tools, an educational word-processing system recently developed for Science Research Associates (SRA).[15] By way of review, we are looking for a tool that is:

> Process-oriented rather than product-oriented—a tool that places as much emphasis on learning to write as on producing a finished composition.

> Devoted to machine tasks that exploit the computer's strengths as a machine while leaving people-appropriate tasks to people.

> Computer-imaginative—designed to take into account the ways in which a powerful software tool affects the nature of the tasks it helps the user to do and changes the ways in which they are done.

Integrated as fully as possible with the instructional process in the classroom rather than, as Taylor described Second Wave tools, standing apart from instruction, merely available for those who know how and why to use them.

In the sections that follow, we shall devote most of our discussion of this new word-processing system for microcomputers to those features that fulfill the criteria listed above.

Computer Management for Integration

When using a conventional word processor, users load the program and begin to enter or edit text, which may subsequently be copied to a different disk for storage. As we have learned, this method of operation has been carried over from the business environment for which word processors were first developed as tools. The business writer is not, however, involved in an instructional process. Nobody needs to see his or her work in progress. Others need access to it only when the finished text is printed and delivered.

The student writer is in a very different situation. In the classroom the writing *process* is most important. Therefore, some means of interacting with works in progress is the most important feature of a true *student* word processor. The teacher—and possibly other students—should be able to see and interact with a student's composition as it is being developed. Conventional word processors are actually inferior to paper and pencil in this respect: Although teachers may collect and view student storage disks on which work in progress resides, it is difficult for them to comment on the plan or draft they see.

The SRA system solves this problem by employing a computer management system that governs the word-processing functions of the system, provides data to the teacher, and provides a mechanism to facilitate the teacher-student information exchange on each student's work in progress.

A teacher, on first entering the SRA system, is taken to the management system's *main menu*. From the menu the teacher can move to the main *class roster* display, to establish the parameters according to which *prints* of students' files are made, or can move to the main *exercises and assignments* display.

The main *exercises and assignments* display presents the teacher with a list of all files that contain writing exercises for students. Up to eighteen exercises—sentences to combine, paragraphs to correct, ideas to organize and so on—may be stored here. From the main display, the teacher may look at exercises already listed, add exercises to the system, and change or delete exercises or assignments.

From the *main menu* the teacher may also enter the *class roster* display, which shows the names of all students in the class. From this display, the system permits the teacher to store names and records for up to thirty-six students, to add or delete students from the roster, to change the spelling of students' names or their passwords, and to delete the entire roster at the end of the term. From this display, the teacher may also choose to see the *student record* of any student in the roster.

The *student record* display first shows the teacher the file names of all the exercises assigned to this student. It permits the teacher to add or delete exercises for this student. (When the teacher chooses to add an exercise, the program takes the teacher to the full list of exercise and assignment files and permits him or her to make choices using the list as a menu.) From this display, the teacher may also control the student's level of access to the word processor (described below). Finally, from this display, the teacher may elect to *inspect* or *comment* on the student's work.

If the teacher chooses to look at a student's file, the program instructs him or her to load the disk on which the student's work is stored. Loading a student's disk from this point in the management system automatically puts the teacher in *comment mode*. When the disk is loaded, the teacher sees the student's menu, which contains the file names of all the exercises the teacher has assigned to the student and all the files the student has created for work in progress (up to eighteen files).

By pressing the letter beside a file name, the teacher is able to *inspect* either the exercise the student has completed in an exercise file or the finished composition or work in progress stored in a student-created file. In either type of file, the teacher may insert *comments* wherever needed. (Later, when the students view their disks, the interlinear comments appear in a contrasting color to differentiate them from the student's work.)

Students also enter the SRA system through the computer management system. Before loading the disk with the word processor program on it and his or her own storage disk, the student inserts the management disk and "signs on" to the system. At this point the management system recognizes and records the student's presence and transfers information about his or her level of access to the system and other system-related data from the management disk to the student's disk. These management tasks are performed transparently, invisible to the student, who is merely cleared and sent on to the word processor. In addition, the management system transfers any exercises the teacher has assigned since the student's last entry into the system, and it sends a message to the student's storage disk that says, in effect, "Mark each student work file in which the teacher has placed new comments since the student last signed on to the system."

From this initializing point, the management system sends students to their individual *student menu* displays. The menu lists all files on their personal storage disk—including both work files they have created and exercise files assigned by the teacher. From this display, students may enter and work on any one of these files. When a student enters a file and begins to edit, the SRA system operates much like a regular word processor, with some alterations we shall discuss in the next section.

Rather than choosing to edit a file, the student may choose from a list of other options on the student menu that permit him or her to create, join, delete, rename, or copy files; reorder the list of files; "unlock" a file (discussed below); or print a file. Each of these options from the student menu display is available with a single keypress. When a file contains teacher comments the student has not yet read, an asterisk appears next to the file name on the menu. When the student has chosen to "lock" the file, an *X* occurs next to the file name: *X* means "access barred."

The value of this kind of mediated, managed access to the word processor in an instructional situation is obvious:

1. Management permits the word processor to be *fully integrated* with instruction. By permitting the teacher to assign, correct, and direct students to revise not only compositions but also assigned *exercises* on the computer, the word processor may become the core of the whole composition curriculum.

2. Management focuses the efforts of teachers and students on *process* rather than *product* by permitting teachers to see and comment on students' work at varying stages and to assign them specific exercises based on their individual needs.

3. Management assists both teachers and students by taking care of routine bookkeeping and other *machine tasks*, but it leaves writing to the students; assigning, commenting, and correcting to the teacher.

Power versus Ease of Use

Our discussion of the SRA word processor's management system illustrated three of the four principal considerations of educational software tools. As we turn our attention to the heart of the system—the word processor itself—let us focus on the remaining concern: computer imagination. That is, how does the tool's design account for the ways in which using the tool changes the nature of the task? To answer that question, let us begin by comparing "what word processors do" to "what student writers need."

In order to represent any advantage over traditional writing methods and media (such as typewriters or paper and pencil), word processors have to be *powerful*. In this context, power means that the tool is able to perform many different operations on a text. But the computer cannot know when to employ each function. The user must tell the computer what to do by pressing keys and inserting directives as he or she writes. Thus, the more powerful the tool, the more keypresses and commands the user must remember or look up in order to use the tool.

Regardless of the medium in which they compose, the big problem for student writers is controlling the writing process. Students have difficulty choosing a topic, developing it, and planning a theme; writing good sentences and fleshing out paragraphs; maintaining unity, coherence, consistency of tone and diction, and so on. Whatever part of their attention students must devote to the manipulation of the medium in which they compose thus represents not only time lost from composition but distractions that threaten to interrupt the creative process. Students, therefore, need as *transparent* a medium as possible in which to do their writing. The perfect student compositional medium would present no obstacles to students, permitting them to devote full attention to their themes and to developing their writing skills.

No mechanical medium—whether computer-based or pencil and paper— can ever completely achieve this goal. But word processors can easily exacerbate the problem because, as we have seen, they increase the user's power and control over the tool (and thus, over the process of writing) only by adding commands and directives that ruin transparency by interposing themselves between the user and the task of composition.

Educators were quick to notice this problem when students began to try to use commercial word processing tools in the classroom. Thus, the aim of the first word processors developed specifically for student use was to become "user friendly," which meant easier to use. The Bank Street Writer is one of the better known exponents of this approach to solving the problem of transparency.[16] Unfortunately, simply making student word processors easy to use so they do not further impair students as they engage in the already difficult task of writing is not enough. Stripped-down word processors seem easy to use at first only because they require students to learn and remember fewer commands and keypresses that control specific functions. As the student writer begins to use these word processors, however, he or she discovers that for many conceptually simple tasks a whole string of "simple" commands must be entered to make the word processor respond. Suddenly, the "simple" student word processor seems much less transparent and much less useful. Ultimately, it is no solution to achieve simple operation at the expense of power and flexibility.

Clearly, what we need is a word processor that is both easy to use *and* powerful—one that makes many different and flexible operations easily available. That's *real* user friendliness. And coming up with a computer-imaginative way to get both at once is imperative for a process-oriented word processing tool designed for student use. The SRA system attacks this problem in three main ways. We have already discussed the first of them in a different context. The *student* part of the management system permits users to perform powerful operations on files by pressing keys from a menu. The student need not remember what key performs what function, because the menu lists both the key to press and the function it performs. The other two ways in which the SRA system combines power with ease of use are not located in the management system but in the word processor itself, and they are equally computer imaginative.

Turning Keypress Conventions into Generalizations

If users only needed to insert text from the beginning straight through to the end, word processors could be a lot simpler to use. But writers must edit their work; they must go back into the text frequently to make additions, deletions, and corrections, and to rearrange a draft's content. When using paper and pencil, this operation is relatively easy. The writer merely picks up a pencil, moves over the page, erases or crosses something out, and inserts new material.

Of course, if the writer makes many or extensive changes, the draft becomes difficult to read; and if he wants to move blocks of text, he must cut and paste the pieces. One of the word processor's chief advantages is that, when the writer makes such changes like this, he can instantly get a "clean copy" that incorporates his changes. Nevertheless, using paper and pencil, these operations are at least *conceptually* easier to grasp and thus more transparent.

They are not so conceptually easy on a word processor. Before the user can actually *make* the desired changes in a text, he must tell the computer where he wants the change to occur. To do that, he moves a cursor, or indicator, over the screen until it is located in the correct place within the text. Then he can add, delete, or move things from that point. But the user must first learn to use a series of directives that control the movement of the cursor, and that is where the transparency problem occurs. If students must learn and use a large number of commands simply to move the cursor on the screen, they could easily be distracted from writing and thinking, which would not occur if they were using paper and pencil. Yet, if the word processor is to provide students with power and flexibility of use, many such directives must be available.

The SRA system solves this dilemma by employing *generalizations* that govern keypress conventions. One such generalization governs "amount of move." For example, if you look at the chart in Figure 8.7, you will notice that the arrow keys move the cursor (the up arrow and down arrow control vertical moves; the left arrow and right arrow control horizontal moves), while the Ctrl and Alt keys add power to keypresses. Thus, left arrow moves the cursor one *space* to the left; Ctrl-left arrow moves the cursor one *word* to

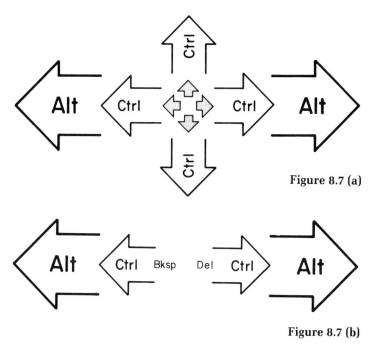

Figure 8.7 (a)

Figure 8.7 (b)

Generalized keypress conventions in the SRA word processing system: (a) shows the conventions for cursor movements; (b) shows how the generalizations extend to the backspace and delete functions.

the left; and Alt-left arrow moves the cursor *all the way* left, to the first character on the line. The generalization is:

> Key = small move
>
> Ctrl-key = medium-sized move
>
> Alt-key = big move

Then, when the student learns to use the *backspace* directive to remove text to the left of the cursor, the same generalization is used:

> Pressing Backspace removes one *character* to the left of the cursor.
>
> Pressing Ctrl and Backspace removes one *word* to the left of the cursor.
>
> Pressing Alt and Backspace removes *everything* on that line to the left of the cursor.

The figure shows that the same relationship exists between right arrow and the *delete* directive (Del), which removes text to the right of the cursor.

Although the figure does not show it, the directives *Home* and *End* utilize the same generalization. Pressing the Home key takes the student to the first character on the screen; the End key takes the student to the last character on the screen. Using the Ctrl key with Home and End give bigger moves—to the first and last characters in the *file*.

Levels of Access

Generalizations help to make directives easier to remember, but they do not diminish their number. Even with keypress generalizations, word processors need many directives to provide power and flexibility, and students have to learn them. Reducing the list of directives students must master makes learning them easier for the student, but that solution is unacceptable because it reduces the power of the system.

If you think about the problem of learning the names and uses of many directives, you will notice that the problem is not how many there are, but that many of them must be learned before the student can interact successfully with the system. Even a young student is capable of learning a large number of operations if they are presented one at a time, if the student can master the use of a few before more are presented, and if he is motivated to learn more because he has succeeded in applying those already learned.

As so often happens, the key to solving the problem of power versus ease of use involves shifting our perspective from Second Wave to Third Wave concerns—away from the *machine* and on to the *user*. This is not a machine problem at all but a problem of interacting with Third Wave users. Once that computer-imaginative insight has been reached, the solution is not difficult.

What we need is a word processor designed to present the directives to users not all at once, but in levels of increasing power and sophistication. The SRA system has three levels:

- The *first level* teaches the basic cursor movements and editing directives. While it permits users to do most editing tasks (excluding only moving big blocks of text around), it emphasizes not the most powerful, but the conceptually *easiest*, way of doing them. Its job is to get students editing, to let them develop the basic skills of word processing in as nonthreatening an environment as possible.
- The *second level* concentrates on efficiency. It teaches students the keypress generalizations and helps them learn to do the same operations they already know in the fastest and most powerful ways possible. It also introduces several new directives (such as centering and underlining text) that extend beyond the basic editing functions.
- The *third level* teaches students more specialized tasks not directly related to editing—superscripts (for formulas), directives for creating

indented lists (for outlines), and so on. When students have mastered this level, they have at their disposal a tool as powerful as most commercial word processors, yet learning to use it was almost painless.

Access to each level of use is controlled through the management system, which permits several options. Teachers can leave the system completely open—permit all students to enter at Level Three with all options available. Teachers can restrict student access to Level One or Level Two and require students to demonstrate proficiency before moving to the next level. Teachers can start students at Level One and leave it to them to decide when they need to move to higher levels.

In addition, the system comes with a series of tutorials for each level of use. These present the new directives, teach the generalizations, provide students with practice, and help them become efficient users. As with access to the levels, the management system permits teachers to ignore these lessons, require them as a condition for entering the next level, or permit students to take them when they need them.

Each of the design characteristics presented above is intended to help solve the "power versus ease of use" problem. In conclusion, remember that this problem is not merely one of user friendliness. The issue is really that of transparency, and it extends beyond mere user friendliness. Only by becoming transparent can a word processor be maximally effective as an *instructional* tool—one that facilitates rather than interposes itself between the student and the processes of thinking and writing. By getting out of the student's way, by removing obstacles that separate thinking from the written expression of thought, the word processor can make its most important impact on the nature of the writing task and best help the student learn this critical skill.

WHAT YOU HAVE LEARNED IN THIS CHAPTER

1. We defined a software tool as a computer program or group of programs that perform a specific task or group of tasks. Tools accept some form of information input from the user and then perform a preprogrammed operation or set of operations on it as instructed by the user.

2. Second Wave tools aim at doing better and faster some task users already perform. Third Wave tools attempt to expand the range of user operations, and they open up new possibilities. Education has an imperative need for Third Wave tools.

3. We discussed several important concerns that affect the power and utility of tools applied in education, the first of which was the difference between

product orientation and process orientation. Because business is product oriented, so are software tools originally developed for a business environment. Education is often process oriented and requires tools that reflect this different concern.

4. Another concern is appropriateness of the task. In order to be useful, software tools in education should be devoted to machine tasks for which the computer is suited. They should avoid the pitfall of imitation by not taking on tasks best left to people.

5. Computer imagination is another essential concern. Third Wave tools affect the nature of the tasks they are designed to perform. A good tool's computer-imaginative design reflects an awareness of this feedback between task and tool.

6. The final concern we discussed was integration. One of the most important features of an educational software tool is the degree to which it can be integrated with the instructional process.

7. We found that the educational potential of software tools is only beginning to be tapped. We discussed a managed word processing system that demonstrates the immediate future of educational software tools.

NOTES

1. Robert P. Taylor, ed., *The Computer in the School: Tutor, Tool, Tutee* (New York and London: Teachers College Press, 1980), p. 8.

2. Ibid., p. 3.

3. Ibid., p. 8.

4. Lillian S. Bridwell, Paula Reed Nancarrow, and Donald Ross, "The Writing Process and the Writing Machine: Current Research on Word Processors Relevant to the Teaching of Composition," in Richard Beach and Lillian S. Bridwell, eds., *New Directions in Composition Research* (New York: Guilford Press, 1984), pp. 381–398.

5. Robert Shostack, "Computer-Assisted Composition Instruction: The State of the Art," in Robert Shostack, ed., *Computers in Composition Instruction* (Eugene, Oreg.: International Council for Computers in Education, 1984), p. 9.

6. Bridwell et al., "Writing Process and Writing Machine," pp. 382–383.

7. For discussion and critique of the *Writer's Workbench* packages, see L. L. Cherry and W. Versterman, *Writing Tools: The "Style" and "Diction" Programs*, technical report (Murray Hills, N.J.: Bell Labs, November 1980) and L. T. Frase, *Writer's Workbench: Computer Supports for the Writing Process*, technical report (Murray Hills, N.J.: Bell Labs, 1980).

8. Bridwell et al., "Writing Process and Writing Machine," p. 388.

9. Ibid., p. 389.

10. Ibid., p. 388.

11. See Hugh Burns, "Computer-Assisted Prewriting Activities: Harmonics for Invention," in Shostack, ed., *Computers in Composition Instruction*, pp. 19–26.

12. See Helen Schwartz, "'But What Do I Write?'—Literary Analysis Made Easier," in Shostack, ed., *Computers in Composition Instruction*, pp. 27–31.

13. Sharon Dugdale and David Kibbey, "Graphing Equations," Computer-Based Education Lesson (Iowa City, Iowa: Conduit, 1983).

14. Martin A. Siegel, Lindsay P. Reichmann, Dennis M. Davis, Elizabeth J. Clapp, Robert J. Stevens, and Robert C. Dixon, "GED Curriculum: Science," Computer-Based Education Lesson (Urbana: University of Illinois, 1983).

15. Martin A. Siegel, J. Michael Felty, and Robert C. Dixon, "Electronic Ink: An Educational Word Processing System," Computer-Based Education Program (Chicago: Science Research Associates, Inc., 1985).

16. Bridwell et al., "Writing Process and Writing Machine," pp. 385–386, 391–395.

9

The Computer in the Classroom

From the beginning we have been saying that, for an educator entering the bewilderingly complex field of CBE as a nonspecialist user, a clear perspective of the field is essential. For that reason we have spent considerable time in previous chapters developing one. But now we have it, and it is time to apply it. In this chapter, we talk about practical classroom choices.

We shall discuss evaluation and selection of educational hardware and software, keeping in mind the notions of *hardware* as a transparent medium for delivering instruction, and *software* that exploits the strengths of the computer as a medium.

Although the costs of educational computing are coming down, they are still high. They include not merely the cost of acquiring computers and instructional software to run on them. They also involve "retooling" teachers, curricula, and even the school's physical plant to accommodate the new medium. The selections you make must therefore be maximally *effective*: cost effective, instructionally effective, and time effective. For these reasons, this chapter's guiding principle is that of "making educational computing worth it."

FIRST THINGS FIRST

The faculty of West Side School wanted to computerize. Neither the principal nor most of the teachers knew much about computers, but they wanted to make a good choice. So they went to Sandra C., the math teacher, because she had a microcomputer at home and could program. (They might have consulted a computer sci-

ence or other science teacher, or even a business instructor who taught some data processing.)

A conscientious person, Sandra took this responsibility very seriously. She read up on small computers and on educational computing, made a thorough investigation of available hardware in the school's price range, went to the local computer stores for "hands on" experience, and made sure ample software was available for the computer she chose.

Delighted, the faculty began their part of the process. They looked through ads and reviews in magazines, talked to teachers in other schools that had computers, went to "courseware fairs" and visited the software vendors' booths at institutes and conventions, and made some choices. They read previews, attended software demonstrations, used checklists, questionnaires, and sets of guidelines to evaluate the software, then made selections based on the highest ratings.

West Side School might well have been pleased with the choices they made, because the faculty approached the tasks of hardware and software selection with diligence and care. But they could have done even better.

It was a bit unfair, for example, to allow Sandra C. to decide on the hardware alone. True, she is the school's "computer expert," and her expertise is valuable. But she was forced to make her machine choices in a vacuum. She was forced into a Second Wave approach to computers, because she did not get the Third Wave user input she needed. She could only try to find the best machine for the money, and because she is a good teacher and has insight into other teachers' needs, she probably made a good choice. She would have been much better equipped, however, if the faculty had spent more time and effort thinking about how they were going to use the machines they bought—how many they needed, where they were to be placed, what they wanted to deliver on them, and so on.

Imagine how much better, too, the final *software* choices would have been if the faculty members had begun their search by describing to themselves as precisely as they could the instructional *uses* they wanted from software. Determining instructional uses is a teacher choice, not a "computer choice." Deciding what you want curricular materials to do in your classroom is a question that transcends delivery medium.

However, instead of determining their needs before going out to look at software, they said, "Gee, I don't know anything about computers. Let's see what is being advertised, what is selling well, and what is getting good reviews." They ended up getting what was "hot"—what was currently attracting a lot of attention. Since these lessons were selling well and got good reviews, they were probably of good intrinsic quality, but the ultimate utility of a package is determined not just by its intrinsic worth but by how well it fits the uses you want to make of it.

The West Side School faculty, in other words, asked only, "Is it a good, well-received lesson?" They should *also* have asked, "Does it do what I want and fit into my plan?" They could not ask the second question, however, because they had not thought about their curriculum needs before going out to pick software packages. They forgot this step, because somehow they just did not think of CBE materials as being "in the curriculum" in the way other teaching materials are.

Notice how the word "uses" keeps coming up in our critique of West Side's hardware and software selection process. They might not have realized they had a problem, but they had one nevertheless: They were attacking a Third Wave problem from a Second Wave perspective. They did not realize, for example, that if you are teaching one child on one microcomputer, you can be available for high-quality interaction with the child and computer whenever it is necessary. If, however, you are a classroom teacher delivering a language arts curriculum to thirty students, each of whom is working individually with relatively little direct teacher interaction, your situation is very different. Each child is in a different lesson, working at his or her own rate, and you are not always immediately available as problems arise.

Or, again, a classroom teacher using a single microcomputer to demonstrate an experiment to a science class is in a very different situation and has a different point of view from a classroom teacher using a few microcomputers to deliver remediation to a few students while the class as a whole does other work with the teacher.

The folks at West Side School had no way to know it, but their selection process suffered from lingering, unhelpful Second Wave attitudes. They were treating hardware and software as if they were independent when, in fact, they are interrelated in Third Wave computing uses like CBE. They were treating educational computing choices as if they were absolutes—cut-and-dried choices—instead of being dependent on the context of use. Their acquisition process contained no means to ensure that they would exploit the strengths of the computer as an educational medium in the choices that they made. Nothing about it alerted them to consider whether they were improving the individualization of instruction or whether they were offering teachers a guarantee of mastery. They are not to blame: They had no Third Wave perspective to apply. But we do.

TAKING STOCK

Our perspective suggests a three-point plan for acquiring educational hardware and software:

1. Take stock of your hardware situation.
   a. What machine features do you need?
   b. How many machines do you need?
   c. Where are they to be situated in the school?

    d. How do current acquisitions fit into the future of computing in your school?

2. Take stock of your instructional requirements.
    a. For what academic subjects do you want to use the computer as teacher?
    b. Where within the curriculum of each subject do you want to use CBE?
    c. What instructional approach do you favor—tutor, tool, or tutee?
    d. When do you want the computer to deliver complete teaching, and when instructional supplements?

3. With that information and those decisions firmly in mind, embark on the processes of selection and evaluation in the same way (and with the same care) that West Side School did.

The first two steps in the process are completely interrelated and must be undertaken simultaneously. They are related to the third step in a different way: They partly determine its results. Let us discuss each.

Taking Stock of Your Hardware Situation

Hardware Features If we could, we would love to say, "Figure out your software situation and needs first, and then buy whatever computer is required to deliver them." We would like to say it because, from the Third Wave user's perspective, machines really do not count—the computer should be merely a transparent medium through which the instruction flows, with no intrinsic significance. It is not practical to take that attitude, however, because you cannot possibly know in advance *all* the programs you are going to want to deliver on your educational computers. You have to make an open-ended hardware selection.

It would be easier if computers were more like cars. Like computers, cars have a lot of available options. But unlike computers, cars' options usually represent "luxuries" that merely enhance the functions of the "basic model," which can do the job perfectly well without them. All cars have engines, but for more money you can have more power. All cars have steering and brakes, but for more money, you can get power steering and brakes. All cars have windows, but for more money, you can get electric window openers. Computer options are not so simple. The options are often no "luxuries," but instead reflect *choices* that exclude some uses while making others possible.

For example, to do efficient word processing, many computers must be equipped with a special card that makes an eighty-character line of text on the screen just like a line of typed text. But once equipped with that card, a computer may not be able to run some instructional programs. Another example: A complex keyboard with programmable function keys adds power (and cost), but it may confuse and intimidate some users with its sheer complexity—and it may *not*, in fact, add value if you never use software that requires these extra keys. Because they are choices, not luxuries, the various combinations of options available on computers mean that there is simply no single perfect hardware configuration. A tradeoff is almost always involved. That is why, unless you know exactly what software you plan to run on the computer—not just now, but for always—you have to buy open-ended hardware. You have to make sure it will run the software you do not yet know you are going to want. And *that*, in turn, is why taking stock of your hardware situation and needs is so critically important—and why West Side School may yet run into problems.

   Nobody, therefore, can tell you what computer to buy, and you should not make that decision in a vacuum, as Sandra C. had to. Your decision should be based on the fullest assessment possible of your current plans and future needs in the areas of hardware and software, which should inform your decision. There are, however, some general guidelines that can help:

1. Although we cannot specify the "top" end of educational computing, we can specify the "bottom" end. For serviceable delivery of high-quality instruction, a computer should have:
   a. Enough internal memory to run sophisticated programs (at least 64K; 128K is better).
   b. A *real* monitor (not a TV set)—either monochrome or color.
   c. At least one floppy disk drive (it should not use cassettes).
2. Probably the toughest hardware problem schools are going to face is obsolescence: "After all the time and money we have spent, how can we take a step *backward* now, junking our equipment to take advantage of the slick new machines now available?" The hardware industry will keep changing. You have to assume that the machines you buy now are not going to satisfy your instructional needs forever. But you can protect yourself against early obsolescence when buying currently available hardware. Make sure that the machines you buy can continue to do something useful, even if you should later decide to switch to some other configuration for your primary method of delivering instruction.

Suppose, for example, you ascertain that the machines you are now planning to buy to deliver instruction can also do word processing, run problem-solving and calculational tools, deliver educational games and reinforcers, do classroom demos, and so on. Their utility will not end if you subsequently acquire a new hardware system to deliver the main part of your instruction.

You will not have to feel you are "taking a step backward" if you decide to acquire other machines. But you have to plan now for this later use as well as for the current one.

Number of Computers   The number of instructional computers in schools varies widely. At one extreme is the school with a single computer that is wheeled on a cart from one classroom to another whenever a teacher wishes to use it. At the other extreme is the classroom with enough computer work stations for at least a significant proportion of students to work independently on a computer at the same time.

The uses teachers can profitably make of computers depend, of course, on the number of computers available. Investing in software that requires each student to spend a great deal of individual time on the computer makes no sense if you have only one computer. If you have several, however, it is a waste of resources not to turn appropriate tasks over to the computer—utilizing it to deliver segments of the curriculum that then may be eliminated from the noncomputerized segment of the curriculum.

Whatever your hardware situation, taking careful stock of it is a critical preparatory step to software acquisition.

Deployment of Computers   We know of three ways schools deploy their machines: "traveling" computers, computers in the classroom, and the "computer center" arrangement. Wheeling computers on carts from place to place as needed is an arrangement nobody really likes. If the computers seldom move, carts are not needed. If the computers are in high demand and travel frequently, the school needs more computers. Deploying computers in individual classrooms—fully at the disposal of the students and teachers who work there—is the best arrangement, but school budgetary restrictions often preclude it. When planning for the future, a highly desirable goal is having at least four computers in each classroom. You can do good things with fewer, but to make a substantial impact on instruction in the classroom, adequate resources are necessary.

Some schools locate the computers centrally, and students travel to a "computer center." Some schools intend this arrangement as an interim solution; others seem to prefer it. It has advantages. While students are in the computer center, each student gets uninterrupted access to the computer. In addition, someone who knows more than the classroom teacher is usually readily available with advice and expertise, which can reassure a computer-shy teacher.

The computer center solution also has disadvantages. When computers are in the classroom the teacher can effectively integrate computer-delivered instruction into the curriculum. When students work in the computer center, however, the teacher does not know exactly what work they have done. The teacher may receive a report of students' progress, but may not know where they began, how far they got, and whether they mastered the content. The proctor in the computer center is not, after all, the classroom teacher.

Sending students to the computer center is like sending them to music class or to gym. The problem is that the material on which students work in the computer center is not separate from the rest of the curriculum, as music or physical education is. Even a teacher who accompanies students to the computer center to see what they are doing will have difficulty integrating instruction delivered and received there with the classroom curriculum. Going to the computer center is almost like going on a field trip within the school. The experience can be valuable, but integrating the computer with the classroom is even more valuable.

Whichever arrangement you choose, computer deployment has a strong effect on the amount and kind of instruction you can deliver on computers.

Avoiding Hardware Traps   We know there is no single perfect hardware configuration. One trap is to let that paralyze you. Even if what you get now is not as good as what will be available in the future, the computer still has much to offer to education. It is important not to be like some people who, expecting further developments in color television technology, are still waiting to buy a color TV. They are partially right—color technology will get better. But meanwhile, look at what they are missing!

Another trap is to get carried away with hardware and its intrinsic capabilities. In CBE now and in the future, the software the machine runs is the more important concern. In this respect you can compare computers to chalkboards. Having an eye-easing green board is better than having an old-fashioned hard blackboard; having a big one is better than having a small one; having one with panels that slide across one another to multiply the amount of board space without increasing the wall area the boards cover—all these improve the technology. But in the last analysis, it is what you *do* with the chalkboard that is vital.

If that is true today, when the hardware industry is in turmoil, it will become increasingly true as standardization is achieved. Remember, we are in the first stages of mass marketing a new technology. Compare today's microcomputer industry to the early days of television. While television today is concerned principally with developing and delivering programs, in the early days the focus was on hardware—getting TV sets into American homes.

Inevitably, however, the emphasis changed from hardware to software— from TV sets to TV programs—and the same is true for CBE. Ultimately, the hardware system used to deliver CBE will matter no more than the choice to publish a textbook in hardcover or paperback. The instruction in the book determines its value for the reader. The package in which it is delivered makes a difference, certainly, but not nearly as important a difference as the content that is delivered. Likewise, the brand and capabilities of a particular

computer have only limited importance in CBE. The other hardware considerations we have discussed—making sure that you have enough computers
to be effective, carefully considering how you deploy the machines you have,
and most important, integrating them into your curriculum in imaginative
ways—in the long run are more important than what kind of computer you
have.

But there are dangers in succumbing to the machine craze. There is a tendency, often seen in schools today, to pin our hopes for educational computing on the mere *presence* of computers in our schools—the expectation that
the hardware itself will "do the trick." But the future of educational computing lies solely in productive use of the machines for teaching, not in just
having computers in the school. Another danger of concentrating too exclusively on machines is that a sense of technical inadequacy can lead you to
abandon control over hardware, so that you acquire computers by accretion
rather than by design. Remember, in education, hardware is only a transparent medium through which instruction flows. The instruction is the critical
part, and that is your area of expertise.

Taking Stock of Your Instructional Requirements

Instructional Approach   Before you begin to consider individual software
programs, it is a good idea to decide which of the computer-based educational
approaches we have discussed is of most interest to you. If what you really
want is a tutee approach, even the best tutor-style programs will disappoint
you, and vice versa. There are good and bad representatives of tutor, tutee,
and tool, but to compare them meaningfully, you must pick the category first
and compare individual software packages within that category. Comparing
tutor lessons to tutee lessons—apples to oranges—just causes confusion.

We have discussed tutor and tutee as instructional *approaches* in previous
chapters and as tools in the last chapter. In the software selection process,
these additional comparisons become important:

- Tutee instruction represents an additional subject added to the curriculum, and thus, requires additional time on the part of both teachers and students. Tutor mode merely delivers instruction in regular
  subject areas, so it adds neither time nor new content to the curriculum; it seeks merely to enhance classroom instruction and/or make
  it more efficient.
- Tutee software is perforce "complete-teaching" software; it stands
  alone, separate from the rest of the curriculum. Tutor software may
  do complete teaching, but some programs can also be used to supplement classroom instruction. Both complete teaching and supplemen-

tal instruction can be valuable. Which is appropriate for your individual classroom is a matter for you to decide.

- Tutee software derives its power from being user alterable. Therefore, both teachers and students must learn how to manipulate the software before, or at the same time as, they use it for learning, and that process requires considerable time. The goal of tutor instruction is transparency. Both teachers and students should be able to use the software with no prior training or experience.
- Both tutee and tutor software seek to individualize instruction. Based on discovery, the tutee mode requires a high degree of teacher interaction—guiding and shaping student discovery. Good tutor instruction seeks to function independently, freeing the teacher for other, high-quality interactions with students not engaged in computer-based activities.
- Instructional outcomes of tutee instruction depend on the particular student (and on the expert guidance of the teacher). If it is to be valuable, tutor instruction should bear responsibility for its own outcomes and should guarantee mastery.
- As they are employed in the instructional process, tools take on the quality of either instructional type. Used by the student alone in an exploratory mode, the tool often functions in tutee mode; used by the teacher to facilitate the presentation of classroom instruction, the tool functions in tutor mode.

All three types of CBE can make valuable contributions to the classroom, but each does something different. Teachers, therefore, need not restrict themselves exclusively to the use of just one type. But to avoid confusion, you should decide which instructional approach you need in software for a particular instructional situation before you start to compare individual lessons. Here is the order to follow: (1) decide what use you need; (2) determine whether a tutee, tool, or tutor lesson would best serve this need; then (3) make your selections from among CBE programs of that variety.

Choices of Subject and Curriculum   In addition to obvious considerations, such as the subject areas for which you want educational software and the age and performance level of the students who will use it, consider the way you arrange your classroom. Specifically, do you prefer to have the class work as a unit, or are you comfortable with small group and/or individual instruction?

Some educational software packages, such as computer-based demonstrations, may be used with an entire class. For example, a biology teacher might use a package demonstrating the passing of characteristics in generations of fruit flies, or a chemistry teacher might use a lesson that simulates an experiment that cannot be performed in the classroom. Some tool-mode software may also be used by a whole class together—for example, the mathematical function plotter discussed in Chapter 8. In the main, however, good educational software is designed to individualize instruction in some way, and thus requires interaction with students individually.

Finally, within a subject area, consider whether you want the computer to teach some segments of the curriculum completely, or whether you want to use it to supplement the regular curriculum. Some software actually teaches a content. That is, it presents everything the students need to know about a content and drills them in the appropriate skills. Other software supplements classroom instruction in a content and is designed for use as remediation, extended practice, or enrichment of material primarily delivered by teacher or text.

CRITERIA FOR EVALUATING EDUCATIONAL SOFTWARE

In our discussion of Third Wave computing in Chapter 2, we saw that computer-based instruction is difficult to create because it must combine *content* excellence and sophisticated *programming* with *computer imagination*. Therefore, when evaluating courseware you should concentrate on each of these aspects.

Content

In evaluating lessons for subject area excellence, your task is most similar to evaluating print materials and other media that deliver instruction. The questions to keep in mind are presented in Figure 9.1.

The figure does not attempt to present a complete set of questions covering the instructional component of CBE lessons. It is meant, instead, to suggest that the process of evaluating courseware for *content* is quite similar to evaluating the content of any instruction. The questions may seem so obvious that they hardly need to be listed.

The problem in evaluating courseware is that it is easy to get distracted from these fundamental instructional considerations by the alluring features of a new, exciting, interactive medium—by "bells and whistles," as they are sometimes called. In the worst cases, designers use bells and whistles to cover up bad instruction, hoping that, when the teacher selects the courseware and the student uses it, both will be so dazzled by the pyrotechnics that they will not realize it is all show and no substance.

Even reasonably good instruction may be hampered by too much indul-

Evaluating Instructional Content

1. What are the goals and objectives of the courseware?

   - Are they clearly stated somewhere?

   - How well does the courseware meet them?

   - Do they fit into your curriculum?

2. Is it good instruction?

   - Is the content well matched to the learners' ability levels?

   - Is it accurate?

   - Is it significant?

   - Does the lesson have clear and sufficient directions?

   - If offline support materials are needed, are they present and sufficient?

   - If necessary, is there a teacher's guide?

   - Where appropriate, does the lesson provide diagnostic pretesting and mastery posttesting?

Figure 9.1

Evaluating instructional content of CBE lessons.

gence in electronic tomfoolery. Here is an example: In order to take the sting out of negative feedback delivered when a student responds incorrectly, some CBE lessons do engaging little tricks, but when the student gets an item right, the computer merely prints, "OK." Not surprisingly, in these lessons students sometimes find getting things wrong more fun than getting them right.

There is nothing wrong with bells and whistles, or with anything that makes learning more interesting and rewarding—provided it does not obscure the instruction, either for the teacher who is selecting it or for the student who is using it. But make sure that you are evaluating the lesson as instruction first. If it is good instruction, little extras will enhance it. If it is not, no amount of razzle-dazzle will improve it.

Programming

You probably feel pretty secure about evaluating the instructional content of CBE lessons. The prospect of evaluating their programming might be scary, but it should not be. Compare it to buying a car. As a driver, you can judge some things perfectly well, like how much pickup a car has for passing, how well the brakes work, how easily it handles, and whether it has a standard or automatic transmission—even if knowing *why* these things work requires a specialist's knowledge.

As when shopping for a car, then, keep in mind two main aspects when evaluating the programming component of courseware: utility (what it does), and beauty or elegance (a matter of personal taste). The main criterion for judging utility is *transparency*, and the main question is, "Does the programming get out of the way and let the instruction come through unimpeded to

Figure 9.2

Evaluating programming in CBE lessons.

Evaluating Programming

1. Check basic screen displays:

   - Are text and information clearly displayed?

   - Is everything easy to read?

   - Are on-screen directions for using the program clear?

   - Is the program clear and logical in the way it presents information?

   - Is it easy to visualize where you are in the lesson at any given point?

2. Check graphics (and other special features):

   - Are graphics clear?

   - Do they contribute meaningfully to instruction?

   - Are they animated?

        If so, does that contribute to instruction?
        Does it take up too much time?

   - Do you like them as much by the time you finish the lesson as you did when you started?

   - (Repeat this process for sound, color, touch screen, light pen, or any other "special effects.")

3. Check user friendliness:

   - When you run the courseware, does it execute all the way through without errors?

   - Try to break it. Can you do it?

   - Does it require coded input of any kind?

   - Can a student get "stuck"? (What happens if you enter an incorrect answer several times in a row?)

the student?" In judging the transparency of a lesson's programming, pay special attention to two factors: how the various screen displays look and work, and how user friendly the lesson is.

Figure 9.2 presents some important questions to ask when judging the transparency of programming. Most of the questions that refer to screen displays are obvious and straightforward, but a concrete example may be useful. We once talked to a University of Illinois student who violently opposed the notion of computer-based education and discovered that her opposition stemmed from a basic music course she had taken, in which a computer lesson was used to teach the names of the notes on the musical staff.

The lesson was a simple drill, and its theory was sound if somewhat unimaginative. It placed a note on the staff and asked the student to type in the pitch name. If the student got the note right twice, it was retired from the drill. If the student got it wrong, the lesson asked the student to "Try again" two more times. If the student still could not figure it out, the lesson gave the answer and returned the item to the stack for subsequent review—a basic flashcard drill.

But the lesson had a simple transparency problem, infinitely frustrating to students, but so trivial from the design and programming point of view that it totally escaped the attention of the developer. The lines of the musical staff were set too close together for the degree of resolution of the computer's screen. The student (who knew the names of the pitches of the staff before she took the class) continually made "performance errors" that were really just misreadings resulting from the screen's ambiguity in note placement. "The stupid machine kept telling me that I should have known that one, to try harder and concentrate," the student told us. "But it wasn't my fault."

She found the experience so frustrating—because it emphasized the rigid, mechanical qualities of the computer instead of exploiting its strengths as a medium—that she rejected the whole notion of computer-based education. The moral is clear. Checking screen displays for clarity, comprehensibility, and visual appeal—in short, for the programming transparency that lets the instruction of the lesson flow through the computer to the student unimpeded—is an easy task, one that requires no specialized training, but it can be an extremely important determinant of the instructional utility of the software.

Graphics   The group of questions regarding graphics and other special effects deserves close attention as you evaluate the instruction. The ability of the computer to generate graphics, change them during the course of the lesson, and animate them is a major strength of the medium, one that is not available in printed materials. As the questions in Figure 9.2 suggest, however, the principal concern is that they contribute meaningfully to instruction. We have already spoken about the dangers of bells and whistles; graphics is the place within a lesson where you will normally find them.

An example might help to clarify the danger of useless graphics. We recently saw a lesson in which a delightful history book for children was translated into a computer-based lesson. The book told a story that was beautifully accompanied by engaging illustrations. The computerized version repeated the story, but the computer on which it was programmed and on which it ran could produce only graphics of simple superimposed blocks of color.

The computer imitation, as you can imagine, was less satisfactory than the book. The lesson's designer/programmer, however, realized this fact and sought to compensate for it by animating the graphics. In fact, he created a graphic character who "spoke" to the student. (The simple illustration's mouth moved as the computer beeped, and the "spoken" text appeared at the bottom of the screen, written out.)

It was an imaginative idea, but it did not work. The animations took a long time to plot on the screen, they were not as attractive as the book's glowing and detailed pictures, and they contributed almost nothing to the lesson. In fact, because they took so long to plot, students soon found the lesson boring. This is an example not just of poor use of graphics but of a CBE lesson imitating a task better left to another medium.

User Friendliness   We know that the nature of user friendliness as an issue has changed a lot in the past few years. Not long ago we would have had to caution you not to settle for lessons that required the use of complicated codes to get access to the instruction. And some early lessons could be destroyed, or at least bafflingly interrupted, by an accidental wrong keypress.

Today, the most pernicious of these old-fashioned specialist computing notions have disappeared. But our discussion in the last chapter showed that as software has become more sophisticated, the user friendliness issue has not gone away, it has merely changed in nature. Today it is helpful to think of user friendliness as an appropriate balance between software power and ease of use. These software qualities tend to vary inversely. The more powerful a piece of software, the more difficult it is to learn to use, and the more complicated it is to use.

That much we know. But how does power versus ease of use affect courseware evaluation? Intrinsically, this new conception of user friendliness as a balance of power versus ease of use is neither bad nor good. It does, however, place more responsibility on the educator selecting courseware. It means questions like, "What's the *best* word processor?" are meaningless. Is the "best" the one that is easiest to use? Is it the one that is most powerful and sophisticated? It is up to the one selecting or evaluating the software to take into account the abilities of the prospective student users and the software capabilities required by the uses they will make of the package or lesson.

If a tool or lesson is advertised as user friendly, you should consider, depending on the students for whom you are selecting it, whether that is altogether good. Bearing in mind that ease of use generally occurs only at the expense of software power or sophistication, you may want something that is a little harder to learn to use and more complicated to use than the "friendliest" package. At any rate, never let anybody present user friendliness as an absolute quality (except in the restricted sense of the bug-free, unbreakable software we discussed). Easy-to-use software that lacks the power to do what you want is just as "unfriendly" as software that is impossibly difficult to figure out.

Computer Imagination

Increasingly, articles and published educational software evaluation tools (such as checklists) have become concerned with a quality often referred to as "imaginativeness" in tutor-style lessons. Ann Lathrop and Bobby Goodson, for example, head their list of CBE lesson evaluation criteria with a section called "Creativity." It asks, among other things, whether the lesson presents "information or instructional activities in a way not easily duplicated with textbooks . . . or other traditional classroom materials."[1] Esther Steinberg proposes three categories to include in courseware review: "(1) suitability of the lesson for the intended population; (2) quality of implementation of unique features of CAI; and (3) observations of student users."[2] In her article "Criteria for the Evaluation of Microcomputer Courseware," Vicki Cohen reminds readers:

> It is important to differentiate between the two kinds of attributes that need to be considered: (1) those that are generic to all media of instruction, and are recommended strategies to use for instructional design; and (2) those that are necessary to consider specifically in the design of software for the microcomputer and potentially affect learning outcomes in a unique way.[3]

Among published checklists, neither the National Council of Teachers of Mathematics *Guidelines for Evaluating Computerized Instructional Materials*,[4] the format of the Educational Products Information Exchange *PRO/FILE* for published software reviews,[5] nor the MicroSIFT *Evaluator's Guide* (developed for the Northwest Regional Educational Laboratory)[6] include "imaginativeness" among their evaluation criteria. The checklist of the California Library Media Consortium for Classroom Evaluation of Microcomputer Courseware does have a single item under the category of general design that asks whether the lesson demonstrates "creative, innovative, effective use of the computer."[7] (The evaluator answers yes, no, or not applicable.)

The quality of courseware that these publications are getting at is something we know very well. It is computer imagination—the degree to which a lesson exploits the strengths of the computer medium to enhance instruction, rather than merely imitating other teaching media in a computer environment. It is the most important quality of computer-based instruction and the hardest to describe in precise terms for evaluation purposes. You may find an imaginative use of the medium literally *anywhere* in a lesson, so to try to generate a list of computer imaginative lesson traits would be futile.

There are many ways for a computer-based lesson to be merely *imaginative*—in the sense of being attractive, engaging, and "cute." But *computer imagination* always directly enhances a lesson's instructional effectiveness in some way, and a lesson need not contain the most dazzling electronic wizardry to be extremely computer imaginative.

In a very real sense, this book may be viewed as an endeavor to present the concept of computer imagination in courseware examples and to teach you, the educational computer user, to become more computer imaginative in your approach to computer-based educational materials. Thus, many of the lessons we have looked at throughout the book may be thought of as instances of the concept of "computer imagination," and they represent the best (perhaps the only) way to describe it. Of course, they do not add up to a definitive list, because the nature of computer imagination defies such an attempt.

It may help to mention some of the things that computer imagination is not:

1. Computer imagination is not "bells and whistles" of the kind that add razzle-dazzle but have no effect on instruction. (We discussed this issue above, concentrating on graphics and other special effects.)

2. It is not awe-inspiring programming effects that contribute nothing to instruction. (Remember our discussion of those lessons, for example, that request user input in short answers when multiple choice or some other format would do? They are impressive, because they make the computer appear to "understand" whatever the student types in, but they are really just complicated programming gimmickry. If it does not contribute to instruction, it is not computer imagination—no matter how wondrous it seems.)

It may also help to recollect some qualities of lessons that have computer imagination. A computer-imaginative lesson is likely to:

1. Individualize instruction
   a. It should behave differently for different students.
   b. It should be adaptive.

2. Contain *meaningful* interaction
   a. It should accept student input in machine-appropriate modes.
   b. It should have immediate, instructional feedback.

3. Guarantee mastery
    a. It should place students accurately in instruction.
    b. It should remediate students with problems, specifically addressing their problems.
    c. It should provide a sound review of knowledge and skills to ensure long-term memory.

It may also help to provide one more extended example of a computer-based lesson that exploits the strengths of the computer medium to teach a concept. Consider how a good textbook introduces the concept of fractions to elementary students. Here is a typical procedure:

1. Start with a sheet of paper (a unit). Fold it once to illustrate the concept of "half." Fold the halves to illustrate the concept of "quarters." Demonstrate that "two quarters" is the same as "one half." Extend the concept to fractions generally.

2. Draw a number line marked off in units as in Figure 9.3a. Transfer the concept of folding the piece of paper into halves to the number line—dividing a unit into halves—as in Figure 9.3b. Continue to expand the transfer by adding quarters and eighths to the divided unit as in Figure 9.3c.

Figure 9.3

Typical textbook initial presentation of fractions.

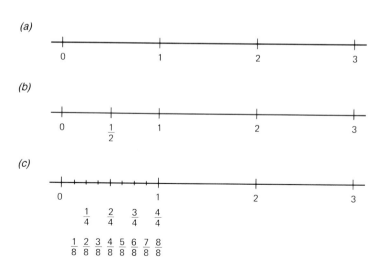

3. Lead students into applying the skill by introducing a procedure like the one represented in Figure 9.4.

The difficulty in teaching the concept is that it depends on students' making a critical minimum difference discrimination. A thing (a unit) *becomes* two halves, four quarters, and so on. The trick to teaching it effectively, then, is to find a way to present the discrimination *dynamically*. The textbook's initial presentation of the concept relies heavily on teacher *action*, because books are not a dynamic medium. The problem arises when students are asked to practice the skill, applying it to other situations. The teacher must bow out and let students do it on their own, but when the teacher leaves, so does the dynamic element of instruction. Thus, the third stage of teaching fractions (represented in Figure 9.4) is less effective than the first two.

Now compare the application segment of the lesson in Figure 9.4 to the computer-imaginative lesson, "Darts," by Sharon Dugdale, David Kibbey, and Barry Cohen.[8] The computer lesson is simplicity itself: It merely instructs the student to "shoot a dart" at any point of his or her choosing on the number line by typing in a number or mathematical expression. The lesson accepts

Figure 9.4

Typical textbook routine for applying the concept of fractions to new situations.

Teacher: Look at this segment. It has been
divided into 3 equal parts. Write a fraction
name for each point: A, B, C, and D.

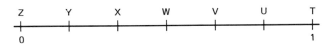

Teacher: How may equal parts now?
Write a fraction name for each point.

Is 3/6 the same as 1/2?
Is 1/6 the same as 1/3?
Is 4/6 the same as 1/2?
Is 4/6 the same as 2/3?

What is a fraction name for 1?
What is another fraction name for 1?

whole numbers, fractions, and decimal equivalents (and, thus, extends its usefulness by providing a powerful means to extend the concept of fractions to decimals). The lesson retains the full dynamic quality of the teacher's presentation, but it lets the student work completely on his own. A shot that misses a balloon is as instructive as a shot that hits a balloon. Students can "zero in" on the balloons, presenting themselves with as many minimum difference discriminations as they need. Unlike the textbook exercises, their feedback is immediate. Figure 9.5a shows a dart shot at 1⅖ that has hit a balloon; Figure 9.5b shows a dart shot at 3⅓ that did not hit a balloon.

The basic design of the lesson is computer imaginative enough, but its full instructional power becomes apparent when you begin to consider the ways students use it. When zeroing in on a target balloon, they can learn important things about mathematical expressions. Looking at the number line, for example, a student may realize that the balloon is "almost to 3 but not quite." She may instruct the program to shoot a dart at "2 + ⅔," but she may also try "3 − ⅓." If that does not quite hit the balloon, students sometimes type instructions like "3 − ⅓ + .1" to produce the effect they desire.

Dugdale also reports that students frequently locate the position of a balloon by doing things like measuring the total number of finger widths between two integers marked on the number line, and then shooting a dart at a fraction expressed in that measurement.[9] For example, if the space between 0 and 1 on the number line is 4 finger widths, with a balloon near 3

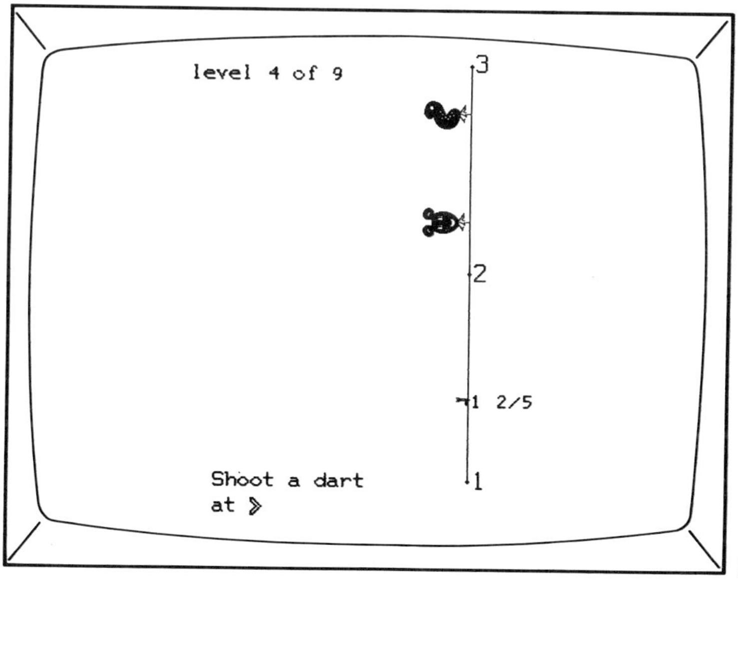

(a)

Figure 9.5

Two cases in the computer-based lesson "Darts" by Dugdale, Kibbey, and Cohen: In (a) the dart has hit a balloon, and in (b) it has not. Copyright © 1975 by the Board of Trustees of the University of Illinois. Reprinted by permission.

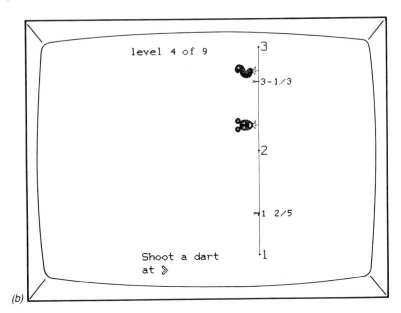

level 4 of 9

·3

→3–1/3

·2

→1 2/5

·1

Shoot a dart
at ⟩

Figure 9.5

(Continued)

(b)

finger widths, the student will shoot a dart at ¾. Or if the space between 0 and 1 measures 4½ finger widths, the student may decide to use ninths, calling each finger width equal to ⅖.

Such behavior can lead to insights about equivalent fractions, but combined with another feature of the lesson, it does something even more valuable: It integrates learning about estimation and approximation with the teaching routine instead of treating it separately in the curriculum. The "correct" answer is any answer that pops the balloon, and balloons appear on the number line at random points that are not always expressible in simple fractions with small denominators. The lesson thus teaches important practical applications related to the concept of fractions: that measurement is not exact, and that the determination of how much accuracy of measurement is necessary depends on the task at hand.[10]

"Darts" is an elegant, economical, and computer-imaginative lesson, but we chose this illustration to demonstrate how exploiting the strengths of the computer as an instructional medium often leads to ways of dealing with subject matter that look very different from an appropriate treatment in other media. It would have been quite possible to construct a computer lesson that let students apply the concept of fractions to new situations exactly as the textbook did in Figure 9.4. Such a lesson could even have been effective. But the treatment in "Darts" is better precisely because of its computer imaginativeness.

The following list of questions will help you to discover the computer-imaginativeness of a lesson when you evaluate it. Because of the nature of computer imagination, a lesson that tests out well according to this procedure may not be the most computer-imaginative of lessons, but one that fails it almost certainly will *not* be very computer imaginative.

1. When you look at a lesson, do not feel that *you* are being tested. Relax, and do not be afraid to make mistakes as you go through the lesson.

2. Go through the lesson at least twice—first as the good student, getting everything right; then as a poor performing student, getting many things wrong. Pay attention to how the lesson *differs* in these two cases. A computer-imaginative lesson will behave significantly differently in each case.

3. When you are making mistakes, try making the same mistake several times in a row to see what happens. A computer-imaginative lesson will include some mechanism to prevent your getting "stuck."

4. Make different *kinds* of mistakes on the same question, and then pay attention to the nature of the feedback you receive. An "imitative" lesson will just say, "No. Try again." A more computer-imaginative lesson will provide corrective feedback. A very computer-imaginative lesson will provide corrective feedback *specific to your particular error*.

5. Pay attention to the way in which *review* of missed items is handled. How much and how often are missed items reviewed? Are generalizations reviewed using flipbook parts that present the same skill in different, closely related instances? An "imitative" lesson will often treat missed items no differently from correctly answered ones. A more computer-imaginative lesson will bring back missed items for review and retire items answered correctly. A very computer-imaginative lesson will use a technique such as increasing ratio review to provide long-term shaping of memory.

PROCEDURE FOR EVALUATING EDUCATIONAL SOFTWARE

Locate Appropriate Software   After taking stock of your hardware situation and instructional needs, generate a list of topics for computer-based lessons and begin to look for available lessons that teach these topics. There are several ways to find out about existing computer-based lessons:

1. Look out for ads, reviews, and manufacturers' announcements in magazines and journals.

2. Books like *Hively's Choice*[10] and *Courseware in the Classroom*[11] give brief descriptions and complete cross-indexing of courseware by subject, performance level, and so on.

3. Listen to what other teachers say about courseware in your subject area. They may own and use programs that might interest you. Do not be shy. Whether you know someone there or not, visit schools that are more computerized than yours and look at what they have.

4. "Courseware fairs," inservices, and other special functions devoted to showing courseware are becoming more numerous and provide the opportunity for "hands-on" experience.

5. Software developers' booths at institutes and conventions provide a similar opportunity to view and interact with courseware.

6. Consortia (if your school or district is lucky enough to belong to one) that own or distribute courseware or act as an intermediary in the courseware acquisition process can provide valuable help.

Obtain Software for Review   You should personally review a copy of any lesson you are considering acquiring. As a means of *locating* potential courseware, any of the methods described above is good. Some, however, turn out to be more efficient in practice because they permit first-hand inspection of the products, and that is vital. You should never fully trust anybody else's opinion of a piece of software. *You* are the user. You know your needs, and you must not only see courseware but work with it yourself to know it is right for you.

A far better approach is to have the courseware on hand in your classroom. You will then be able to preview and evaluate it at your leisure. Also important, you can try it out with students. We know of three main ways in which schools can get hold of courseware to use:

1. Some companies make copies available either on approval or with risk-free return privileges. This is preferable but not always possible. Often the supplier is concerned that the software could be copied and then returned for refund.

2. Some of the bigger courseware publishers make demonstration disks available. They contain snippets of the company's courseware that provide a better example of how it looks and "feels" than any print medium or prose discussion could. Some disks are interactive, so you can get an idea of how the courseware works.

3. You may also be able to borrow a disk to review in your classroom or with your students—from another teacher, another school, or from a consortium to which your school belongs.

With Courseware in Hand, Conduct Your Evaluation   Each of the criteria discussed in the previous section—content, programming, and computer imagination—should be evaluated in at least one pass and often several passes through the program. In addition, you may wish to use an objective evaluation tool, such as one of the many published checklists that are available. You have to be careful with checklists, however. Courseware evaluation is not a cut-and-dried procedure—not an automatic, machinelike process that yields absolute results. You cannot total a lesson's "debits" and "credits" and come up with a "bottom line." The criteria for evaluation that a checklist or any tool proposes may apply to most or all lessons, but the weight they get will vary from instructional use to instructional use and from teacher to teacher. A checklist's format has no convenient way to reflect this. In fact, checklists often pose these problems for courseware evaluators:

1. *Checklists often seem to focus on qualities that are irrelevant to the software in question.* A checklist item, for example, that asks whether "responses to errors made by the student are helpful or sarcastic" makes little sense if the teacher is attempting to evaluate the Logo program discussed in Chapter 3 (which makes scant use of error messages) or a word processor. Or if a software package is intended to provide remedial drill on a basic skill for a low-performing student, how important is a checklist item that asks whether the program "stimulates students' creativity"?

2. *Checklists often make unequal qualities appear to be equal.* Answering yes, for example, to the question, "Is feedback to student errors helpful and adequate?" is surely much more important than answering yes to a question that asks whether "the software makes interesting use of color."

3. *Checklists often ask questions that are too vague or general to be helpful.* A checklist item that asks whether the program "exploits the computer to its full capabilities" is too broad. Questions like, "Does the content have educational value?" or "Is the program age-appropriate for learners?" are self-evident.

4. *Checklists often seem to present contingent qualities as if they were absolutes.* Is it always desirable, for example, for an educational software package to be "related to standard textbooks," as some checklists ask? The "right" answer depends on how you plan to use the software.

One final point. J. Richard Dennis makes an observation about evaluating courseware in comparison to evaluating other instructional materials that provides a helpful concluding thought to our discussion of the process of evaluation:

Computerized instructional materials also require evaluation, perhaps even more than text materials, since computer lessons frequently must function relatively independent of human intervention. In using a text, or even a set of exercises in a text, teachers frequently will alter, augment, or eliminate pieces of the material. Sometimes this is done on a rather spur-of-the-moment basis, with only intuitive justification for the change. Such manipulation is not nearly so easy (if possible at all) with computerized materials.[12]

Dennis's point is clear. However important evaluation is to the selection process in teacher-delivered media, it is more important in computer-based instruction—especially when you plan to let students spend time working on it by themselves. You cannot help it along. To make a significant impact on instructional effectiveness in the classroom, CBE, more than any other instructional materials, has to be excellent.

WHAT YOU HAVE LEARNED IN THIS CHAPTER

1. Since educational computing is Third Wave computing, it is important to begin your process of hardware and software acquisition by taking careful inventory of the uses you will make of the machines and of the needs of users. (It is also important to avoid too exclusive a focus on machines and machine capability.)

2. The costs in money, time, and effort to acquire hardware and software and to retool teachers, curricula, and schools for CBE are high. To justify these costs, educational computing must increase instructional effectiveness dramatically. How hardware and software choices maximize instructional effectiveness is thus the main question to keep in mind in the selection and evaluation process.

3. There is no such thing as a perfect hardware configuration. Users' needs vary, and hardware choices always involve trade-offs. Still, machines acquired by schools for educational use should have at least these minimum capabilities:
   a. Sufficient internal memory to execute relatively sophisticated programs
   b. A real monitor, not a TV set
   c. Floppy disk drive, not cassette, loading

4. For adequate instructional effectiveness, schools should aim for at least four computer work stations in each classroom whose teacher wants to use CBE.

5. To make effective software choices, you cannot compare tutor, tool, and tutee software to one another. Decide which category you want for a given task, then evaluate software *within* that category.

6. For maximum effectiveness, decide whether you want students to work individually, in small groups, or as a whole class, then choose software designed for that configuration.

7. Some lessons provide complete teaching; others are intended to supplement offline instruction. Both can have value, but effectiveness depends on deciding which you want, then choosing courseware to deliver it.

8. Since CBE is a blend of *content* expertise and *programming* expertise united in *computer-imaginative* ways, evaluate prospective courseware on these three criteria:
   a. *Content.* Do not let electronic wizardry distract you from a tough-minded evaluation of the content accuracy and educational significance of a program.
   b. *Programming.* The user's concern with programming should be focused on *transparency*: the degree to which the functioning of the lesson gets out of the way and permits the smooth delivery of the instruction.
   c. *Computer imagination.* Lessons can be imaginative in many extraneous ways. *Computer* imagination, however, always:
      (1) Increases instructional effectiveness in some meaningful way, and
      (2) Makes the lesson perform differently for different students in a way that is appropriate to their individual needs.

9. Consider user friendliness as a balance between software's power and its ease of use. The software that is easiest to use is not necessarily best, because it has less power. To maximize effectiveness, consider your student users' needs and abilities and pick the appropriate level of complexity.

10. When acquiring educational hardware and software, follow this procedure to maximize instructional effectiveness:
    a. Take careful stock of your instructional situation and requirements.
    b. Locate software that accords with those needs and teaches what you want.
    c. Always examine educational software first-hand (and watch students using it if possible), employing an evaluation tool (such as a checklist), if desired, as you evaluate it.

11. Remember that much of the educational software you acquire will have to do its job on its own without the help, clarification, or further explanation you can give to other media. Thus, if it is to be effective, it must be excellent. Evaluate very carefully.

NOTES

1. Ann Lathrop and Bobby Goodson, *Courseware in the Classroom* (Menlo Park, Calif.: Addison-Wesley, 1983), p. 57.

2. Esther R. Steinberg, "Reviewing the Instructional Effectiveness of Computer Courseware," *Educational Technology 23* (January 1983): 17.

3. Vicki Blum Cohen, "Criteria for the Evaluation of Microcomputer Courseware," *Educational Technology 23* (January 1983): 9.

4. William Heck, Jerry Johnson, and Robert Kansky, *Guidelines for Evaluating Computerized Instructional Materials* (Reston, Va.: National Council of Teachers of Mathematics, 1981).

5. *EPIE Micro-Courseware PRO/FILES* are published by Educational Products Information Exchange and Consumers Union, Box 839, Water Mill, N.Y. 11976.

6. MicroSIFT, *The Evaluator's Guide for Microcomputer-based Instructional Packages* (4th printing) is published by the International Council for Computers in Education, University of Oregon, 1787 Agate Street, Eugene, Oreg. 97403.

7. The California Library Media Consortium for Classroom Evaluation of Microcomputer Courseware, "Courseware Reviews 1982" and "Courseware Reviews 1983" (50 reviews each, $10 each) are available from San Mateo County Office of Education, 333 Main Street, Redwood City, Calif. 94063.

8. Sharon Dugdale, David Kibbey, and Barry Cohen, "Darts," Computer-Based Education Lesson (Urbana: University of Illinois, 1975, 1976, 1977, 1978). An Apple version is available from Control Data Publishing Company, 1982.

9. Sharon Dugdale, "Computers: Applications Unlimited," in V. P. Hansen and M. J. Zweng, eds., *Computers in Mathematics Education*, 1984 Yearbook (Reston, Va.: National Council of Teachers of Mathematics, 1984).

10. Sharon Dugdale, "There's a Green Glob in Your Classroom!" *Classroom Computer News 3*, no. 4 (March 1983): 40–41.

11. Wells Hively, ed., *Hively's Choice* (Elizabethtown, Pa.: Hively's Choice Publications and Continental Press, 1983).

12. Lathrop and Goodson, *Courseware in the Classroom*.

13. J. Richard Dennis, *A Teacher's Introduction to Educational Computing*, Illinois Series on Educational Application of Computers, Number 2e (Urbana: University of Illinois, College of Education, Department of Secondary Education, 1979), p. 2.

10

Attacking the "Courseware Problem"

In this chapter we will first analyze the reasons why so little good courseware is available. Then, using the insights we have developed, we will examine ways to increase both the quantity and quality of excellent educational software.

Although this chapter's content includes matters that most teachers as individuals cannot expect to affect directly, some knowledge of the topics discussed is nevertheless extremely important for informed consumers. The more you, as a Third Wave educational computer user, know about important factors controlling the courseware market, the better immediate software decisions you can make, the better long-range planning you can do, and the better chance you will have of making your needs and desires felt in the marketplace.

THE COURSEWARE PROBLEM

The last chapter dealt with the topic of courseware excellence from the teacher's perspective—with the problems of identifying needs and acquiring the products that fill them. This chapter also treats the topic of courseware excellence, but it is viewed more from the perspective of producers than consumers. It is as if in the last chapter we held courseware constant—assuming for the moment that excellent courseware was available in sufficient quantity, and the trick was making sure teachers and schools knew how to select it properly. Unfortunately, as this excerpt from Alfred Glossbrenner's *How to Buy Courseware* well documents, excellent courseware is not widely available:

> There is a problem with educational software. A problem, and a promise. The problem can best be illustrated by the initial results of a study begun in 1983 by the Education Products Information Exchange, a nonprofit organization based in Watermill, New York, and Consumers Union. The project enlisted the aid of some 300 teachers to evaluate educational programs. As reported in the Wall Street Journal, "Of the initial 50 programs reviewed, only a fourth got a grade of 60% or better." Other professional educators are less precise but more to the point. "The quality of educational software today," says one, "ranges from poor to horrendous."
>
> That's the problem. The promise is best illustrated by projections contained in Personal Computer Educational Software Market Report, a study produced by the highly respected Future Computing Company based in Richardson, Texas. Future Computing projects that the educational software market will grow by 71% a year, from a 1982 market of $70 million to a 1987 market of $1 billion. Those figures don't mean much until you realize that in 1982, approximately 2.4 million educational software packages were sold. By 1987—the year of the billion dollar market—the number of packages is expected to top 34 million, 24 million of which will be bought for use at home.[1]

In this chapter, we propose to examine the causes of this "courseware problem" and to discuss what can be done about it.

Several simple explanations of the courseware problem have been offered, but none is adequate. There is some truth to all of them, perhaps, but they are oversimplified and dance around the central issue. One favorite is the "chicken and egg" scenario, which goes like this:

> Software developer: *We don't have good courseware, because we can't afford it. It costs a lot of money to develop, and the market has not defined its tastes. We could spend a lot of money producing something nobody would even want.*

> Teacher: *How do you expect us to know what we want, when we have so few good options from which to choose? You're supposed to be the experts. Give us some good choices, and we'll show you what our tastes are.*

Excellent software is indeed expensive to develop, manufacture, and distribute. The base costs compare to textbooks and other print material, but courseware has a much greater research and development cost, because the computer's potential as an instructional medium is well understood by neither the educators who will use it nor the authors who develop the instruction. Nevertheless, preliminary research indicates that computer delivery can increase instructional effectiveness dramatically.[2] Combined with the reduced cost per student to deliver it, this increase in effectiveness makes CBE a potential bargain for schools. And what about the $70 million spent developing software in 1982? Clearly, *somebody* is willing to spend some cash before the market defines its tastes!

Thus, an explanation of the courseware problem based on cost factors—like the "chicken and egg" scenario—is not sufficient. One can hardly help siding with the teachers: Given the potential for increased effectiveness at reduced cost, it seems very likely that excellent courseware would entail minimum risk to the developers.

Another favorite explanation of the courseware problem centers on the issue of hardware/software compatibility:

> Software developer: *It's not a trivial matter to convert software designed for one machine to run on another. Hardware varies in many ways—from those the user sees, such as the different types of screen displays and keysets, to invisible ways, the operating systems and programming languages. And because it's not a trivial undertaking, it is expensive. If hardware were standardized, it would become cost effective to develop excellent software. We're willing to work within the limitations imposed by any hardware system—as long as it is just one set of restrictions. How can you expect us to satisfy the demands of every possible machine?*

Again, that explanation has some force, but it is not adequate. If our problem were that good courseware was available inequitably—for only a few brands of computers, for mainframes but not for micros, for expensive machines but not for cheap ones—it would have more merit. The problem, however, is that regardless of machines, the quality of courseware is low. Compatibility is not the real problem; there are other forces at work to impede the development of excellent CBE.

One of the weakest arguments concerns teachers' fears:

> Software developer: *We could be building excellent CBE, but teachers are afraid of it. They want to use computers, but they don't want them to do too good a job. After all, think what that could mean to their own job security!*

Needless to say, those who offer that explanation for bad courseware do not use it on teachers—at least not more than once! We have run into some teachers who still resist the inroads of computers, but the source of their reluctance is entirely different. Some teachers feel that computers in the classroom will augment an already dangerous tendency to mechanize and depersonalize the educational process. They are not at all worried that the computer will *replace* them; their feeling is that it is a costly device that will contribute nothing to those elements of teaching that are most important.

Teachers' real fears of educational computing and job security have much more to do with retooling. Many fear that, to be employable, they will have to acquire a new set of difficult and highly technical skills—ones for which they are not well suited. If the notion of Third Wave computing, with its shift in emphasis away from the machine and onto users and new uses, does not gain more force in education, these fears may be well founded. More likely, however, unless we concentrate on becoming "drivers" instead of "mechanics," the computer will become merely another educational fad.

Understanding the Courseware Problem

As we said, these explanations for the courseware problem dance around the central issues without facing them. They do that because those who offer them have not acknowledged the essential difference in perspective between Second and Third Wave computing, which we have tried to develop in this book. Because we espouse that perspective, we can state the basic underlying causes of the courseware problem directly and clearly:

- *Lingering Second Wave attitudes.* "Getting our schools computerized" still too often means buying computers first and worrying about what to do with them later. This machine emphasis is carried over from Second Wave thinking, and its inevitable result is a software crisis.

  We have to understand that in Third Wave computing the machine itself is unimportant; the uses to which it is put (which are determined by the software it runs) are the critical concerns. And we have to conceptualize that software from a perspective that recognizes the nature of the Third Wave user, who is not a hobbyist or amateur professional—not a "mechanic"—but a "driver."

- *Lack of computer imagination.* We still view the computer merely as a new educational technology when we should shift to the realization that it is a new instructional *medium.* Effective use of a new medium depends on identifying and exploiting its particular strengths. In this area, computer "experts"—Second Wave experts—have no more indication of how to proceed than classroom teachers. Because of their strong rooting in Second Wave thinking, they are often conceptually not even as well off as the computer "illiterate" teachers who depend on them, and for whom their Second Wave attitude has so little regard.

  It is not, in other words, that the people who know how to make excellent educational software just are not doing it for some reason. It is that nobody really knows *what to do.* As long as we depend on computer "experts" to produce products for us to consume, we cannot get excellent courseware. Educators as professionals have to intervene somewhere. To get excellent courseware, we have to find a way to bridge the gap between those who know about computers and those who know content and pedagogy. We have named this insight "computer imagination."

These are the basic underlying causes of the courseware problem, but each segment of the educational computing community experiences them differently and contributes to the problem in its own way. An effective plan to redress the problem thus requires us to examine the contributions of schools, hardware manufacturers, educational publishers (and other software developers), and university CBE researchers.

Schools' Contributions

Schools succumb to Second Wave thinking in two main ways. First, they are making major investments in hardware before good software exists to run on it. They do it innocently, because they have been persuaded by "experts" that the educational potential of the computer resides in the machine itself. Nevertheless, their innocent act contributes mightily to the courseware problem by creating a powerful *market vacuum*.

The presence of large numbers of machines in the schools ensures that, good or bad, courseware will be developed to justify the schools' hardware investment. The school market is so "hungry" that the quality of courseware actually ceases to be an issue in the short run. No matter what is developed, schools have to buy it, because they already have machines that have to be used. Opportunities for the unscrupulous and for "quick kill" courseware profiteers abound in such a market. Even well-intentioned courseware developers feel tremendous pressure to produce quickly and cannot control quality or imaginativeness as they would like. The long-term effect of the market vacuum may be to abort educational computing before it has a chance to develop its full potential.

Second, teachers, again innocently, too often "buy the idea" of hobbyism, which is the quick Second Wave answer to the dearth of excellent courseware and to the prevalence of awkward, ineffective, and unfriendly software. So-called authoring systems that permit teachers to build their own instructional lessons—within the system's stiff, mechanical, and unimaginative constraints—are not the answer to the courseware problem. The teacher is neither a programmer nor an instructional designer. Teachers are too busy to take on these tasks, which are the province of trained experts. Telling teachers unsatisfied with available courseware "to do it themselves" may get the hardware sales representatives off the hook, but its long-term effect on the instructional effectiveness of CBE is disastrous.

Programming courses and computer literacy courses, which teach teachers and students to become "amateur professionals" on the computer, are also attractive, because they represent an excuse to use a school's otherwise idle, expensive machines. This lingering Second Wave attitude toward users must be overcome if computers are to have a significant impact on instructional effectiveness. Attending classes also may diminish the urgency with which the *real* concern—that of producing excellent courseware—is felt. It is nice to tinker with the machines, and programming and computer literacy courses may be worthwhile, but what we really *need* is excellent courseware.

Manufacturers' Contributions

It is tempting to think, "*These* are the culprits! These are the nasty Second Wave experts who know better how to make a buck pushing machines on unsuspecting educational users!" Not true. The attitudes and interests of the hardware people do contribute to the courseware problem, but they are victims, too.

Those in the computer industry know that the computer has fantastic educational potential. When they "sell" schools on the importance of owning the machines they manufacture, they are not being dishonest. They are not even dishonest when they neglect to ask educational customers if they have a clear idea of how they intend to use the computers—whether they know what courseware to buy. They just do not perceive that to be their "department." From their point of view, it is too bad if educators do not realize that Third Wave computing is more a proposition of software than hardware. Besides, what would computer manufacturers tell you? They know less about what constitutes good education than you do. Nevertheless, their strong emphasis on the machine and concomitant neglect of the software component are major contributors to the courseware problem.

They are, perhaps, being dishonest to the extent that they arrogantly propound hobbyism: "Don't complain that my machine won't do what you want. It *can*—you just can't make it. It is your fault." The courseware problem may not be all *their* fault, but neither is it all *yours*. In fact, all this buck-passing does not get us closer to solving the courseware problem, which would benefit computer manufacturers and distributors as much as it would educators.

If the hardware manufacturers had less influence on educational users, their "it is not my department" attitude would be fine. Unfortunately, they sometimes do get into the development of educational software, and their products contribute significantly to the courseware problem. The courseware they develop tends to reflect their machine emphasis; it shows off the capabilities of their hardware attractively but often has little instructional value. Its very imaginativeness thus inhibits computer imagination, because their position of authority in the computer field creates a feeling that "slick is good." They are not equipped either to produce or develop excellent instructional software.

Educational Publishers' Contributions

Textbook publishers feel victimized by the courseware problem. They feel that educational software ought to be their domain. Courseware may be floppy disks and not print, but the disks contain instruction, and that is their territory. They are used to dealing with authors and handling the editorial process; they have in place instructional distribution networks and contacts with teachers and school systems. Publishers feel that they are better able to control the educational quality of software than are computer manufacturers. Their problems are: (1) they have no control over the hardware on which whatever software they developed would be run, and (2) they do not fully understand the computer as an instructional medium. Unfortunately, that has not kept them out of the courseware development market—or from contributing to the courseware problem.

Like the hardware manufacturers, publishers' courseware tends to emphasize their strong suit. Because they lack an adequate understanding of the potential of the computer medium, their products often tend to be "computerized textbooks." That emphasis is reflected in how many publishers go about developing courseware. Their staff of instructional designers in one room converts print instruction to computer designs; a staff of programmers in another room turns these designs into programs. Computer imagination is practically nonexistent in such a process. Just as the hardware people end up with wretched instruction that looks very good on the computer, publishers end up with decent instruction that does not take advantage of the medium. Excellent instruction, however, requires computer imagination, and computer imagination is a blend of both: sound content and pedagogy with exploitation of the medium's particular strengths.

Publishers contribute to the courseware problem in another important way. Uncertain about both the tastes of the educational computing market and its effect on sales of the print materials that are their stock in trade, publishers tend to develop courseware that augments their textbook curricula: "Buy our series"—they say. "It's better than theirs because it is accompanied by computer disks!" Though that is a nice sales point, it has a strong negative effect on courseware excellence because it tends to keep CBE ancillary to print instruction—exclusively supplemental in nature. As long as it is an "add-on," CBE will never achieve the potential that can make the investment in hardware and software pay off for schools. One aspect of courseware excellence means having full, self-standing, effective instruction. Only that can free the teacher, reduce the delivery cost while enhancing instruction, and make educational computing worthwhile for schools.

In an excellent, pithy article in the *Journal of Computer-Based Instruction*,[3] Francis Fisher explains the publisher/manufacturer courseware development issue very clearly:

> The educational publishers seem to assume that their experience in supplying printed textbooks to schools equips them to produce courseware for the new electronic technology. With print, however, the publishers generally commission an author or receive a manuscript from someone who is familiar with the pedagogical principles involved in both the presentation of the subject matter and the use of print media. With electronic courseware, publishers do sometimes receive submissions from the new cottage industry of courseware authors. But in the main, these are small efforts; programming a substantial work is generally beyond the resources of single individuals. So the publishing firms themselves have, by and large, become authors. As authors, however, they are without experience with the pedagogical possibilities of the computer and tend to focus on getting their products on the market quickly to meet the demands of a computer-hungry public before they lose their place in the education market. As a result, the publishers frequently end up by just putting their own textbooks on line. The result is similar to the early educational-television efforts in which programs consisted of a teacher sitting in front of the camera, with no exploitation of the medium. The result was a talking head. Likewise, if you program a textbook onto a computer, you end up with nothing but a moving book.
>
> Computer manufacturers, on the other hand, understand how computers can store data and perform large computations, the purposes for which the machines were originally designed, but are even less likely sources of innovation in the use of the computer for teaching than are publishers. Indeed, some manufacturers sense no need to guide innovation in courseware development; they wrongly assume that the schools know enough about computer-assisted education to specify how it should be designed.[4]

Fisher's discussion rightly points out additional concerns that affect publishers and hardware manufacturers alike, and over which they have no control. Rushing to "fill the void," responding to the market, minimizing risk, ensuring short-term profit—these are unavoidable concerns, but they are short-term and short-sighted ones, not likely to contribute to a resolution of the courseware problem.

University Courseware Developers' Contributions

Exempt from the market and profit pressures that thwart the computer industry's and publishers' efforts, university-based courseware developers are free to concentrate on excellence, yet they too contribute to the courseware problem. First, they ignore it. In the face of the market vacuum discussed above, Fisher claims that university developers "tend to be academic in outlook and unconcerned with the business of producing a marketable product."[5] He is not suggesting that university CBE specialists give up their concern for quality and rush "to fill the void." No one begrudges time spent in research that translates into the excellent courseware we so badly need. Fisher's remark indicates impatience with university professors, who do not seem to realize that an expedient, effective solution to the courseware problem affects their future as deeply as the business sector's. Instead, academics behave as if approaching the courseware problem with a sense of urgency were somehow unseemly. We do not ask them to give up their standards, but we *do* ask them to realize that the problem is big, immediate, and requires their concerned commitment. This is no time for ivory towers!

In their defense, university researchers have some justification for treating the market vacuum as if it were not their problem. The business sector profits if the market void is filled with courseware they develop; university researchers often do not. Perhaps university researchers need a larger share in profits if they develop excellent courseware. Then their sense of urgency would increase—not just because of the money they could make, but also because of the commitments they would have made. They would be "in the game"—there is nothing like a contract deadline to quicken the imaginative faculties.

The *scale* on which university researchers work in their courseware development efforts also contributes to the courseware problem. In the main, university CBE researchers usually write courseware in small development groups, and their lessons are delivered on the same small computers that the schools use. Their research is underwritten by small grants for short periods. These factors are completely outside the control of the developers, but they have strong impact on the courseware that is developed. Not only do they result in small-scale products, but they constrain our thinking about the very nature of CBE and its potential in our schools.

If the only courseware our best developers are ever allowed to conceptualize is on a scale too small to affect instructional effectiveness in our schools in any significant way, the courseware problem is not just serious—it is fatal. Among all developers, university researchers must conceptualize what CBE is to become—and not be forced to labor within the delivery constraints imposed on the consumer market by the current state of technology and distribution.

Thus, one part of the answer to the courseware problem is to fund research on an appropriate scale. We need funding for courseware development, but we also need funding for research into computer imagination—for investigating the strengths of the medium and the instructional techniques for tapping them—even when such research is not specifically directed toward the production of courseware products.

Another part of the solution is to take the professions of computer-based instructional design and programming *much* more seriously. Few of those who are producing the best, most computer-imaginative educational software devote a significant amount of time to training the next generation of CBE professionals. Some universities have a few courses in the design of computer-based education, but graduate programs offering advanced degrees in CBE are still scarce. Even noted CBE developers in many cases hold appointments in educational psychology or other areas of education, signifying that

CBE is not treated as an academic specialty in its own right, but as a kind of hobby in which any faculty member with an interest is permitted to dally. Some journals and professional associations devoted to CBE are emerging, and that is a good sign. The situation will improve when the remainder of the hobbyist flavor that sometimes pervades the literature disappears, and CBE takes itself seriously enough to consider creating standards and shaping policy.

A final problem that affects university courseware development is one that affects education generally. The double-edged sword of pluralism plays an important role in the courseware problem. Educators disagree on almost everything. In fact, there is probably only one thing we agree on—that every-one has the right to do his or her own thing. We have learned our lesson through bitter experiences. It seems that every time we buy into a big move-ment—every time we "put all our eggs in one basket"—something bad hap-pens. Like open classrooms. Or new math.

Pluralism is thus necessary, but it is not exactly *good*. It has benefits, but it exacts a price. In the case of CBE, it is particularly dangerous. There is little danger of any single *instructional* point of view in the field of CBE coming to predominate and destroy the others. The danger is that, while educators fight it out and cannot decide, lingering Second Wave attitudes toward computers are pervading the approach to school computerization by default. Reality is not waiting for us to make up our minds. Our pluralist commitment is evis-cerating our capacity as a profession to lead at a time when our leadership is sorely needed. We do not need "one way" to approach the development of courseware, but we do need a firm, clear, and strong commitment to a Third Wave approach to educational computing.

Resolving the Courseware Problem

Our discussion of the various facets of the courseware problem permits us to draw certain important conclusions:

- Courseware is a big problem. All segments of the educational com-puting community—manufacturers, publishers, users—contribute to it and are affected by it in interlocking ways. The expense entailed in resolving the problem is large—both for producers and consumers. We need to produce courseware on a whole new scale—not just more packages but bigger, more ambitious packages.
- The problem is nobody's fault. Both producers and consumers are victims. But because of the ways in which they are constrained, both also contribute to the problem.
- The problem will not go away by itself. The interrelated nature of the facets of the courseware problem have the various segments of the

educational computing community deadlocked. The problem cannot just work itself out—someone must take it on.

- The courseware problem is urgent. The advent of the microcomputer has created a ground swell of interest in nonspecialist computing both in and out of schools. The computing fad currently carries such force that we often begin to speak in terms of potential but end up talking inevitabilities. The only inevitability about computer-based education—at least for this generation—is that we must solve the courseware problem or computers will end up in the closet with the opaque projectors.

The solution is a simple question of economics. Schools are getting good Second Wave *machine* value from computers now—power and flexibility, good machine potential for a good price. What they are not getting is good Third Wave *use* from their machines. But schools are Third Wave users. Computing is worth their investment only if it does what they need. Thus, the future of educational computing depends on a viable practical resolution of the courseware problem. It is time to consider just what practical steps we have to take.

First, the most practical solution to the courseware problem is the one that addresses the most pressing educational needs.

There are all kinds of things that CBE *could* do, and we should get around to doing all of them. But given the urgency and complexity of the courseware problem, we must establish some priorities. If we are talking *practical* solutions, we have to work first on developing software that addresses the most pressing needs and the widest student population. Only in this way can educational computing producers and consumers realize a reasonable return on their investment.

Increasing instructional effectiveness is clearly the most pressing educational problem facing our country today. The National Commission on Excellence in Education, in *A Nation at Risk: The Imperative for Educational Reform,* defined and provided solutions to the problems afflicting American education. The commission wrote:

> The people of the United States need to know that individuals in our society who do not possess the levels of skill, literacy, and training essential to this new era will be effectively disenfranchised, not simply from the material rewards that accompany competent performance, but also from the chance to participate fully in our national life.[6]

The educational software we want to develop first—the "practical solution" software—is that which is directly intended to increase students' knowledge and skills and that succeeds in doing so.

During the course of this book, we have discussed many different kinds of educational software with many different goals. The type that most directly addresses the pressing need of increasing instructional effectiveness is tutor-style courseware—educational software that uses the computer *to deliver* instruction. If we are talking practical solutions to CBE's urgent and complex problem, we must concentrate first on developing excellent tutor-style courseware, not because it is intrinsically superior, but because it addresses the practical issue most directly.

There is nothing *wrong* with improving students' computer literacy, with training children to program computers, with providing rich electronic environments packed with powerful ideas that students may discover as they wander in it freely. Nor is there anything wrong with using authoring systems or simplified languages to produce our own electronic "ditto sheets," or with making use of any direction educational computing takes. But these activities do not address the pressing need of increasing instructional effectiveness, which alone, among possibilities for computer use in our schools, has a chance of providing sufficient return on investment to justify the costs involved for producers and consumers. Tough, effective, instructionally sophisticated courseware does that—and that is what we must *first* concentrate on developing.

Second, the most practical solution to the courseware problem is the one that best accommodates Third Wave modes of computer use.

Educators can learn a valuable practical lesson here from "personal" business computing—word processing, report generation, spreadsheeting, and other executive functions, which are often referred to as management information systems (MIS). This kind of computing, though in the business sector, is also Third Wave computing and has as its equivalent our courseware problem. The business problem is much easier to address, however, partly because the programmers who build MIS software have a better understanding of business uses and partly because development efforts are not plagued by the equivalent of the complex relationship between manufacturers, publishers, university educators, and educational users. In other words, *their* courseware problem is simpler, and they are beginning to solve it.

One manufacturer's solution may be simply illustrated by the development of the Apple Macintosh computer. (Other companies have developed and are developing similar computers.) What is different about the Macintosh has almost nothing to do with *machine* qualities. It is not offering "more power and more memory in less space for less money!" or any of the other small-computer qualities manufacturers were pushing just a short time ago. The Macintosh does have some extended machine capabilities over previous Apple models, but that is not what is important about it. The big differences are: (1) the machine itself is designed from the point of view of nonspecialists—with their needs and desires in mind, and (2) the Macintosh concept is not "computer" but "computer plus software" as a single entity.

In simplest terms, the small-computer market for business managers and executives (the Third Wave component of business computing) has with the Macintosh formally admitted that Third Wave users are going to be "drivers" rather than "mechanics." Apple and other companies tried the other, lingering Second Wave approach. They even tried *giving* computers to executives. But they found that only a few executives wanted to learn to interact with unfriendly machines on the machine's own terms. Those few want to make a hobby of computers—to become hobbyists—and that is fine. But many executives, with neither the time nor inclination to become hobbyists, greeted the "vast, incredible potential" of their new desktop computers with a big yawn. Until they could "drive" it, they were not interested. Educators should learn from that!

A practical solution to the courseware problem is thus to concentrate first and most on developing CBE that respects the nonspecialist status of Third Wave educational users—teachers and students. We are not yet as ready to admit it as Third Wave business users and the computer market that serves them are, but the computer will have a significant and lasting impact on educational effectiveness in this country only if we treat users as drivers. We can compel all students to take computer literacy courses; we can even require them to study programming—just as once we required that they learn Latin. Of course, you have to search far for a Latin speaker today.

Third, the most practical solution to the courseware problem is the one that produces courseware on a scale large enough to have a significant impact on educational effectiveness.

Understanding *why* this step is necessary is not the problem. The problem is (1) understanding *how* to accomplish it, and (2) *accepting* the practical solution, despite our strong commitment to pluralism in approaches. In order to produce large-scale CBE curricula, to increase instructional effectiveness, and to address the complex and interrelated facets of the courseware problem that have deadlocked the segments of educational computing, we need new, centralized, organizational structures of large size and with substantial power and funding—centers similar to the regional educational development and research centers now in existence in other areas of education.

CBE DEVELOPMENT CENTERS

The concept of development centers in CBE represents the application of computer imagination at a structural, organizational level. It proceeds from the notion that we have not just more or bigger problems in CBE than in education generally, but that CBE's problems are of a different kind. Existing educational structures have a bootstrap problem: Before they can address new issues effectively, they must find a way to alter their point of view enough to see the differences as qualitative. Only then will they be equipped to tackle the interdependent issues here described. The concept of a development center, in contrast, proceeds directly from the assumption of qualitative difference.

Some might argue that development centers represent a drastic, difficult, and perhaps too highly structured approach to solving the courseware problem. Centers would cost a lot of money, and that implies a restriction of alternatives. Relatively few such centers could be established—in comparison to the many, essentially independent approaches and solutions that now characterize the field. We had better, in other words, be pretty sure of our chances of success before putting all our eggs in one basket.

Centralization certainly carries with it risk, but there is also a trade-off benefit. To the extent that the issues discussed in this book are, in fact, interdependent, the *only* effective way to resolve the problems is to take a new organizational approach. In other words, despite the cost, development centers have a potential for payoff that independent, isolated research cannot hope to offer.

Goals and Emphases

In order to address the interdependent issues discussed above, CBE development centers might combine three spheres of activity:

Development In addition to developing individual lessons that incorporate sophisticated instructional design features to exploit the strengths of the computer as an educational medium, development centers could provide a setting in which entire computer-based curricula, incorporating computer management and online testing, are possible. They could also facilitate *production* of these curricula for implementation in schools. They would thus combine the best of both worlds—the sophistication of an academic setting with the distribution potential of industry—taking the best university laboratory insights and applying them in integrated curricula for wide dissemination.

The development of integrated curricula, in turn, could lead to the development of sophisticated computer management, testing, and evaluational utilities that are *linked* to instruction. (Developed independently, such software packages can have only minimal connection to instruction.) One of the key insights into realizing the educational potential of computers rests in this ability to *integrate* instructional components. This kind of integration well illustrates the ability of development centers to translate the concept of computer imagination to the organizational level. In traditional educational settings, management, diagnostic testing, and mastery operate independently, simply because no mechanism exists to link them effectively to instruction. The computer has the potential to interrelate them, but doing it effectively requires an organizational setting that facilitates it. Development centers, in other words, could make possible fundamental changes in the nature and delivery of instruction. Such changes are impossible when instructional components are developed in a precomputerized organizational setting.

Research   Development centers would encourage the discovery and development of new instructional uses of the computer through research in computer-based instructional design and programming solutions. Research of this kind is certainly possible without such centers, but they could facilitate it in important ways. In addition to the opportunities to link instructional components, centers could also unite subject area experts from a wide variety of fields with expert CBE designers and programmers. If CBE is ever to transcend the situation in which courseware in math and science instruction represent its highest achievements (because most of those who understand the computer well enough to design sophisticated lessons are experts in these subject areas), development centers are necessary.

Development centers would provide forums for more direct and integral discussion and for more creative pooling of insights than do annual meetings and publications. The close association and free exchange of ideas provided by a center in which scholars can interact, coordinate, and combine their efforts have the potential to move the field of CBE and the current state of courseware development ahead at the same rate that schools are investing in hardware.

Development centers would facilitate the practical as well as the conceptual side of research. Instructional design consultants and expert programmers would be present, for example, to counsel and provide help to the researcher in translating insights into functioning courseware, and the center would provide a mechanism (in the form of a laboratory school) to test and evaluate research.

Finally, the research capability of such a center would provide a means for investigating other issues related to the field of CBE—such as discussions of policy and the cultural impact of computers on education. A center could be a forum for discussing and resolving issues of distribution, the protection of authors' rights, and so on.

Teaching   The presence of scholars, instructional designers, and programmers required by the developmental and research branches of a CBE development center would greatly facilitate the center's teaching function. The graduate programs in computer-based instructional design and programming that centers make possible, for example, would mean that a mechanism would be in place for providing graduate students with laboratory training and field experience. In addition to graduate programs, the center could also perform wider educational tasks:

- Offering courses that develop computer imagination and provide training in computer use for educators and education students who are not specializing in CBE
- Developing text materials in computer literacy for the university at large and for the community
- Offering inservice training programs and seminars to teachers in the field
- Providing a center of activity and involvement for university faculty who are interested in computers and education

Laboratory School

An important part of the center would be a fully computerized laboratory school. Although the center would probably strive to develop materials that were ultimately deliverable on the hardware schools actually own, the development process would be greatly facilitated by the presence of a linked computer system. With such a system the developers at the center would have the opportunity to monitor students in instruction, to invisibly collect very precise data on lesson operation and student performance, and to get comments on lessons from student users sent automatically to the lesson developer. They would also have the capability to fix bugs in the lesson instantly.

Perhaps most important of all for its impact on solving the courseware problem, such a link between lab school and development center would permit developers to go far beyond the ordinary field test procedures for the center's products. A fully linked computer system would make possible a very tight and very easy to implement *formative evaluational cycle*. The impact of such a cycle on basic research in instructional effectiveness would be immeasurable.

WHAT YOU HAVE LEARNED IN THIS CHAPTER

1. The most serious problem facing computer-based education is the lack of sufficient excellent courseware packages.

2. Reasons often given for the courseware problem are inadequate because they fail to take Third Wave computing issues sufficiently into account:
   a. In the "chicken and egg" scenario, software developers claim teachers have not told them what they want, while teachers claim that developers have not given them a choice.
   b. The *incompatibility* argument is that excellent software awaits standardization of hardware components.

    c. An argument based on *teachers' fears* claims that truly excellent software threatens teachers and consequently will not sell.

3. The real underlying causes of the courseware problem are:
    a. Lingering Second Wave attitudes in educational computing that emphasize machines over uses and divert educational users into hobbyist roles, and
    b. A lack of computer imagination, not just in currently available courseware but in the courseware development process itself.

4. Each segment of the educational computing community must share responsibility for the courseware problem, and each experiences its effects differently.
    a. *Schools* contribute by buying hardware in large quantities before adequate software exists, thus creating a powerful market vacuum that invites quick, ineffective solutions and opportunism among unscrupulous software developers. However, schools suffer from a great need for educational software, which developers are unable to produce.
    b. *Hardware manufacturers* push hobbyism on educational users and develop flashy software with little instructional value to sell machines. However, manufacturers lack a distribution network, have insufficient knowledge of content and pedagogy to develop good software, and are unable to dictate tastes to the education market.
    c. *Textbook publishers* have distribution networks and an editorial process in place, but they know little about the strengths of the medium and produce instructionally sound software that often fails to exploit the computer medium effectively. Their packages are often just "electronic books" that also add to the courseware problem because they are ancillary to the publishers' print media. However, publishers suffer from an inability to control the hardware that would deliver the excellent courseware they might develop.
    d. *University researchers* contribute to the courseware problem by ignoring the schools' urgent need for the excellent courseware that they are in the best position to develop. However, researchers suffer from inadequate funding and institutional support and lack of a way to share in the profit from their development efforts.

5. One practical solution to the courseware problem would be to create CBE development centers capable of:
    a. Producing CBE that maximizes instructional effectiveness.
    b. Producing CBE that respects the nonspecialist status of educational computer users.
    c. Producing CBE on a scale that can be truly effective.

6. CBE development centers might have three goals:
    a. *Development* both of excellent instructional lessons and fully integrated curricula

    b. High level *research* on computer-imaginative uses of the medium

    c. *Teaching*—preparing the next generation of CBE instructional designers and programmers

7. With fully computerized laboratory schools, CBE development centers could make possible the long-desired goal of effective formative evaluation of instruction.

NOTES

1. Alfred Glossbrenner, *How to Buy Software* (New York: St. Martin's Press, 1984), p. 530. Copyright © 1984 by Alfred Glossbrenner. Reprinted by permission of St. Martin's Press, Inc.

2. Glossbrenner, on p. 531, cites a study on computer-assisted education: U.S. Office of Technology Assessment, *Informational Technology and Its Impact on American Education* (Washington, D.C.: U.S. Government Printing Office, September 1982).

3. Francis D. Fisher, "Professional Report: Computer-Assisted Education: What's Not Happening?" *Journal of Computer-Based Instruction* 9 (Summer 1982): 19–27.

4. Ibid., p. 23. Reprinted by permission.

5. Ibid.

6. The National Commission on Excellence in Education, *A Nation at Risk: The Imperative for Educational Reform* (Washington, D.C.: U.S. Department of Education, April 1983), p. 7.

11

Possibilities

This chapter deals with the future of educational computing. We will describe some of the exciting courseware developments that lie not far down the road. But our principal concern is to address the future impact of CBE on our schools and our society by extrapolating the effects of the courseware development we discussed in the last chapter.

A QUESTION OF IMPACT

The last chapter was about the serious and mundane present:

- About the courseware problem that is so big and so all-pervasive it could actually kill computer-based education before it gets a real start.
- About forcing ourselves to concentrate on maximizing instructional effectiveness instead of giving free rein to our creative imaginations, producing and consuming new and wonderful computer insights calculated to delight and charm CBE developers and their colleagues as much as (or even more than) children.
- About having to settle for the modest goal of delivering effective instruction in regular, traditional subjects rather than creating expensive but exhilarating electronic environments or giving our children a computer apiece and letting them discover powerful ideas and deep understanding on their own.

Perhaps the courseware problem is big and potentially fatal; perhaps we have to get tough and practical; perhaps we need the kind of "no nonsense," task-oriented educational software development centers described in the last chapter—at least for the present. But what about the bright promise for Third

Wave computing, in education and outside it, that everyone talks about? Is not this excessive commitment to practicality and cost effectiveness almost diametrically opposed to the grand promise heralded for the computer age in the popular press and media?

While we were working on this book, the *Wall Street Journal* printed an article on nonspecialist computing nearly every day, and *Time* broke a long-standing tradition by naming the personal computer "Man of the Year" in 1982. Does the approach to solving the courseware problem described in the preceding chapter indicate a lack of faith in the future? Does it restrict the future of educational computing to an electronic version of the same dull educational structure we have now and are dissatisfied with? We may need the modest, practical, down-to-earth approach discussed in the last chapter for the present, but in *this* chapter, let us talk expansively about the future! Let us examine the solution to the courseware problem described in the last chapter from a future perspective to determine whether its present practicality actually endangers the bright future of CBE by committing us to a useful but ultimately too restricted course of development.

Let us begin by posing two questions:

> What would happen if we actually solved the courseware problem as it was formulated in the last chapter?

> If we got enough excellent courseware in academic subjects and delivered it in schools like the laboratory school described in the last chapter, what effect would it have on curricula, on schools and society, and on the computer literacy of students?

Impact on Curricula

When Janice Johnson's alarm rang at seven o'clock Tuesday morning, she was already up and ready for school. Seated at the computer in her room, she was using a word processor to put the finishing touches on a short story due that day in Creative Writing II at City High. If you read the story, you would be impressed and might not guess that Janice was just seventeen—what used to be called "a senior" back when high school had grades.

One of the most sophisticated features of Janice's story was the way it used "flashback" techniques. That was Janice's own idea; she was proud of it. She thought of it the week before when she was using the same word processing package on the big computer at school to prepare a chemistry report and decided to move a passage up several paragraphs. Adapting the technique to creative writing was a small cognitive leap. She wrote the story straight through, then experimented by moving parts of it around. The word processor made the changes technically easy and encouraged her experimentation. If it had not worked out, however, she knew she could always fall back on the straight narrative order that she had saved on her backup disk.

You also would be impressed with *how* Janice wrote—not at all as one would write using paper and pencil. If you looked at the screen as she worked, you would see that each sentence started on a new line, and that paragraphs were separated by blank lines. When she wanted to change a sentence, she could delete the old version easily, without splitting lines. And when she wanted to move paragraphs around, they were easy to spot.

That little time-saving trick was not Janice's invention, however. Her friend Jennie showed her how to do it when they were working together on the school newspaper. Janice was at home; Jennie at school. Jennie needed editorial advice, so she called Janice up and told her to link their computers for a conference. When Janice made her computer a slave to Jennie's, she noticed Jennie's strange data entry format, asked about it, and Jennie explained. Afterward, both girls began using the technique. (So did Bob, who had taught Jennie in the first place.)

For a teacher, the most interesting thing about Janice's story was how well written it was—far beyond the level of most seventeen-year olds, almost wholly free of grammatical and syntactical problems. If you asked her English teacher, Steve Smith, about that, he would be happy to explain why.

"Let me explain first how our computer-based writing package works," he would tell you eagerly. (It is one of his favorite topics of conversation.) "At its heart is a word processor especially designed for school use. It allows the students to enter their work and edit it just as they would on a regular word processor. They can use it on the terminals at school, or they can work on floppy disks in their computers at home and then copy the disks into memory when they get to school. The difference between our package and a regular word processor, however, is that after the student has signaled his or her readiness, I can view the completed piece in blocks of text as the student composed it, one line at a time, or in paragraphs with wide spacing between the lines for comments. In either of the latter two formats, I can make corrections right on the computer.

"That saves me a great deal of time: I find that I can make more and better comments on students' compositions than I used to. It also saves the kids a lot of time, which is even more important. I used to want to ask them to spend a lot of time on a composition, rewriting, experimenting, really polishing it. I didn't have the heart to do it, though, because I knew how hard they worked just on the mechanics of typing or drafting the clean copy. I knew it would dishearten them to make changes and then have to retype or recopy it. Now that editing is so easy, they are willing to rewrite, and I don't feel guilty asking them to, because the additional time will be devoted to instruction, not mostly to recopying material that was all right in the first place.

"In fact, I'd be willing to say that with this system, our efficiency—the time in instruction kids actually spend on writing rather than on production tasks like copying or typing—has *doubled*. We cover so much more about *writing* in the writing classes now. I'm especially pleased when they bring half-finished or merely sketched-out pieces to me and we can build them together. In fact, we often do that in class: We flesh out an essay strategy together, and they learn writing by doing it instead of talking about it.

"By the way, it's given them—and *me!*—a whole new outlook on the usefulness of *outlines* in writing. I just *know* they often used to write a composition first and make up the outline afterward. Now, using the computerized writing program, they "jot down" main points, examine them, reorder them, and bring them into class for criticism and tightening. When they have a plan they like, they can go right in on top of it in the word processor, gradually flesh out the central ideas with supporting arguments and illustrations in short phrases and fragments without worrying about style. Then, when it looks good, they can rework the intermediate structure, transforming fragments and phrases into complete sentences.

"That part of our computerized writing package—the word processor/correction component—has enabled Janice and all my students to write better, but the package has more! Come to my classroom. It won't take you long to notice that we almost *never* talk about grammar!

"Teaching grammar used to be extremely vexatious, even though it's necessary. Every student needs instruction on some grammar skills, but no two kids seem to have the same gaps in their grammar background. Thus, besides being boring, grammar instruction was always repetitious to at least some of the students. Consequently, they hated doing the exercises as much as I hated teaching them.

"A special feature of the computerized writing curriculum, however, is that it is coupled with a complete set of mastery-based writing skills modules. Now when I notice a grammar problem in a student's writing, I simply key it and assign it, telling the computer management system to route the student into the remedial practice and instruction he or she needs. When the student has come to criterion, the management system automatically sends me a note.

"By the way, if I ever key that skill for remediation again, the management system reminds me that I have assigned it before. At that point I have several options: One, I can work with the student privately. Two, I can closely examine the student's performance during previous sessions in the remedial lesson—requesting a summary of scores on the drills, a summary of items most commonly missed, or even an item-by-item record of performance. Three, I can examine the student's previous compositions, searching them by the correction key that signifies the individual skill being remediated, looking for patterns and improved performance. Finally, if necessary, I can assign additional, perhaps more basic, kinds of remediating instruction that's also available on the system.

"It's kind of funny. To look at these lessons individually, you couldn't imagine how much they have improved the quality of my course. They are not fancy looking; they don't dazzle the student with flashy graphics or gimmicks. They just teach dull content straightforwardly and efficiently. Students can get through them quickly and painlessly, so that they can return to the exciting, fulfilling part of the course—the writing. Modest and practical as the grammar modules are, however, they have had a tremendous impact on my course, because they have freed me to teach the real content of the course and have freed the students to work on it.

"If we had spoken a couple of years ago, I would have scoffed at using computers to teach writing. Then I only thought in terms of the machine itself. I knew that computers could not think or judge writing, so I couldn't see any use for them in an English classroom. Oh, I'd seen some individual drill lessons on basic writing skills, but I wasn't impressed. I finally accepted computers when I saw how these simple, practical lessons, incorporated into a sophisticated, integrated writing curriculum, dramatically increased effectiveness by maximizing students' independent use of time in instruction.

"Now I'm a firm believer in computer-based instruction. How could I not be? My students are writing better than ever; I finally get to teach what I like to teach and what only I—and no machine—*can* teach. As proud as I am of the computerized writing package, though, I have to admit it's not mine alone. Since it's a part of the school's instructional computer system, all the teachers use it. I use the "teacher comments feature" to make stylistic corrections on English assignments, but I know that Fred Peterson, the history teacher, uses it to make substantive comments in his students' assignments, too."

Meanwhile, Janice finished her short story, popped the disk from her computer, and set off for school. When she arrived, she went to the physics lab for class, but she had a few extra moments, so she put her disk into the computer and copied it into her English workspace for Mr. Smith to look at. When she signed on, she discovered she had a few notes. A couple were personal notes—one from Cindy, who was having boyfriend problems; one from her boyfriend, Steve. Another was an automatic note from the school computer, telling her to meet Mr. Peterson, the history teacher, at two o'clock.

Fred Peterson's advanced American history course was almost wholly individualized. It consisted mainly of readings and exercises that tested her understanding of concepts, along with projects that students worked on in pairs or small groups. The computer management system kept track of each student's individual progress and updated Fred every day. Whenever he felt a student needed it, he just called a meeting.

But the meeting announced in Janice's note was of a different kind. When he set up the curriculum, Fred built in points at which he wanted several students to get together with him to discuss critical concepts in the course content. The management system kept track of students' progress in the course, and when at least four students had reached or passed one of the critical points, it consulted each of their schedules and Fred's, scheduled a meeting, and automatically sent them a note to that effect. Janice's note read:

To: Janice, Tim, Stan, and Darnell

Please bring your notes to Mr. Peterson's room at 2 p.m. and be prepared to discuss the political impact of Thomas Paine's writings on the American Revolution.

Janice also had a note from Laurette d'Alembert, a high school student in France who was her "pen pal." As part of a French course, she and the other members of her class established a note file linked to a school in Paris where the students were studying English. The linked note file enabled them to practice their language skills, receive help from one another, and exchange information about their countries—not the kinds of things they read in books, but what kids their age thought and did and liked. The experience inspired Janice to find out more about France, because she really liked Laurette.

Janice skipped Laurette's note, however, because physics class was about to start. Mr. Novak, the teacher, was more of a traditionalist than Mr. Peterson in the history department. True, the physics curriculum, like most of the others in the school, was broken up not into chapters in a textbook but into small, mastery-based instructional units that were delivered individually. But Mr. Novak liked to use the computer for the interactive demonstrations and simulations that substituted for lectures in his course, and he wanted students to be working together on the same topic he was demonstrating. Often his demonstrations were drawn from the experiments the students did in class. Many of these were simulations, but some were not.

Janice enjoyed physics. She liked manipulating real things in an orderly fashion and found that easy to conceptualize. What she did not like was math—at least when she had gone through the math modules in the high school curriculum. Janice's friend Cindy did not understand that. For her math was easy and physics hard.

Luckily for both girls, however, the separateness of math and physics was not very pronounced at City High. The computer management system "remembered" the parts of algebra that had given Janice trouble earlier. When concepts in physics arose that used them, the management system routed her into algebra review units that moved from the concrete physics examples Janice liked to the abstract math that had given her trouble. The system worked just the opposite for Cindy. When she had trouble with physics problems, the management system jumped her out to math lessons and worked from the abstract to the concrete. The two friends often sat side by side in the physics lab, working on the same course content at the same time, yet, if you looked over their shoulders, it might take you a while to realize it. The instruction the computer delivered looked very different for the two students.

After physics, Janice had a free period and went to the library to respond to Laurette's note. When she signed on to the computer there, she was delighted to find a note from Mr. Smith telling her that her short story had been selected for the city-wide literary magazine, to which students from all four of the city's high schools contributed. Excited and pleased, she punched up *The Quill* on her terminal and saw her story there in the index with the others. (*The Quill*, of course, is an electronic magazine.) What pleased her even more was that other students had commented on the story, and it had only been online for an hour! One response was lavish praise; another praised the story but offered some constructive criticism; a third took issue with the second response. Laughing, Janice experienced the thrill of accomplishment. In the city high schools' computerized learning environment, success often was measured by how much other students commented on one's efforts. As she left for lunch, Janice reflected happily, "Hey! This one just might get a string of twenty-five responses!"

By telling this story we intend to make two points. First, the curriculum of City High is fictional and futuristic in only one respect: At this time we lack the courseware, management, and utilities mentioned. The hardware is available, although some of it is now costly because it is not mass produced and there is no big demand for it. Between the time we write these words and the time you read them, hardware capable of doing everything in our story will probably be available at feasible cost. It will most likely have been developed for business uses, but it will be easily transportable to an educational environment.

The software discussed in the story is not fancy or futuristic either. Development costs, both in time and money, would be high, but it is conceptually very feasible. The centers we proposed could turn out such practical, tough, straightforward software with surprising speed and efficiency. The key to its effectiveness is not years of research but a commitment to Third Wave modes of computer use—individualized, content-centered, complete teaching curricula aimed exclusively at maximizing instructional effectiveness.

The fictional English teacher in the story, Steve Smith, put it correctly: Individually, the software packages are unprepossessing, but their combination into managed, integrated curricula shows computer imagination. The *real* computer imagination involves attacking the courseware problem on a scale large enough to ensure effectiveness. To actualize the potential of CBE we do not need to revamp our educational system from the ground up to accommodate the computer. All we need are lots of good, solid, nonflashy instructional packages that focus on the student as *user* rather than as computer whiz kid.

Notice there was no using the computer to tap into the corporate records of Fortune 500 companies, no complicated, hobbyist or semiprofessional skills, and *no programming* involved in any of the City High curricula. Everything that Janice and her friends needed was in the software. All they did was *use* it—just as a driver drives a car. (And so did their teachers!) Think of all the time these students and teachers would have wasted diligently studying the BASIC language and learning about binary arithmetic in computer literacy courses! If CBE is to have an impact on educational effectiveness in this country, computer literacy is not going to provide it. It is time to stop thinking in terms of machines and start thinking in terms of users. It is time for the Second Wave to move on to the Third Wave in educational computing.

Impact on Schools and Society

In our City High scenario we concentrated primarily on a single student. Now shift your focus. Imagine there was not just one Janice Johnson but millions of them.

Janice was not significantly different from most high school students. She was not brilliant. She was not a computer whiz, different from other kids because of the novel way she thought or because of special insights that working with computers had given her. Rather, she was a perfectly normal girl who was learning at her fullest potential. Whatever insights, special skills, and individual talents she possessed emerged because she was learning regular subjects with an effectiveness that far outstripped what is possible in a classroom where one teacher faces twenty students with textbooks. The only thing that the computerized curriculum gave her was truly effective instruction that did not drastically change her or the way she thought. But by teaching her effectively, it dramatically increased her options.

In the information society we are entering, it is not knowledge of computers that will help students succeed; it is just *knowledge* that will make the difference between success and mediocrity. A curriculum like that produced by educational software development centers for schools like City High has tremendous potential, because it takes each student from wherever he or she is and begins a steady, solid process of increasing mastery of the knowledge and skills successful members of our society need. It has no trick or gimmick beyond its capacity to individualize instruction for each student in complete teaching lessons that guarantee mastery. It leaves teachers free for high-quality interactions with students. It increases all students' options, and it continues to do so as long as they stay in the curriculum.

The same content-based instruction works for the slowest students, enabling them to go as far as they can in an infinitely patient and tireless instructional environment, and for the bright students, who move quickly and draw insights as Janice did. Because of its straightforward, mastery-based approach, it could end functional illiteracy in this country at the same time that it produces a crop of future scientists, technical specialists, and leaders. We need neither blinding flashes of extraordinary computer wizardry nor new modes of teaching and learning that emerge somehow from an understanding of computers and the way they work. We need only teach the same subjects we have always taught, but much more effectively.

If anything, the kind of instruction we saw in City High poses a problem for schools just because of its dramatic increase in efficiency and effectiveness. Francis Fisher explains the problem well with an analogy to computer-based training programs in industry:

> *Efficiency in teaching is welcomed in industrial training programs, computer manufacturers point out. "If a sales training program that used to take eight weeks requires only two weeks with computer-assisted methods, any sales manager can figure to the penny how much he has saved. What is the matter," they ask, "with the schools?"*
>
> *If an algebra course that used to take 16 weeks takes only five with the computer, the school has not a saving but a problem: what to do during the other eleven weeks allotted for the course? It seems that the tasks we have assigned to our schools are measured not just in educational output but also in the day-care terms of hours to be spent inside a school building. Of course the time saved in learning algebra could be put to use learning some more of the many things there are to learn, but expanding a curriculum costs money.[1]*

The story of City High provides at least one possible answer to Fisher's question for the schools. We emphasized the difference in the way Mr. Peterson, the history teacher, felt comfortable dissolving the traditional classroom structure almost entirely while Mr. Novak, the physics teacher, felt that students still had much to gain from working as a class. The conclusion is that effective courseware of the kind we have described makes no absolute demands on the structure of the school day. But it implies something more important. It is probably unlikely that the structure of the school day or of curricula will have to be changed by computer-generated administrative fiat. Simply making a truly user-oriented instructional system available to teachers will engender its own curricular adjustments—extensive in some classrooms and schools, more modest and careful in others.

We could, however, extend Fisher's logic and ask as well, "What does society do with a superabundance of qualified people, products of a truly efficient and effective educational system, who expect to be remunerated and challenged commensurately with their potential?" Take Janice, for example. As we said, she is an ordinary kid, but years of interaction with teachers and other students using computer-imaginative software tapped her creativity. She discovered she had some writing talent, but more important and more basic, she developed insightful *ways* of thinking. She became a resourceful, creative thinker.

As she and millions like her, who have knowledge and mastery of skills and who know how to think creatively, leave school to seek employment, we will witness the real effect of solving the courseware problem. We are not prophesying doom—implying that our present society has no place for creative thinkers. Nor are we painting an Arcadian picture of a future where everyone is smart, happy, and contented, placidly going about their creative, fulfilling work tasks. We cannot say precisely *what* the impact of a high level of instructional effectiveness will be on the culture. Our point, however, is that the last chapter's modest, practical, even seemingly *unimaginative* solution to the courseware problem may actually have a far more revolutionary effect on our society than more exciting-sounding approaches that attempt to stretch kids' minds by forcing them to interact with computers on the machine's terms.

Computer Imagination versus Computer Literacy

At the beginning of this chapter, we resolved to make the practical, straightforward approach to solving the courseware problem, which stresses the maximization of instructional effectiveness, accountable to the future of CBE in two ways. We first demanded to know whether practical and cost effective approaches have as great a potential for long-term impact on education and society as more costly, less readily implementable, but more exciting-sounding, more computer-oriented (i.e., machine-oriented) approaches to CBE. We have suggested that the cultural impact of truly effective courseware in adequate quantities probably surpasses the capabilities of many more seemingly novel approaches.

Now we are ready to address the second challenge, which we can specify more precisely:

> While sufficient quantities of practical courseware that deliver instruction in the traditional subjects may be able to have a significant impact on education and society, will they not ultimately do our students and our society a disservice by preserving outmoded preelectronic ways of thinking in what is rapidly becoming a computer culture?

In other words, the ultimate problem with courseware directed to nonspecialist users in traditional subject areas may turn out to be that it ignores the important task of enhancing students' computer literacy. Surely, that is a big problem—one that transcends the short-term gains in increased instructional effectiveness in our schools and higher test scores for our students. Is it not ultimately a method for making them very good at the *wrong things?*

Let us address that important charge by looking not at education but at the changing nature of our culture, for which whatever educational system we implement must prepare our children. Toffler's now familiar *The Third Wave* is almost wholly devoted to sketching the differences between our current industrial society and the postindustrial society for which computer literacy is so important. An analogy he uses succinctly characterizes the difference.[2]

Toffler cites Donald Conover, general manager of corporate education for Western Electric, who compares Second Wave workers to classical musicians and Third Wave workers to jazz improvisers. Classical musicians take a prewritten composition and play it exactly as the composer has indicated. Jazz improvisers, in contrast, have to be ready to "think on their feet." They must be attuned to other musicians in the ensemble and decide what to do next based on what is happening in the unfolding performance.

According to this musical analogy, the single quality that best characterizes the difference between the Second and Third Wave work environments is rapid and constant *change*. Consequently, the qualities Toffler suggests are most important in Third Wave workers are adaptability to change: the ability to pace oneself, to take initiative, to work individually, and to think creatively.

While Toffler's description of how patterns of work are changing is compelling, it is interesting to note that none of the qualities he mentions as characteristic of work environments or workers has anything to do with computers or knowledge of computers. More important, a thorough grounding in programming or the ability to understand computers on their own terms would not be of any particular use. It is true that we are entering a computer culture. It is not clear that to live successfully in such a culture we need to be "computer literate" in the usual sense of the term. In fact, if what Toffler says is true, an entirely different range of worker attributes would be most important. Perhaps, therefore, it is those who wish to teach our students more about computers as machines who may misunderstand the conceptual needs of present students destined to be future workers and producers in our society.

Our description of the City High curriculum mentioned no computer literacy course. Nor, while it probably had them, did it make programming courses central to curriculum in any way. Instead, the software—lessons, communications facilities, and computer management system at City High— was transparent and respected the nonspecialist status of educational users. That does not mean that students did not learn valuable things about interacting with computers. It just means that they learned to be excellent "drivers" rather than amateur "mechanics."

What the City High students learned was not computer literacy but user virtuosity. Janice and her friends prepared themselves for a new work environment by *using software* in powerful ways as they acquired knowledge and skills in regular academic subjects. We spoke of the tricks Janice invented and picked up from her friends—about how she made the word processor function more efficiently for her; about how the computer-based communications sparked her interest in the history and culture of other countries; about how the curriculum automatically presented physics in the way that worked best for her, and thus, enhanced her ability to approach difficult problems creatively. We saw how the computer encouraged consultation and cooperation among students while teaching them to be responsible for themselves and to set their own pace. In sum, we saw that educational software designed for maximally effective use by nonspecialists increased *adaptivity* in Janice and her friends. Janice was prepared for a Third Wave world, not because of what she knew about computers, but because she was a virtuosic user of computers.

When the time soon comes that it is possible to carry the entire contents of the Library of Congress around in a briefcase-sized computer, the problem we will face is not one of knowing how to build the data base we carry, but how to get at the information it contains in imaginative, efficient ways. As it increases our command of the knowledge and skills we need, this capacity to lead us into creative use of an awe-inspiringly powerful new medium is surely the chief value and best destiny of the computer as teacher.

NOTES

1. Francis D. Fisher, "Professional Report: Computer-Assisted Education: What's Not Happening?" *Journal of Computer-Based Instruction* 9 (Summer 1982): 19–27. Material quoted from page 25 reprinted by permission.

2. Alvin Toffler, *The Third Wave* (New York: William Morrow & Company, 1980), p. 401.

Index

Abelson, Harold, 106
Alessi, Stephen M., 145
Apple computer, 59, 214–15
Ausubel, David P., 120
Avner, R. A., 62, 75

Baker, Frank, 56
Bank Street Writer, 169
Barnes, Hank, 145
Beach, Richard, 174
Beethoven, Ludwig van, 3
Biehler, Robert F., 107, 120
Biology curriculum, 66–67
Bridwell, Lillian S., 151, 153, 155–56,
     174–75
Bruner, Elaine C., 144
Bruner, Jerome, 111–14, 121
Burns, Hugh, 158, 175

California Library Media Consortium,
     191, 202
Chabay, Ruth, 59, 61, 75
Chemistry curriculum, 59–63
Cherry, L. L., 174
Ciskey, Mark, 75
Clapp, Elizabeth J., 56, 175
Classification systems:
   global, 41, 47–56
   goal-oriented, 41, 68–70
   instruction-oriented, 41, 59–68
Cohen, Barry, 64, 75, 195–96, 202
Cohen, Vicki Blum, 191, 202
Computer
   as instructional medium, 19
   as "tool," 68–69, 147–74
   as "tutee," 69, 107–20
   as "tutor," 68, 107–20, 123–44
   -based education development
       centers, 215–18
   -based testing, 49–50

data processing, 4–5
deployment in schools, 182–83
educational users, 10–13
educational uses, 19, 71–73
-film comparison, 24, 36–37
flashcard drills, 32–33, 59–68, 136–37
functions, 20–21, 70
   vs. teacher functions, 34–35
future in education, 221–32
games, 60
graphics, 189–90
hardware, 7–10
   selection of, 180–84
hobbyism, 13–15
imagination, 13, 25–26, 141–42, 157–
     59, 191–97
lessons:
   Bone, 66–67
   Capitalization II, 45–46
   Chemaze, 61
   Chemical Formulas and Equations,
      60
   Darts, 187, 195–96
   Doubling, 126–29
   Elements, 59
   Exploring Simple Graphs, 94
   Graphing Equations, 160–62
   Mouse, 62
   Reading Comprehension, 132–34
   Skywriting and Spider Web, 62
literacy, 16–17
-managed instruction, 50–56
programming, 13–15, 63, 81–92, 187–
     90
programs:
   Bank Street Writer, 169
   Electronic Ink, 165–73, 175
   ELIZA, 20
   EPIE Micro-courseware PRO/
      FILES, 191

Computer (continued)
  programs (continued)
    GED Curriculum: Science, 163–65
    LOGO, 43–45, 77–106
    MicroSIFT, 191
    PCP Language Skills Curriculum,
      45–47, 126–29
    PCP Reading Comprehension
      Curriculum, 132–34
    PLATO Curriculum Project, 44–47
    SRA word processor, 165–73, 175
    SRA Writing Skills:
      Punctuation, 30–31
  revolution, 1, 6
  simulations, 62–63
  social history, 2–6
  software development, 203–18
    contributions of:
      educational publishers, 209-10
      manufacturers, 208
      schools, 207–8
      university courseware
        developers, 210–12
  software tools, 151–65
    and computer imagination, 157–59
    evaluation, 186–91, 197–200
    integration of, 159–65
    machine vs. people tasks, 154–56
    product vs. process, 151–54
    selection, 179–80, 184–86
  specialist vs. nonspecialist, 6–7, 10–13
  tasks:
    Second Wave, 1–2
    Third Wave, 1–2, 6–10
  -teacher comparison, 34–35
  -textbook comparison, 24–25, 35–36,
    42
  "thinking" vs. teaching, 22–23
  tutorials, 60
  user-friendly, 10–13, 16, 190–91
  word processors, 151–54
    functions, 152
Computer-based Education
    Development Centers, 215–18
  laboratory school, 218
  lesson development, 216–17
  research, 217
  teaching, 217–18

Conover, Donald, 230
Corrective Feedback Paradigm, 33,
    136–37, 139–40
Courseware—See Computer software;
    Instructional software.
Cuban, Larry, 120
Culture:
  Second vs. Third Wave, 108–14
Curriculum—See also Computer
    lessons; Instruction.
  language, 45–46, 126–29
  mathematics, 64, 80–88, 95, 160–62,
    187, 195–96
  reading, 132–34
  science, 59–62, 66, 163–65
  writing, 30–31, 166–68, 170–73

Data processing, 4–5
Davis, Dennis M., 175
Dennis, J. Richard, 56, 199–200, 202
Dewey, John, 109
DiBello, Louis V., 144
diSessa, Andrea, 106
Dixon, Robert C., 39, 56, 144, 175
Dugdale, Sharon, 64, 75, 95, 106, 143,
    160–62, 175, 195–96, 202

Education—See Instruction;
    Curriculum.
Educational Products Information
    Exchange, 191, 202, 204
Electronic Ink, 165–73, 175
ELIZA, 20

Felty, J. Michael, 39, 75, 144, 175
Fisher, Francis, 209–10, 220, 229,
    232
Flashcard drills, 32–33, 136–37
Frase, L. T., 174

GED Curriculum: Science, 163–65
GEMS System, 51
Gilpin, John, 95, 106, 143
Global System of Classification, 41, 47–
    56
Glossbrenner, Alfred, 204, 220
Goal-oriented System of Classification,
    41, 68–70

Goldenberg, E. Paul, 96, 106
Goodson, Bobby, 191, 202

Hardware—See Computer.
Harvey, Brian, 96, 106
Heck, William, 202
Hively, Wells, 202
Hobbyism, 13–15
Hollerith, Herman, 4–5

IBM, 4
Individualized instruction, 28–31, 117–
    19, 123–44
  accurate placement, 129–30
  distributed practice, 135–37
  instruction sequencing, 137–40
  variable instructional content, 131–
    35
Instruction—See also Curriculum.
  adaptive, and student, 26
  adaptive, and teacher, 27
  child-centered, 108–14
  content-centered, 114–17
  discovery learning, 111–14
  individualized, 28–31, 117–19, 123–
    44
  long-term retention, 32–33, 136–37
  -oriented System of Classification,
    41, 59–68
  paired associate, 32
  remedial, 31
  sequenced, 137–40
  teacher-centered, 110–11
    vs. computer-delivered, 34–35
  tutor-style, 123–44
Instructional:
  feedback, 31, 136–37, 139–40
  games, 61
  media:
    textbooks, 24–25, 32, 35–37
    films, 24, 36–37
  software development, 203–18
    contributions of:
      educational publishers, 209–10
      manufacturers, 208
      schools, 207–8
      university courseware
        developers, 210–12

software tools, 151–65
  and computer imagination, 157–59
  integration of, 159–65
  machine vs. people tasks, 154–56
  product vs. process, 151–54
  styles, 110–19
International Council for Computers in
    Education, 202

James, William, 67
Jaquard loom, 4
Johnson, Jerry, 202

Kansky, Robert, 202
Kean, Elizabeth, 59, 75
Keislar, Evan, 120
Kibbey, David, 64, 75, 160–62, 175, 195–
    96, 202

Language curriculum, 30–31, 45–46,
    126–29
Lathrop, Ann, 191, 202
Learning:
  child-centered, 108–14
  content-centered, 114–17, 123–44
  discovery, 111–14
  individualized, 117–19
  Periodicals Group, 60
  teacher-centered, 110–11
Lessons, computer:
  Bone, 66–67
  Capitalization II, 45–46
  Chemaze, 62
  Chemical Formulas and Equations,
    60
  Darts, 187, 195–96
  Doubling, 126–29
  Elements, 59–60
  Exploring Simple Graphs, 94–95
  Graphing Equations, 160–62
  Mouse, 62–63
  Skywriting and Spider Web, 63
Liu, Albert, 56, 144
LOGO, 43–45, 77–106
  "powerful ideas," 96–97

McDonald's, 11
Machine Age, 2, 5

Maelzel, Johannes, 3
Mathematics:
    curriculum, 63–64, 80–88, 95, 160–62, 187, 195–96
    mathophobia, 79–80
Mayeda, James, 75
Misselt, A. Lynn, 39, 144
Montessori, Maria, 109

Nancarrow, Paula Reed, 151, 174–75
NASA, 5
National Commission on Excellence in Education, 121, 213, 220
National Council of Teachers of Mathematics, 191
Neill, A. S., 109
Newton, Isaac, 2
Northwest Regional Educational Laboratory, 191

Pac Man, 2
Papert, Seymour, 43–45, 56, 77–106, 137, 145
PCP Language Skills Curriculum, 45–46, 126–29
PCP Reading Comprehension Curriculum, 132–34
Piaget, Jean, 80
PLATO System, 71
Programming, computer, 13–15, 63, 81–92
Programs, computer:
    Bank Street Writer, 169
    Electronic Ink, 165–73, 175
    ELIZA, 20
    EPIE Micro-courseware PRO/FILES, 191
    GED Curriculum: Science, 163–65
    LOGO, 43–45, 77–106
    MicroSIFT, 191
    PCP Language Skills Curriculum, 45–47, 126–29
    PCP Reading Comprehension Curriculum, 132–34
    PLATO Curriculum Project, 45–47
    SRA word processor, 165–73, 175
    SRA Writing Skills:
        Punctuation, 30–31

Reading curriculum, 132–34
Reichmann, Lindsay P., 175
Richman, Ellen, 18
Ross, Donald, 151, 174–75

Scholastic Aptitude Test, 49
Schwartz, Helen, 158–59, 175
Science curriculum, 59–63, 66, 163–65
Science Research Associates, 30–31, 165–73
Seastrand, Phil, 75
Shostack, Robert, 153, 174
Shulman, Lee S., 120
Siegel, Martin A., 39, 75, 144–45, 175
Silver, Dorothy, 145
Smith, Adam, 3
Smith, Stanley, 59–63, 75
Snowman, Jack, 107, 120
Software—See Computer.
SRA word processor, 165–73, 175
SRA Writing Skills:
    Punctuation, 30–31
Steinberg, Esther R., 191, 202
Stevens, Robert J., 145, 175
Stevenson, G., 57

Taylor, Robert, 68–69, 75, 147–49, 174
Teacher:
    -delivered vs. computer-delivered instruction, 32
    functions vs. computer functions, 34–35
    role vs. computer role, 20
Thayer, Vivian T., 120
Toffler, Alvin, 1, 18, 108–9, 120, 230–32
Tools, 147–74

Versterman, W., 174

Watt, Daniel, 106
Weir, Sylvia, 106
Weizenbaum, Joseph, 20, 39
Word processor, 151–54
    functions, 152
Writer's Workbench, 155–56
Writing curriculum, 30–31, 166–68, 170–73

About the Authors

Dr. Martin A. Siegel, a professor of Educational Psychology at the University of Illinois at Urbana-Champaign, is a pioneer in the instructional design of computer-based education. He is an international lecturer and consultant in the field. As Assistant Director of the Computer-based Education Research Laboratory, Dr. Siegel directs a team of instructional designers, researchers, programmers, and evaluators. He has authored over 500 hours of microcomputer and PLATO courseware in reading comprehension, language arts, computer management, and word processing systems.

Dennis M. Davis is a specialist in computer-based education, a teacher, a musicologist, and an author. Mr. Davis is a member of the PLATO Education Group at the Computer-based Education Research Laboratory and has taught rhetoric at the University of Illinois at Urbana-Champaign. He is a consultant for firms designing computer-based instructional materials and has written a number of computer lessons and books.